I0799928

Historic
Canada

Saint John West

Volume II

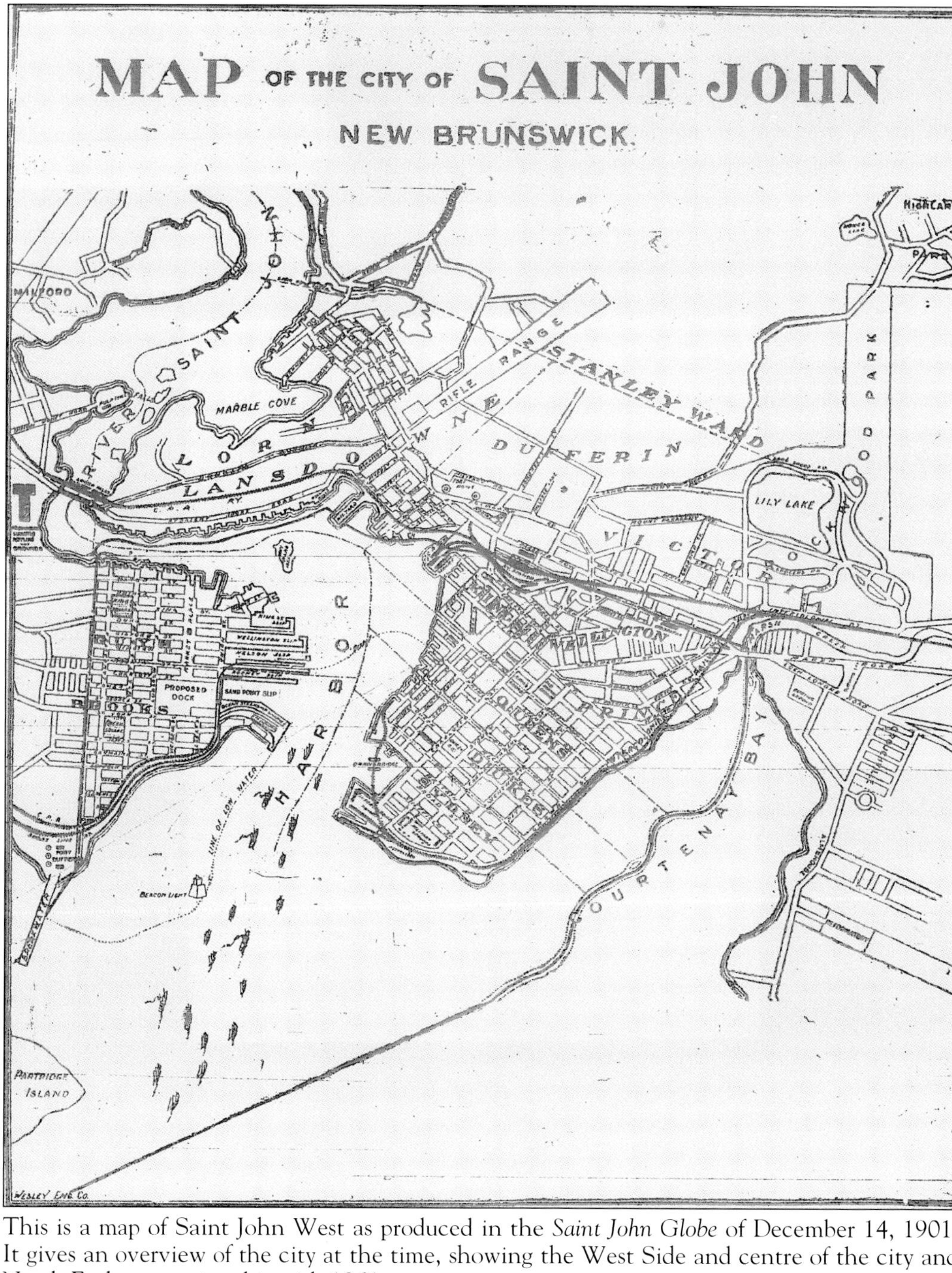

This is a map of Saint John West as produced in the *Saint John Globe* of December 14, 1901. It gives an overview of the city at the time, showing the West Side and centre of the city and North End, comparing this with 1861.

Historic
Canada

SAINT JOHN WEST

VOLUME II

David Goss and Fred Miller

ARCADIA
PUBLISHING

ISBN 978-0-7385-0166-2

Published by Arcadia Publishing
Charleston, South Carolina

Printed in the United States of America

Library of Congress Catalog Card Number: 96102403

For all general information contact Arcadia Publishing at:
Telephone 843-853-2070
Fax 843-853-0044
E-mail sales@arcadiapublishing.com
For customer service and orders:
Toll-Free 1-888-313-2665

Visit us on the Internet at www.arcadiapublishing.com

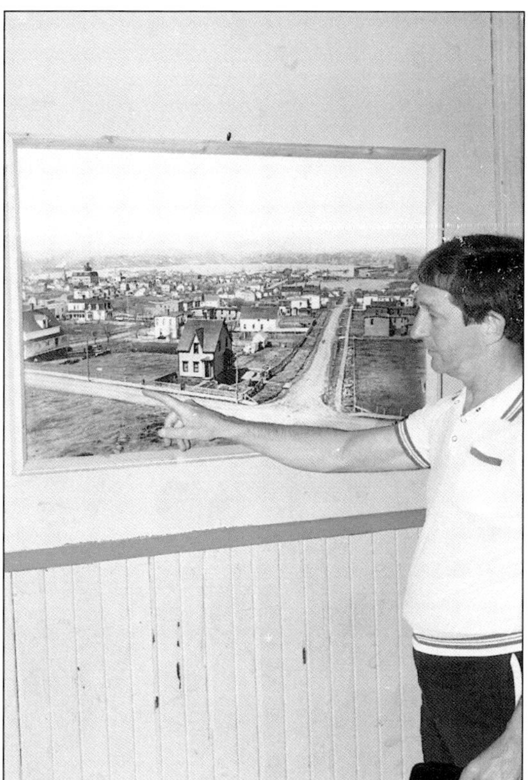

Fred Miller takes a look at one of the earliest photographic images of his beloved West Saint John. (Courtesy David Goss.)

Contents

INTRODUCTION

Soon after Fred Miller and I completed the *Saint John West* book, the question was asked: "When will the next book be out?" Well, Fred and I were so overwhelmed by the instant success of the first book that we said: "We'll get at it right away." However, that was not to be.

Pictures started coming in from people who had seen the first book and realized that they had an image worth sharing after enjoying the photographs and descriptions we had put together for *Saint John West and its Neighbours*. And the pictures just kept coming and coming, and we kept thinking we better take just a bit more time, because great things were showing up, and we just figured there was more to come. So, we kept setting the pictures aside. Both of us got onto other projects for a while, so for one good reason after another the date to begin working on another book kept getting pushed back. Then, tragically, on December 2, 1997, Fred died. It was completely unexpected and a great blow to all of us who knew him.

It was some months before I could get back to looking at the pictures that Fred had collected. We were getting calls about them, so at West Side days in June 1998, we set them all out (as had been done for years) and asked folks to come and pick up what they had given Fred, or to come and identify the people and places in the photographs they wished to leave with us. We didn't have a lot of success with that process so I began to sort through them and compare them to Fred's notes, visit folks who could fill in some gaps, and decide what to use from Fred's collection and from what I had collected.

It soon became obvious that the thrust of the new book should not be pictures that had been taken in the Saint John West area by the Port Authority or the Harbour Bridge Authority or other public agencies, but, rather we should concentrate on all those family pictures that provided a look at Saint John from a very personal viewpoint. These stretched back to the turn of the century and actually go through 1997, as you will see in the double page spread of the centre, which shows the last West Side Days Parade that Fred Miller was involved in.

That, then, is the main difference of this book from the previous one on the area. Although we are still covering the same geographic zone, from City Line to the waterline, about 90 percent of the photos chosen for use are those that were taken by amateur photographers. It is their scrapbooks that have provided this look at Saint John West, and thus, they have shaped the stories that are being told.

Fred kept lots of notes, but they were just that . . . little notes to check this, or call about that. There were many names (we've included all we could find), but only a few had phone numbers. Some of the pictures had complete identification, but most had no clue to their identity or doner. I knew from working with Fred in the past that such information was filed in his head, or he knew just who to call to get the facts. Thus, it has been very difficult to identify the people in the photographs, and in many cases, to be certain who the donors of the photos were. Though an honest effort was made to do both, it has not been possible to fully label every person and photo I have chosen to use. I expect to hear, "If you had asked me, I could have told you," but after conducting dozens of interviews, I was still left with many unanswered questions, and just had to get on with meeting the publisher's deadline.

In a future edition, if there is one, I will make any corrections and further identifications as requested. I hope that you will enjoy this book. I have used "we" many times in its compilation because Fred and I held several planning sessions, and I made use his notes and the documents he collected. In addition, I have felt Fred watching over me as I selected photos and could almost hear him saying, "Ah, that is a good one, Dave."

That was so important in those times when it seemed like the job would never get done . . . or get done right . . . and such times come frequently when putting any compilation like this together.

But now it's in your hands. On the whole, I think it looks good and provides lots of new information on the area. I offer it in tribute to a Recreation co-worker of many years, a lifetime friend, and a man who many have called "Mr. West Side". His memory, in part, will be kept alive through the pictures and the stories he collected, which have been preserved in this latest volume.

—David Goss
February 22, 1999

Acknowledgements

As noted in the introduction, it proved difficult to identify all the photographs. Those that were possible to identify are noted in the text following each one. Many remained unidentified, and many that Fred collected were not usable as no information could be gleaned about them. Even though they were good images, it proved impossible to say for certain where they were taken or who was involved in them. Among Fred's notes were the names of a great number of individuals he had contacted over the years. I have included these in the acknowledgements as I know Fred had spoken to them, and indeed some of the photographs may belong to them.

Within the text will be found the names of some persons who provided specific information on some of the photographs. As well I would like to mention the public agencies who assisted in this and the previous book project, namely, the Saint John Public Library, the West Branch Library, and U.N.B.S.J. library, where I was able to get assistance in researching the background of some of the photographs. Information was also sought and received from Harold Wright, Terry Keleher, and my father, Abe Goss, and it proved invaluable. Fred's notes and documents, which he had collected over the years, were also of great assistance in the captioning of the photographs, as were the two Government of Canada Local Initiative Studies, compiled in bound volumes in 1983 and 1984 by students under a Summer Works Program.

I would also like to acknowledge Terry and Irene Keleher for checking over the final draft, and Derek Goss for typing and correcting the manuscript. My wife's great patience when I get involved in these projects is also so important. Thank you Donna.

If I have missed anyone I will gladly correct it in a future printing of *Saint John West and its Neighbours, Volume II*.

These are the names exactly as they were found among Fred's notes.

Jim Adams
Ron Anderson
Elizabeth Beatteay
Gordie Blaine
Kim Boucher
Mrs Eileen Boyd
Joe Briggs
Mary Brown
Don Burchill
Richard Burpee
Earl Campbell
George Cameron
Harry Campbell
Geraldine Carleton
Jackie Carson
Doug Carter
Gary Childs
Mrs Cleveland
Polly Clifford
Dale Clinton
Vivian Cormier
George Craig
Glendon Curwin
Jim Donner
Florence Donovan
Ann Doucette
Alice Drillon
Victor Duffy
Gerald Dugay
Winnifred Dykeman
Ken Dykeman
Doreen Elliot
Ken Estabrooks
A. Flemming
Larry Fox
Dan Galbraith
Brian Galbraith
John Gow
Joe Green
Sylvia Hamm
Ed Harned
Mrs Hemmings
Mrs Higgins
Don Jones
Doug Kerwin
Velma Kierstead
Jim Kirkpatrick
Gordon Laskey
Mrs Glen Lee
Kiley Cobham
Terry McSorley
Gordon Miller
Don Moore
Hazen Walton
Art Nice
George Norris
Lorraine Parsons
Albert Perry
Ron Prosser
Marg Randall
Ivan Richard
Doug Richardson
Mrs Clarence Ring
Bill Savage
Hector Savoie
Dutchie Schell
Nelson Spencer
Florence Sullivan
Grant Tilley
Karl Tippett
Mrs Frank Trecartin
Theresa Walsh
Peter Walsh
Betty Walsh
Tom Waring
Noel Wittrien

One

From the Hills and Higher: An Overview

Whether it was called Carleton, West Saint John, or Saint John West, and whether the people who lived there were referred to as Algereens, Blue Rockers, Carletonites, or most commonly, West Siders, those who inhabited the streets below City Line on the western peninsula of Saint John had immense pride in the area of the city from which they came and were very proud to be called any of the above names.

Those outside of the area may not have understood that a true West Sider had to live between the harbour and the City Line. That's because it was not an official boundary until 1953, when residents west of City Line, in the area that was known as Beaconsfield, and Fairville decided to form their own city. Tradition says they counted their citizens, and, having come up short of the needed 10,000, added on the 1,700 patients housed in the Provincial Hospital for the Insane, and thus had the numbers for the new city, which they called by the old name for the parish, Lancaster.

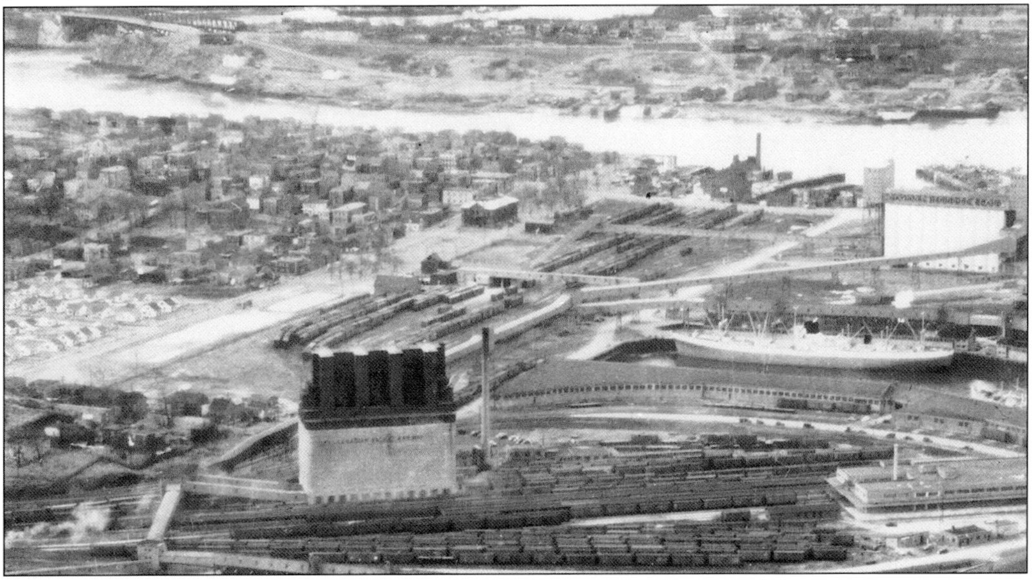

We begin our journey with a picture of the port in 1946, possibly one of the most prosperous eras the area would enjoy. Certainly no one at that time could see the opening of the St. Lawrence Seaway and the changes to come with airline travel and containerization that would drastically effect the port operation in Saint John West.

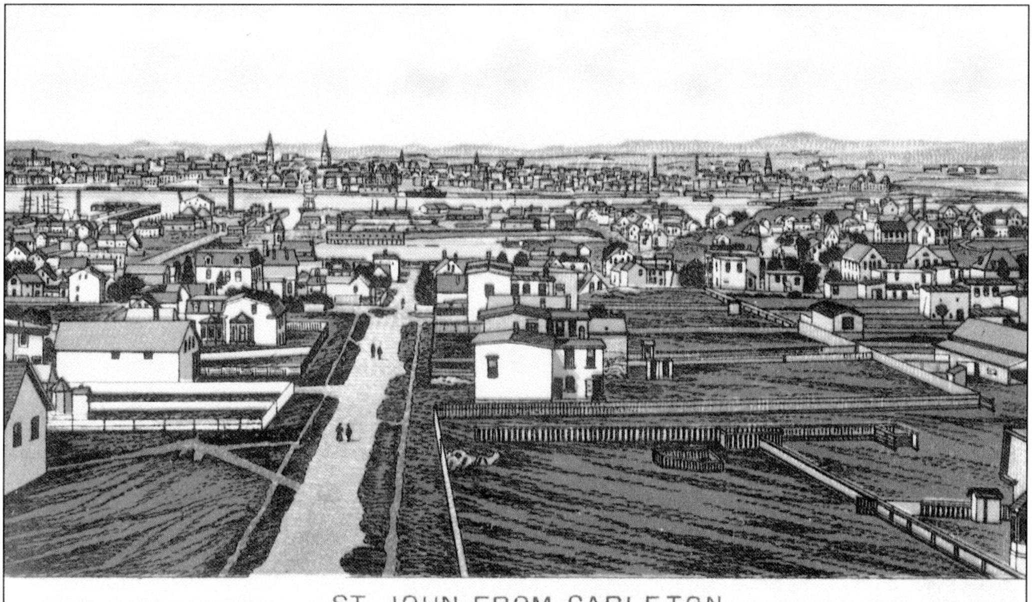

ST. JOHN, FROM CARLETON.

This sketch is titled "Saint John from Carleton," but it might be better titled, "Carleton from Tower Hill," as it depicts Martello Road and Tower Street and the Millpond of Saint John West much more prominently than the streets of the centre of Saint John, which are across the half-mile-wide harbour.

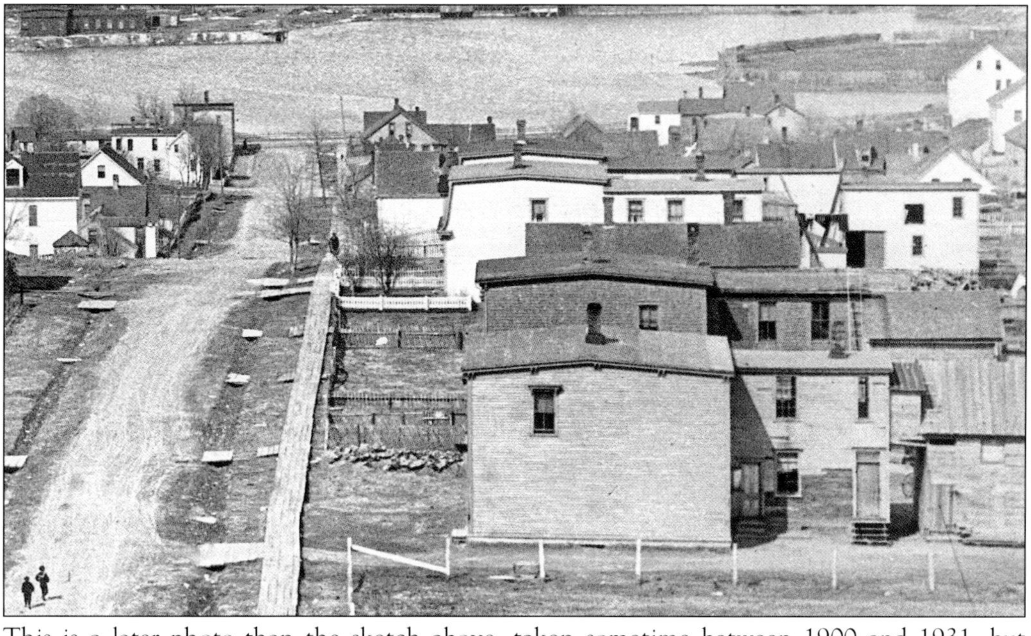

This is a later photo than the sketch above, taken sometime between 1900 and 1931, but again it features Martello Road leading down to the edge of the Millpond. Note the board sidewalks. Some of the Maritime vernacular-style and mansard-roofed-style houses still stand in 1999. Just beyond the Millpond was the wooden Immigration Building through which many new Canadians passed before the Second World War. Its brick replacement still stands, but immigrants do not use it as they no longer arrive by ship.

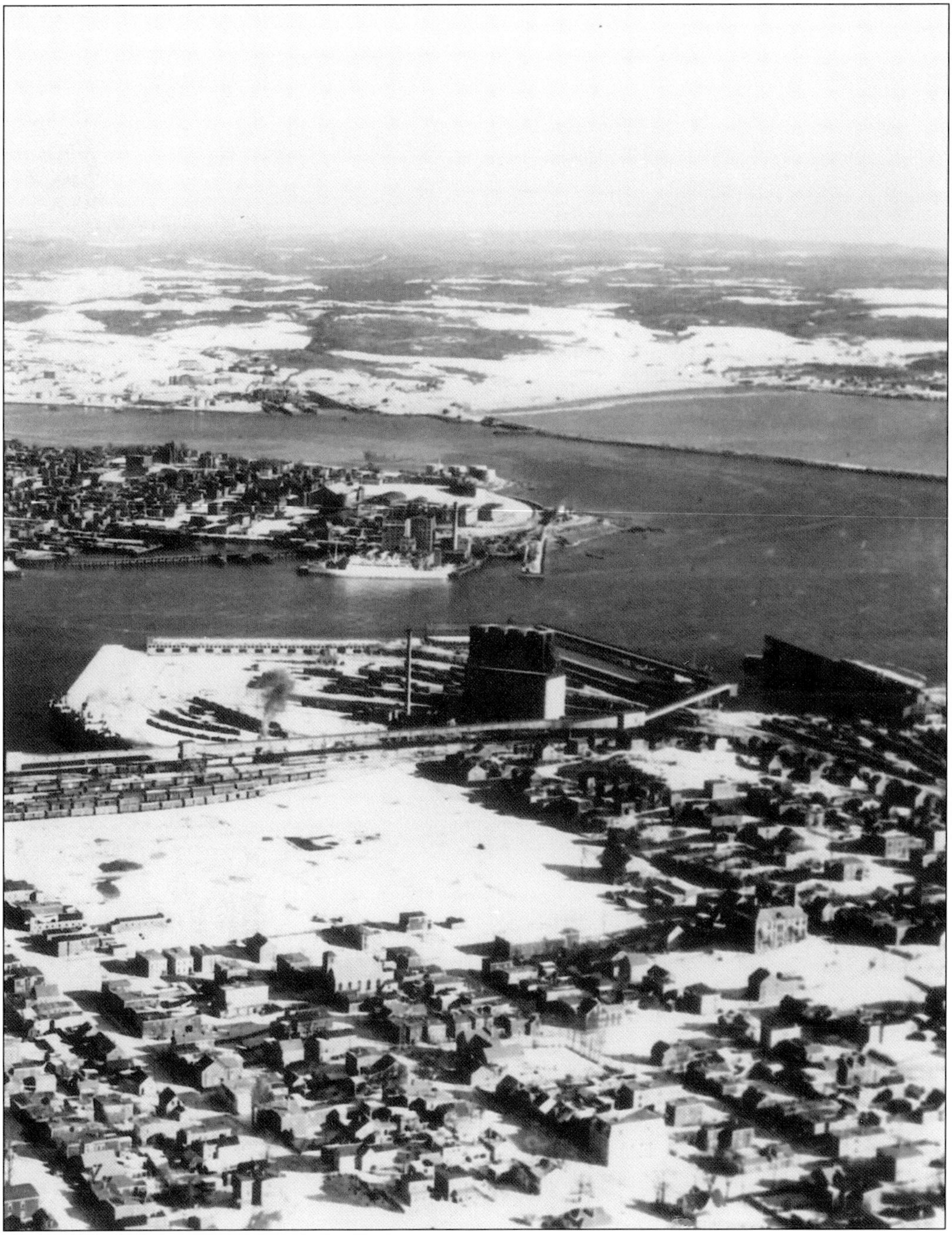

This aerial picture was taken over Martello Tower shortly after the Millpond was filled in as part of the Port redevelopment from 1927 to 1934. In the foreground of the picture is the area known as "Beaconsfield," spoken of in the introduction. Below that is Brooks Ward of Saint John West. Across the harbour in the middle cluster is the South End of Saint John, and on the horizon is Courtenay Bay and Crouchville, now Saint John East.

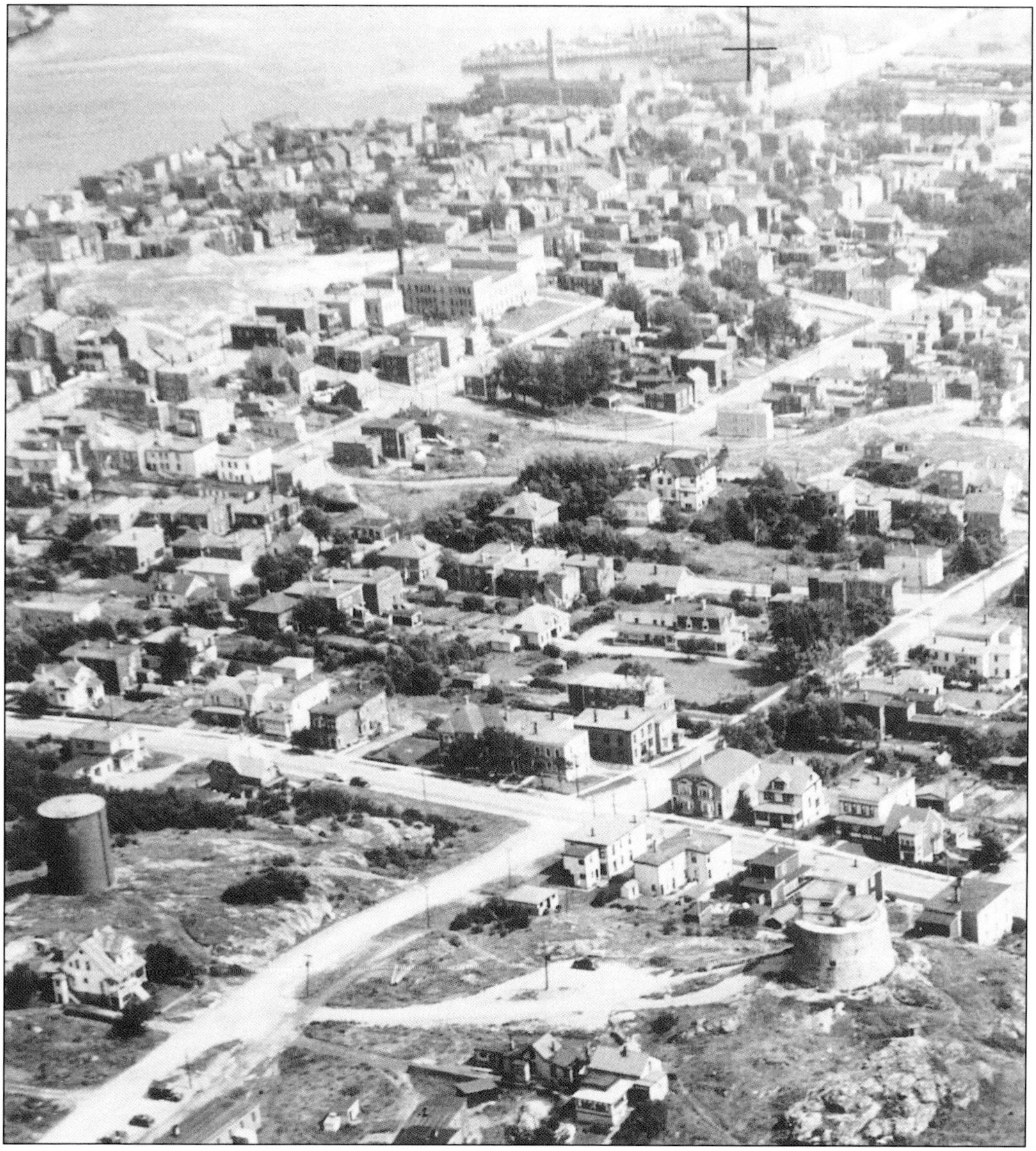

Again we're over Martello Tower but swung in the opposite direction overlooking Guys Ward. This Second World War-era photo shows Martello Tower prominently with the fortifications that were added during that era. To its left is an Army hut, one of many at locations like Fort Dufferin, Courtenay Hill, Winslow Street, and lower St. John Street that served as temporary living and work quarters in this era.

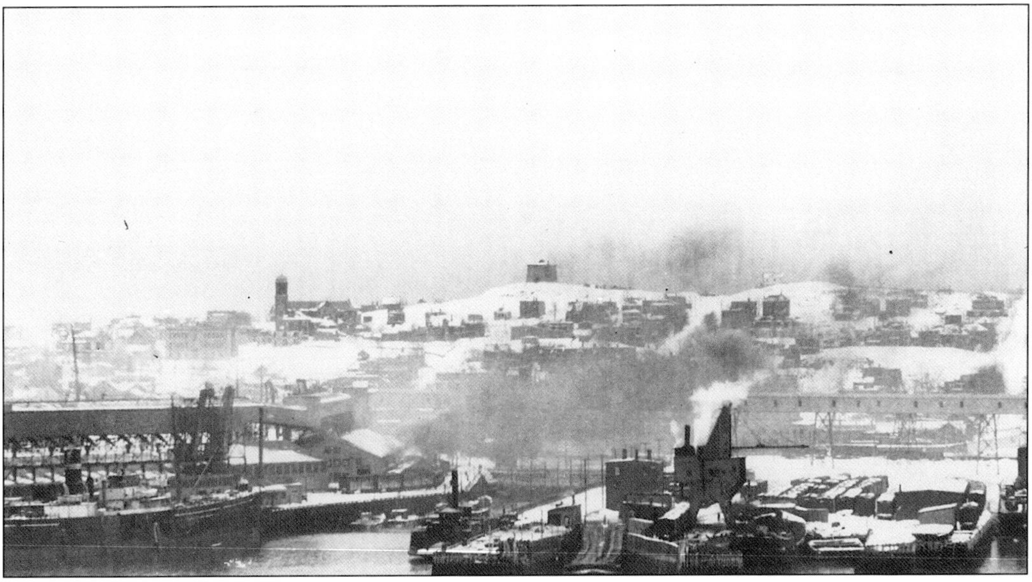

Now we reverse the shot of Saint John West with an aerial view from over the harbour looking back at Martello Tower to Brooks Ward on the left and Guys Ward on the right. We look up the mouth of the ferry terminal at Rodney Slip with the cluster of houses being the reverse view of page 10. Older maps refer to the area as Albert Ward, a designation that disappeared with numbering of the wards.

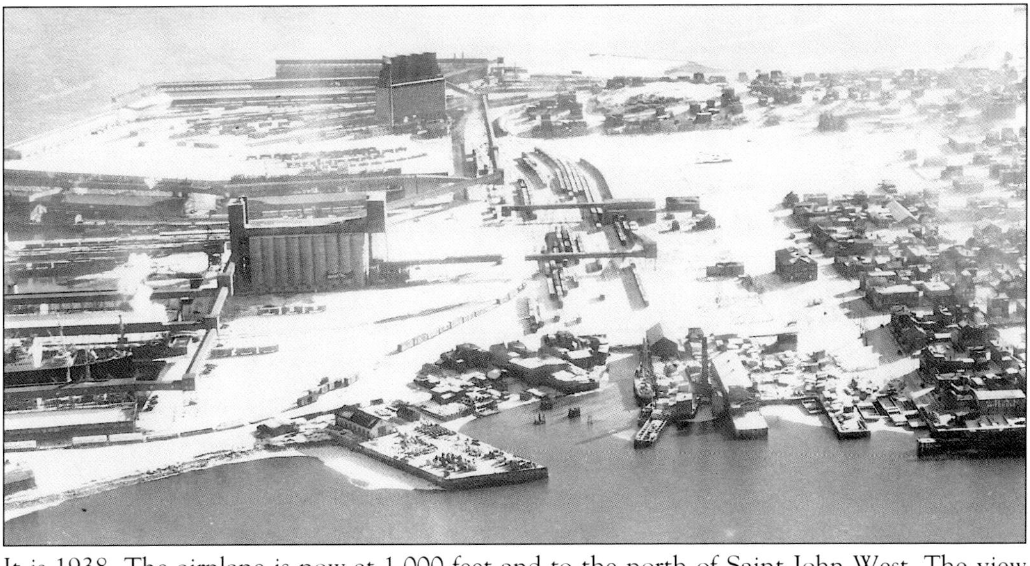

It is 1938. The airplane is now at 1,000 feet and to the north of Saint John West. The view shows the Carleton Public Hall of 1863, which was the only major building that survived destruction of Lower King and Union Streets when the port was redeveloped. It stands in sharp contrast to the barrenness on the north edge of the Millpond, which, after it settled, would be laid with track and dotted with houses as part of the redevelopment.

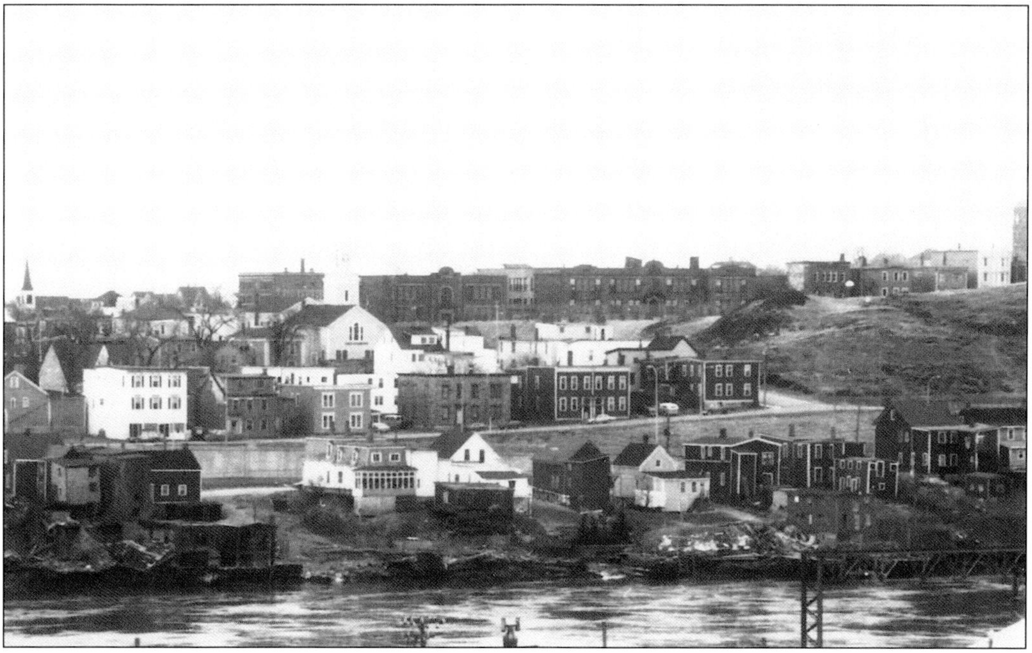

From the hills of Douglas Avenue looking south we have a view of Saint John West in 1970. The throughway (Highway #1) has been partially opened to traffic. The photo shows Prince Street, Courtenay Hill, the New Albert School, and three West Side churches including St. Jude's spire to the left, octagonal St. George's tower in the centre, and the Byzantine cap of Assumption on the far right. All suffered a loss of parishioners, but none as much as St. George's in the heart of the highway changes and loss of 80 properties.

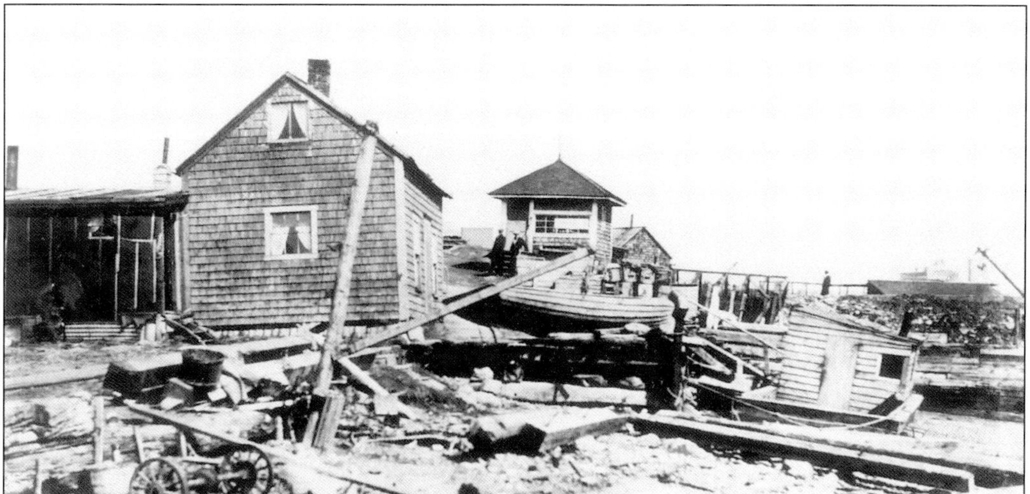

One of the landmarks of the West Side that disappeared and has been forgotten by many was Navy Island, which was separated from the mainland by Buttermilk Channel at the foot of King and Middle Streets. It housed a dozen families at one time and had almost as many ghosts until it disappeared as part of the Port redevelopment in the 1930s. It now supports several of the piers of the bridge. See photo on page 93 for one of the piers being built on the island. (Courtesy of Harold Wright.)

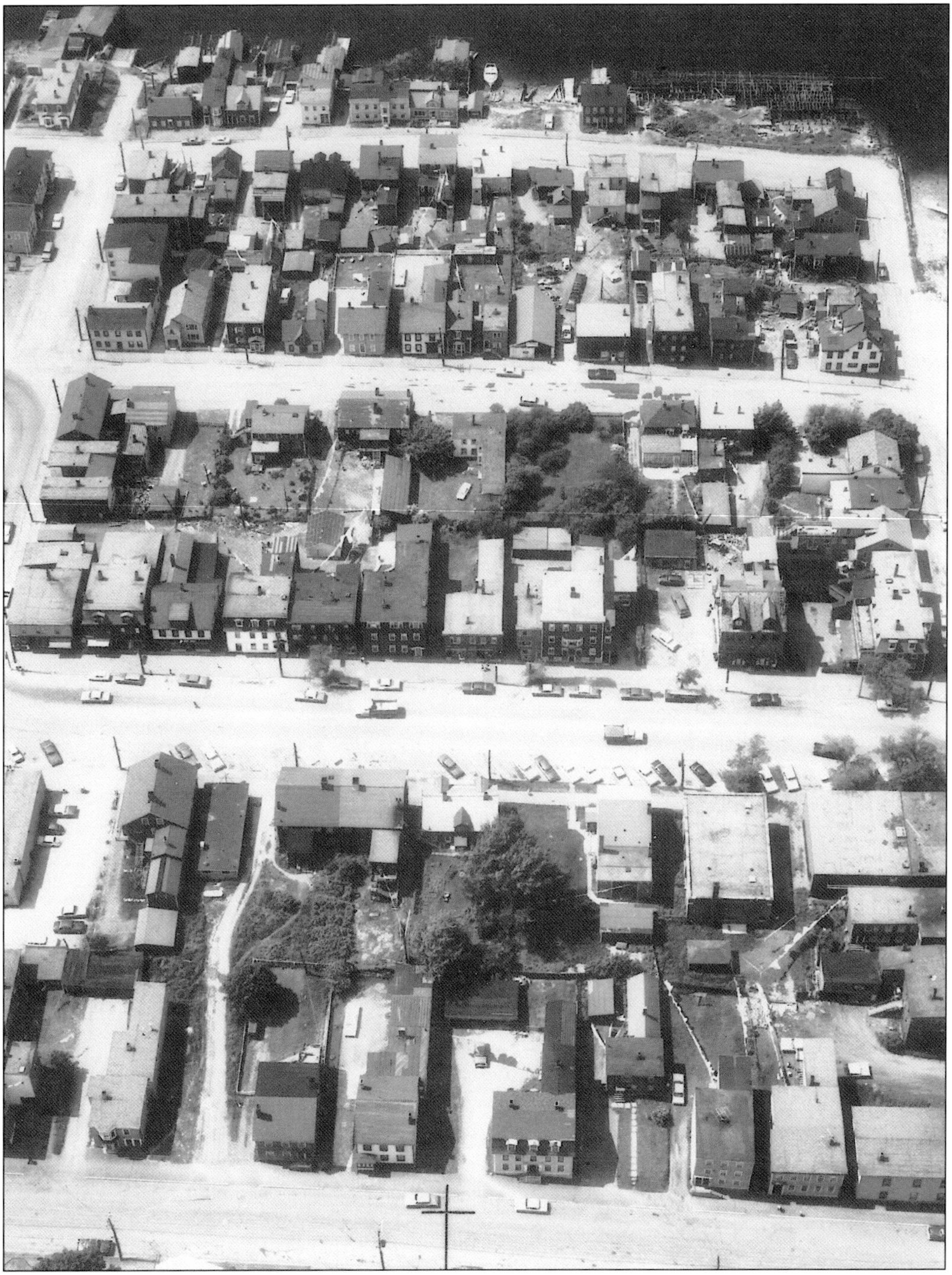

The tightly clustered wooden buildings of Saint John West are clearly seen in this aerial photo taken around 1966. The border of the picture is formed by Ludlow Street to the left, Duke Street at the bottom, Market Place at right, and by Riverview Drive at the top. From 1932 till 1960 this scene would have changed little, but, with the building of the throughway, the demolition of the top third of the structures pictured here occurred.

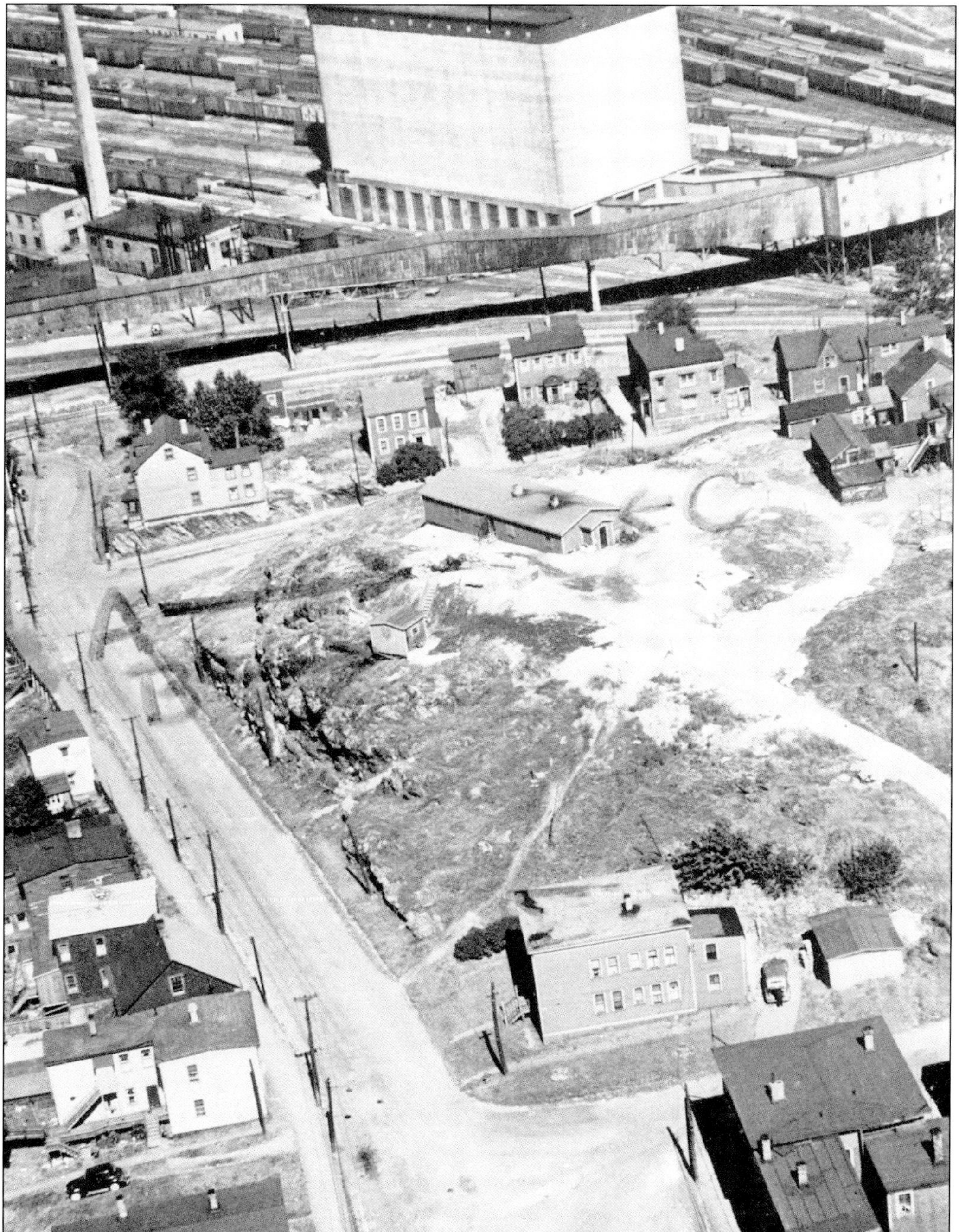

Blue Rock Hill is one of four outcrops that provide great vantage points of Saint John West. It is shown here in an aerial view from 300 feet, on May 9, 1943, at 2:58 p.m. For the remaining photos we will rely on buildings or hills for our vantage points, and local photographers for our pictures. The building labeled "C" is Army property—later converted to three apartments.

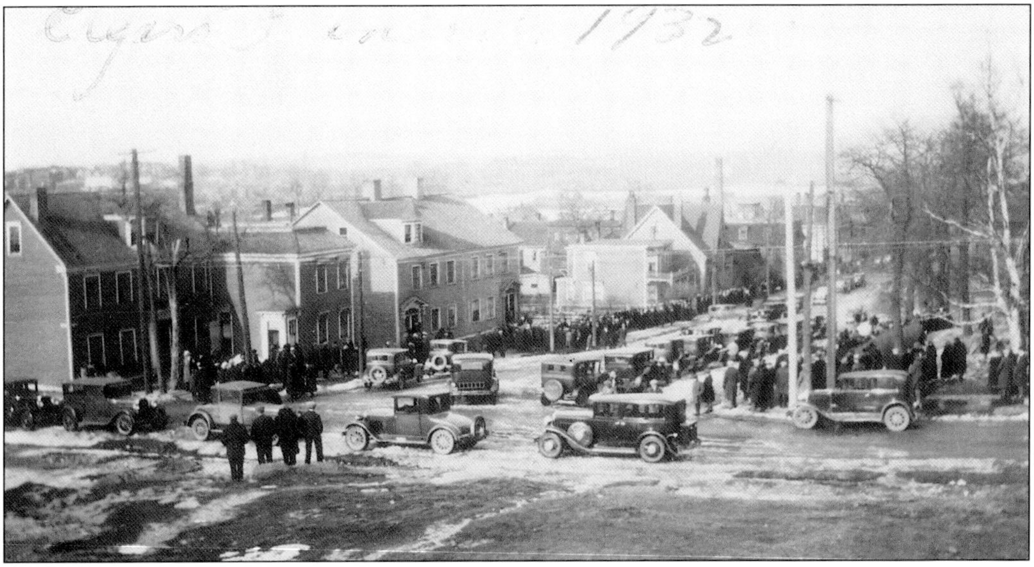

Here are two photos taken from the heights of Courtenay Hill on Duke at Watson. Edgar Carvell's funeral on March 7, 1932, is pictured above as the mourners move up King Street to pay their respect. Carvell was a fireman who lived at 331 King Street and served at #6 station, immediately across the street. He contracted pneumonia and died in a week despite being only 30. His wake was held at the family home. Carvell was a popular member of the community. He had seven sisters and one brother, and he belonged to the Golden Rule Lodge of the Odd Fellows. (Courtesy Gerry Maxwell.)

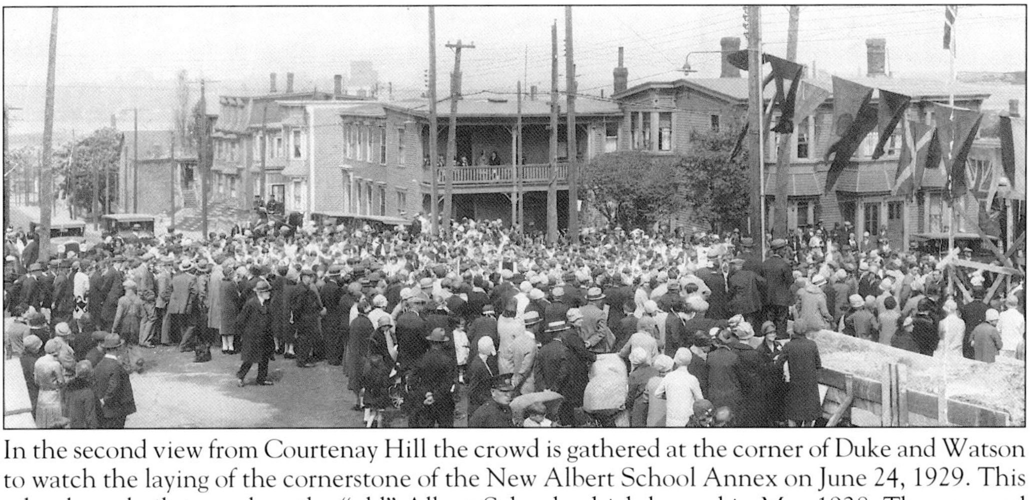

In the second view from Courtenay Hill the crowd is gathered at the corner of Duke and Watson to watch the laying of the cornerstone of the New Albert School Annex on June 24, 1929. This school was built to replace the "old" Albert School, which burned in May 1928. The new and old schools were torn down in 1999. (Courtesy New Albert School Archives.)

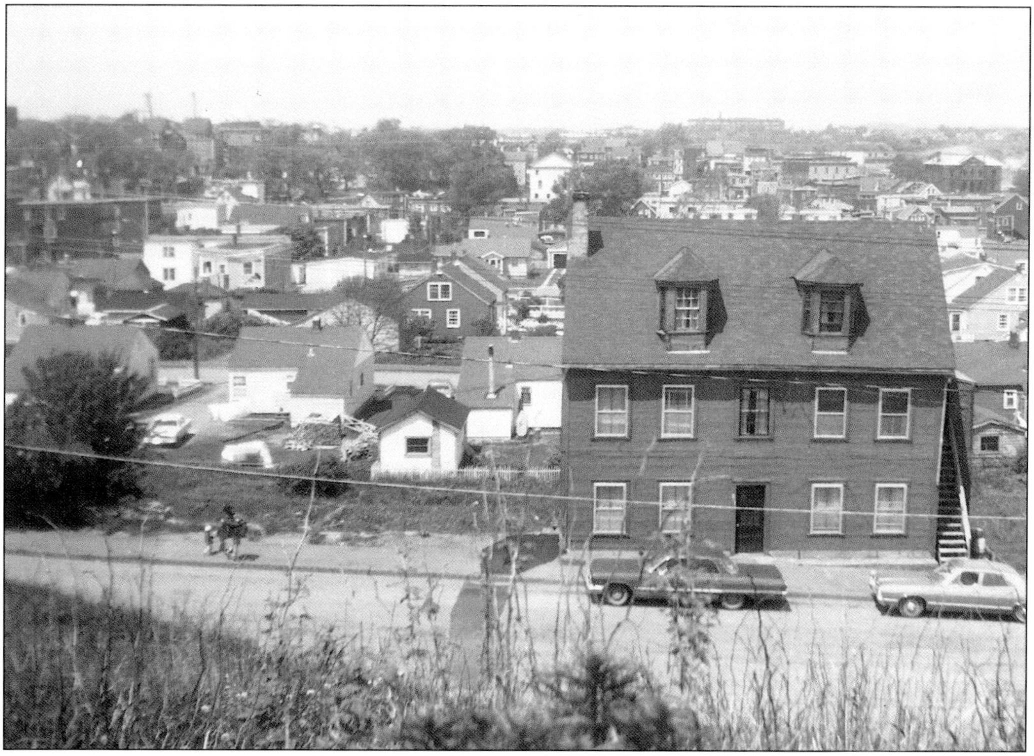

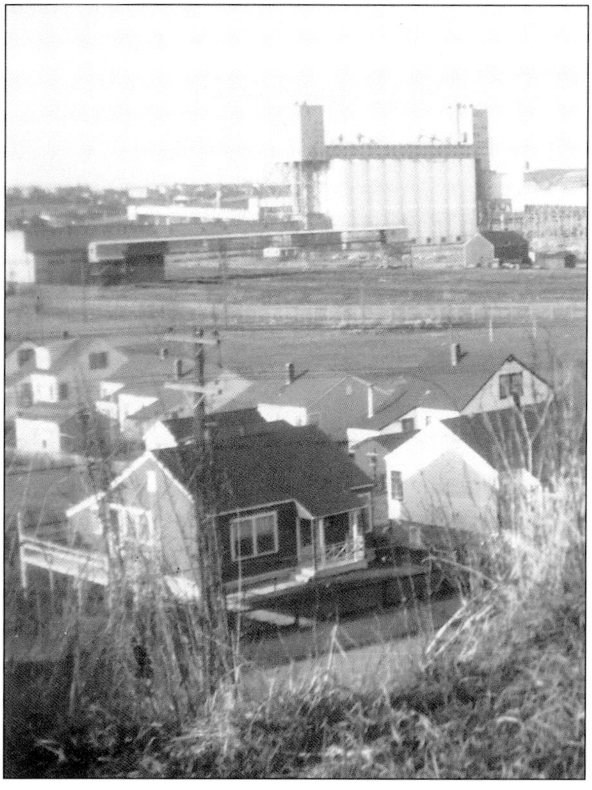

The so called "Red Onion," the home pictured above, is a mock Georgian-style home built on the edge of the Millpond by a local workman who copied the style from grander homes in the centre of Saint John. It is one of the oldest and biggest homes of the area and contrasts sharply in age and style to the bungalows built in the Millpond in 1946 (lower photo) to assist resettlement of returning veterans. Both these photos were taken from the other major hill in Saint John, which was Blue Rock. See the aerial view of the hill in the photo on page 16.

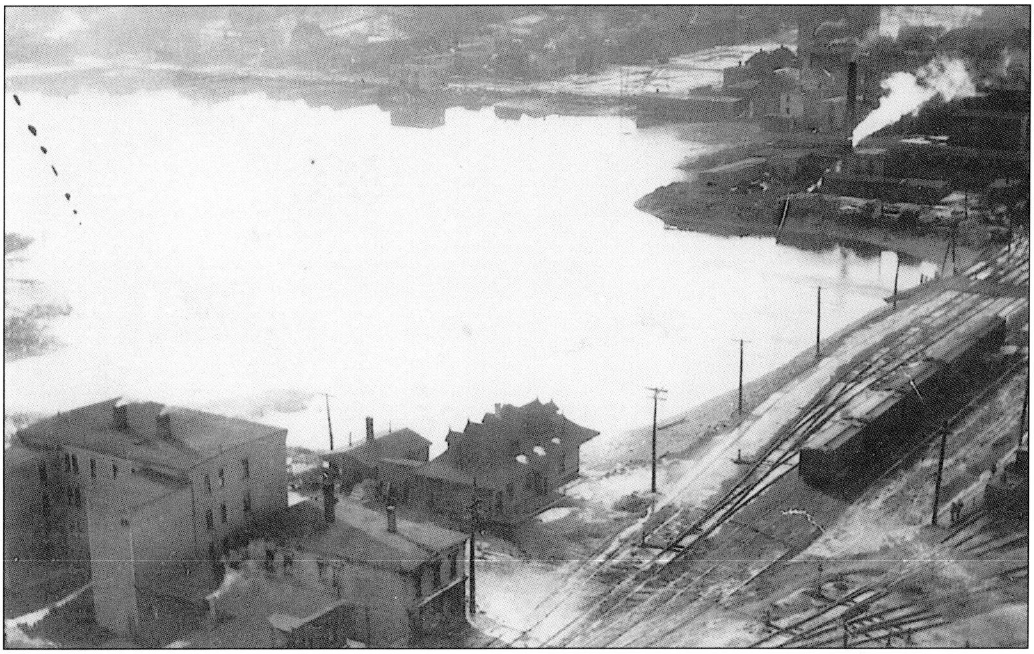

On the Sand Point Wharf, west of the Blue Rock Hill, the first Canadian Pacific wooden grain elevator was built in 1896. It provided the vantage point in 1919 for this shot of the Millpond with the CP Steamship Office (note the traditional Chateau-style roofline they used from sea to sea) on its shoreline. On the corner of St. John and Union Streets is Percy Barnes's store just to the left of the steamship office.

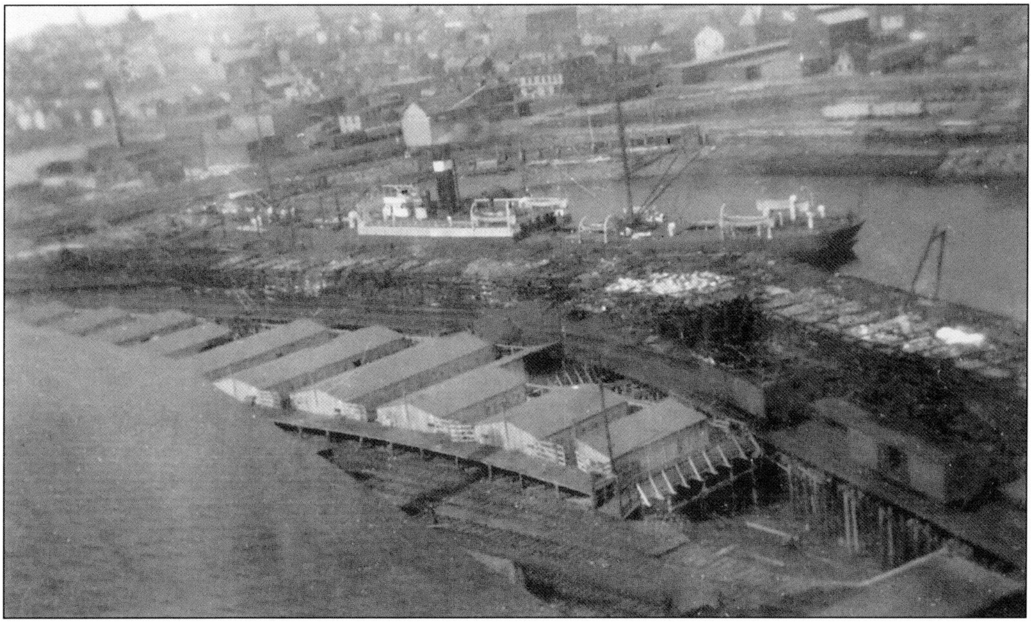

It is believed Cecil E.R. Strange used the same vantage point from atop the grain elevator to picture the ten cattle sheds adjacent to Sand Point slip. Horses and cattle were one of the more unusual cargoes that moved through the port until the mid-1950s. For a closeup view of the horses, and those who worked with them, see page 80. (Courtesy Robert Taylor.)

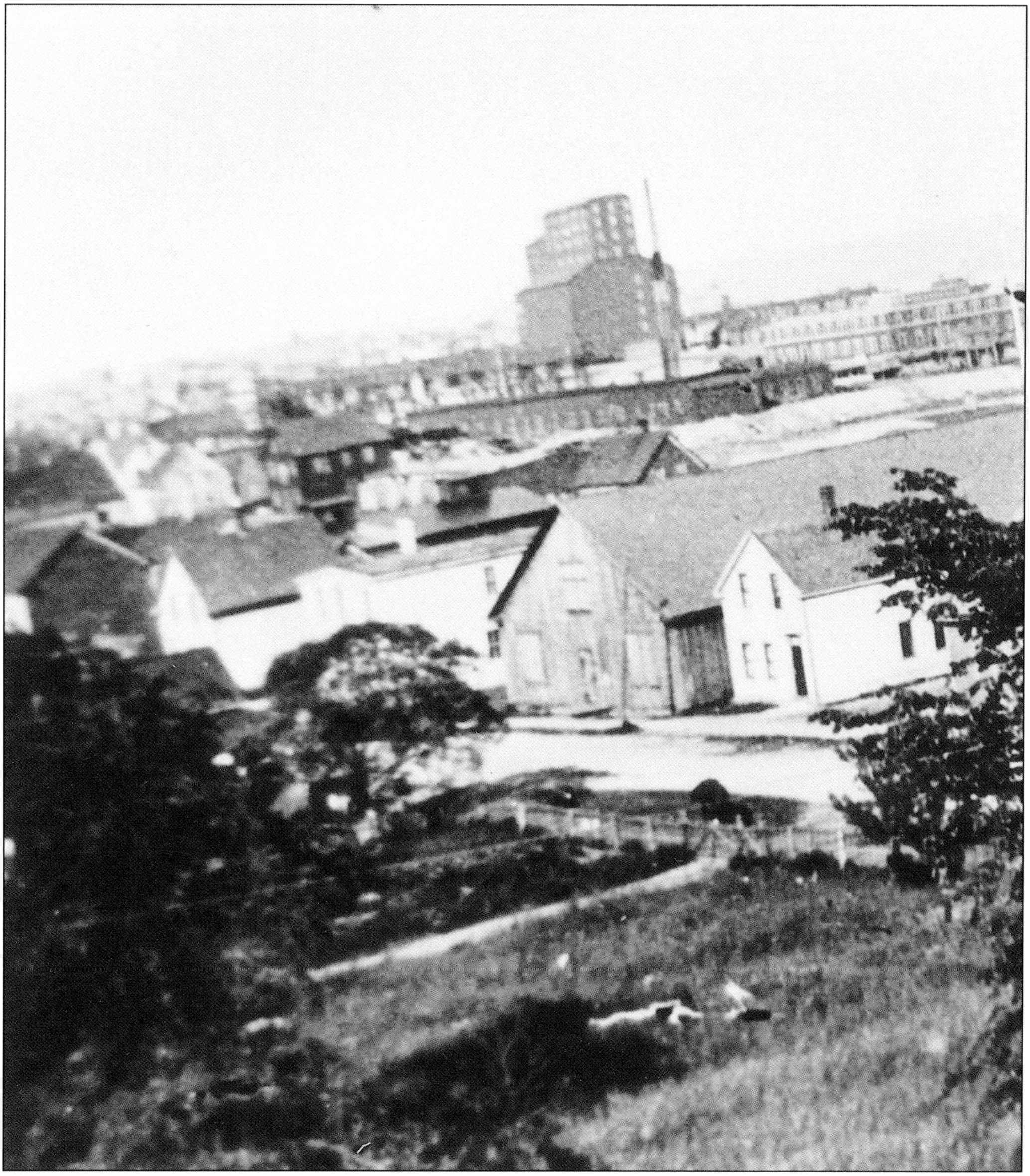

Strange also took this shot, which, in the background, shows the grain elevator he'd used for the previous photo. It was taken from his back bedroom window of 156 Guilford Street at Ludlow where he lived. He made his living as an insurance agent, but we're fortunate that, like his neighbour A.V.F. Duffy, who lived just a few blocks south on Ludlow, his avocation was photography. Both left behind many interesting images of Saint John West. This is one of the few we found that showed the curling rink, the second building on Winslow Street. (Courtesy Robert Taylor.)

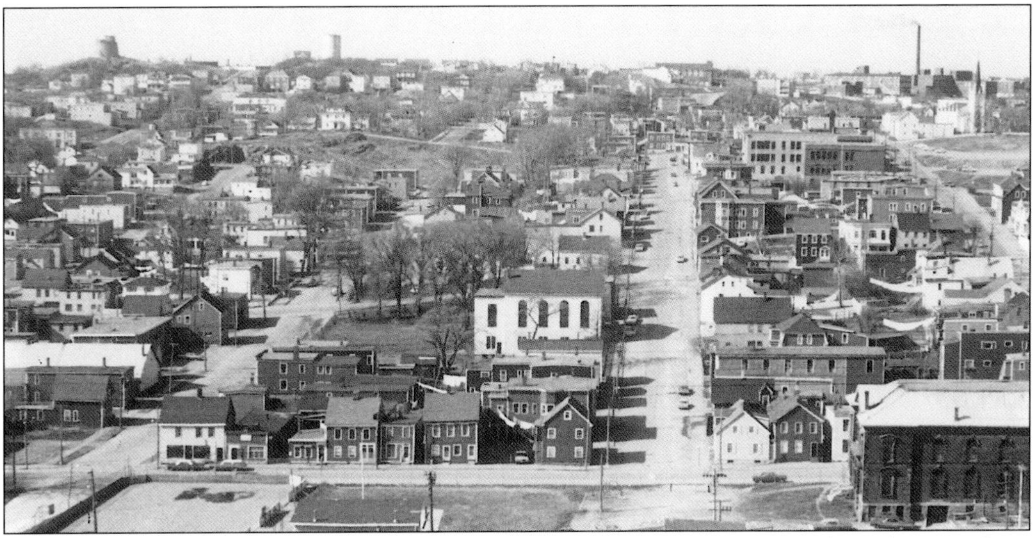

In 1971, Malcolm Somerville was working for the National Harbours Board patching roofs on the grain elevators. The 200-foot-high structure was perfect for a series of photos that would give a panoramic view of his hometown. This one looks directly west and up Guilford Street. Some of the buildings shown have disappeared, including the Carleton Church in the centre, Kirk Church to the right, and the D.V.A. Veteran's Hospital on the upper horizon.

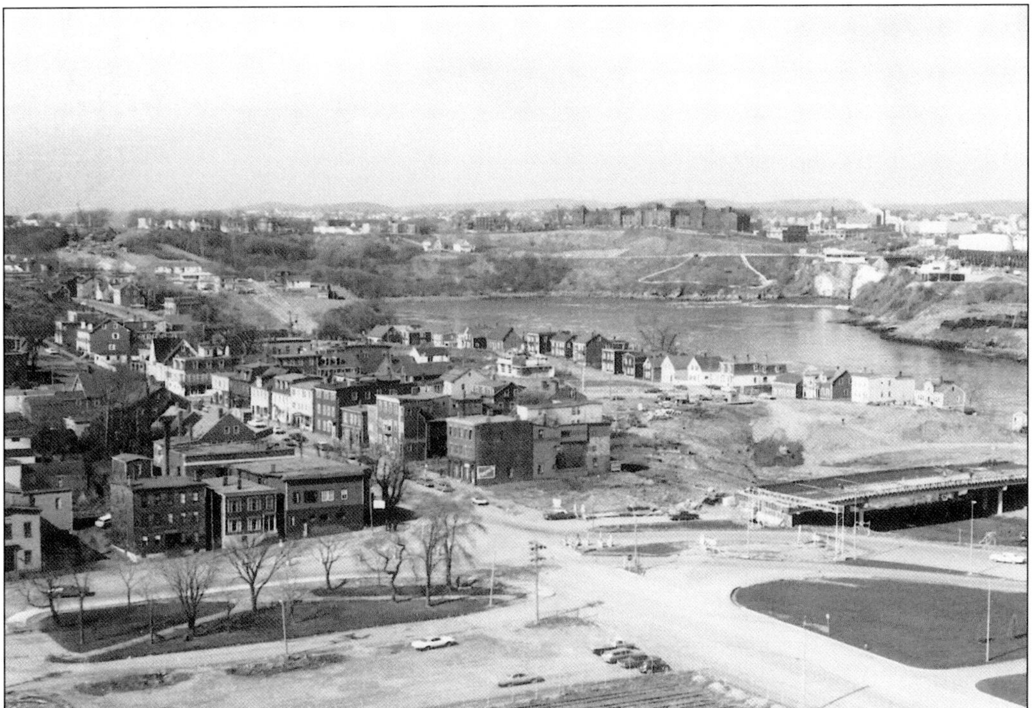

The Harbour Bridge underpass is shown under construction in this second view by Malcolm Somerville. In the lower right corner is the Harbour Bridge entrance, and beside it traffic can be seen headed for the bridge, which was completed in 1968. See page 88 for more of Mr. Somerville's photos from atop the grain elevator.

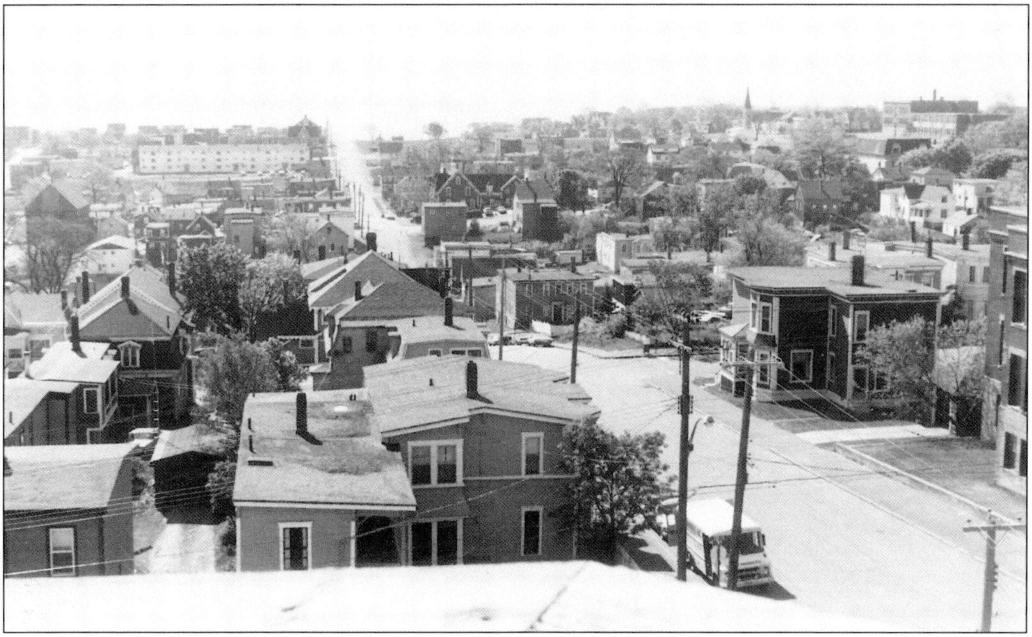

Five years after Malcolm Somerville's trip to the top of the grain elevators, David Goss was atop the octagonal tower of St. George's Church on Watson Street, and he took the two photos on this page. This one is of Watson Street looking towards the south and the Bay of Fundy. Dr. Pendrigh's home at 219 Guilford Street, the last of the West Side resident doctors, is in the immediate right centre beside the New Albert School Annex.

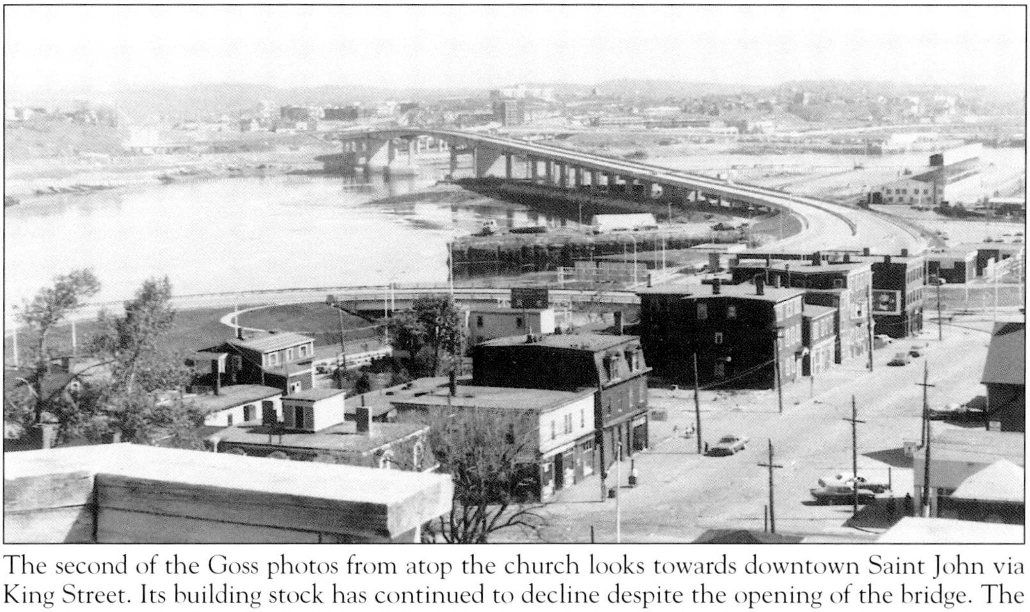

The second of the Goss photos from atop the church looks towards downtown Saint John via King Street. Its building stock has continued to decline despite the opening of the bridge. The growth potential foreseen for Saint John West from the bridge development, such as motels and restaurants, never materialized to any great degree. A Tim Horton Shop, a grocery store (which failed), and four new apartments have been built on the street since the bridge opened to traffic on August 17, 1968. In 1973, the Bank of Nova Scotia moved from 206 King to a new building at 105 Ludlow.

Two

The People of Carleton and Their Work

Most residents of Saint John West found their work within a few blocks of their homes. Many were employed on the railroad or found part-time work at the port. These employers will be featured in a later chapter. In this chapter we will show the many other types of jobs that West Siders had both full time and part time. It is certainly not inclusive, for few workers would have had cameras, and if they did it was unlikely there was time in the 60-hour work week to take photos.

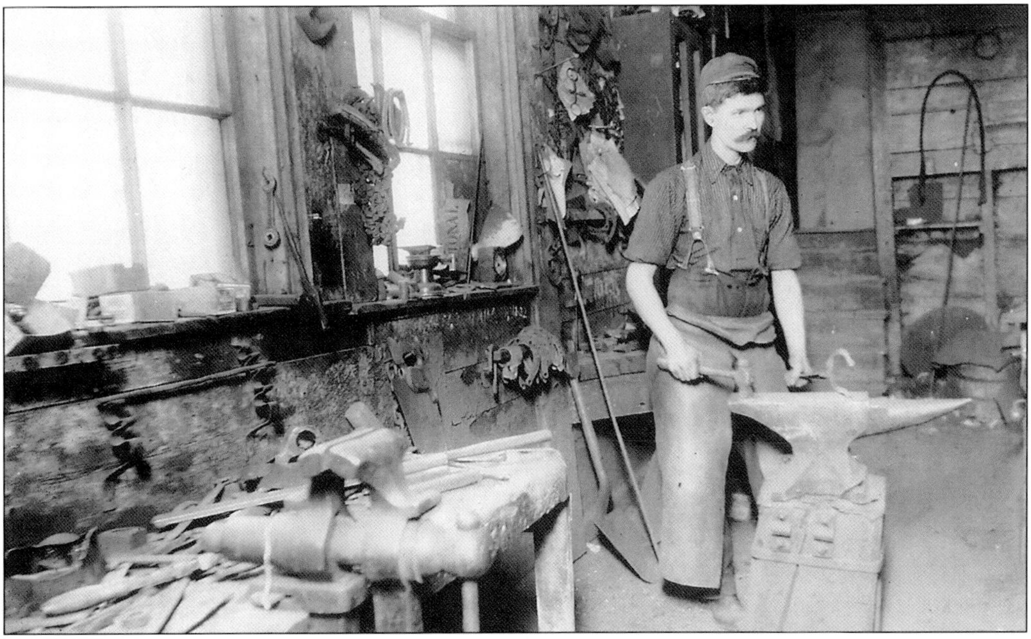

Blacksmith James Trainor worked at the Union Foundry, and his wages in the early part of the century would have been $2 per day. That would have been sufficient to take care of what was normally a family of six or more. (Courtesy of Harold Wright.)

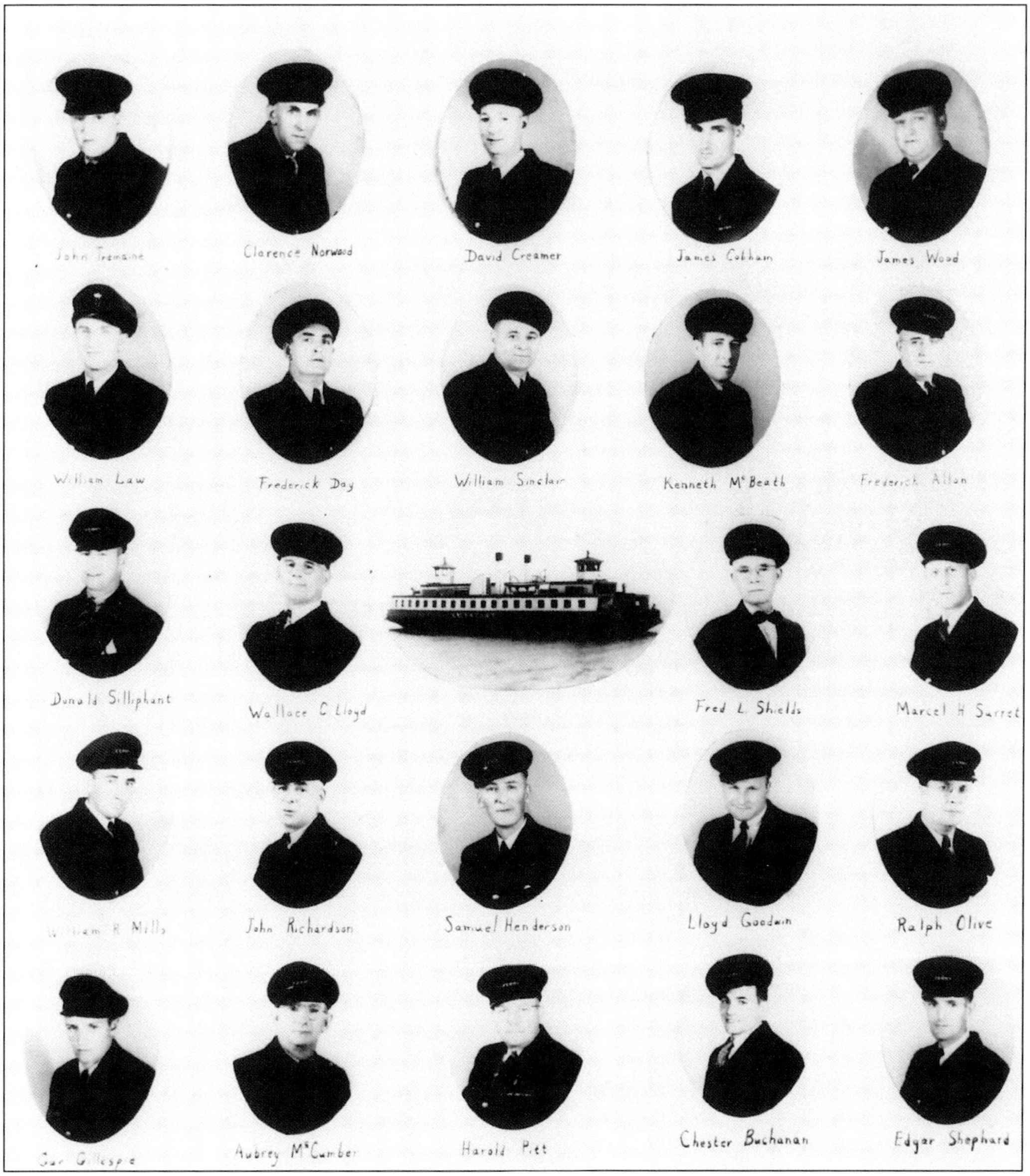

These gentlemen were the operators of the ferry *Loyalist*, the last ferry to serve the people of Carleton. Ferry service was promised when the city was set up in 1785 and first consisted of row boats across the harbour. By 1839, the first of the larger ferries was put in place for the growing number of foot passengers, and then still larger ferries for passengers and automobiles were put into service. The *Victoria* was the 1839 ferry, then the *Lady Colebrook* in 1841, the *Prince of Wales* in 1860, the *Ouangondy* in 1870, the *Western Extension*, also about 1870, the *Ludlow* in 1905, along with *Governor Carleton* (1905–1911), and the final ferry, the *Loyalist* in 1933, until service ended on June 30, 1953.

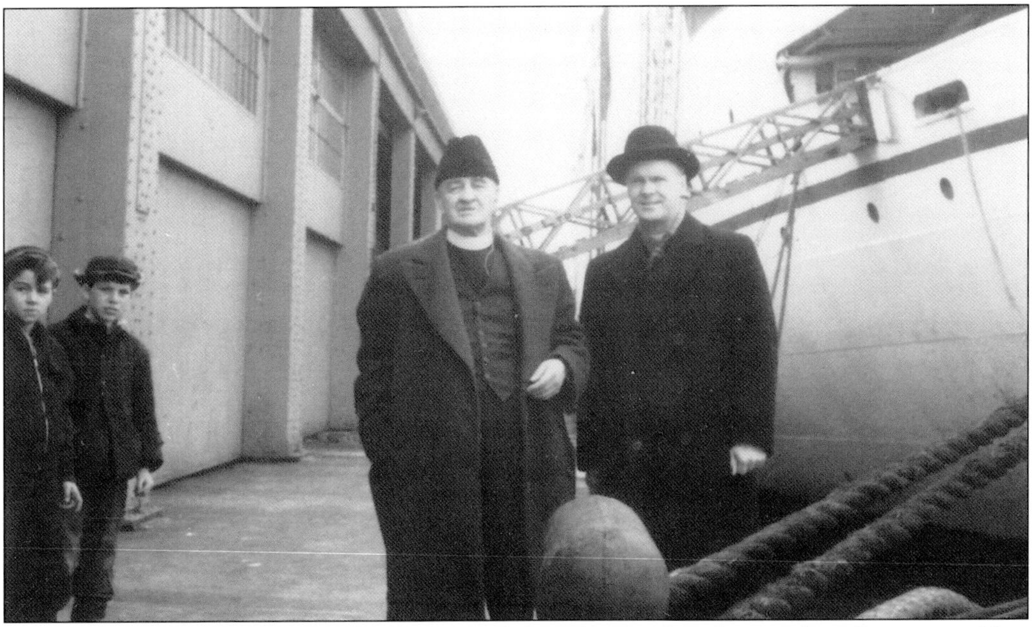

Above, Canon Haigh, with collar, emigrated from England and arrived in Gagetown, New Brunswick, before settling in Saint John as the Rector of St. George's Church in 1932. He served the parish and the community tirelessly until 1966. As an emigrant, he was particularly interested in visiting the seamen, and counselled them regularly. He would also be called for prayers if there was an accident at the port, a frequent occurrence among those who worked with slings, as shown below in the hold of the ship.

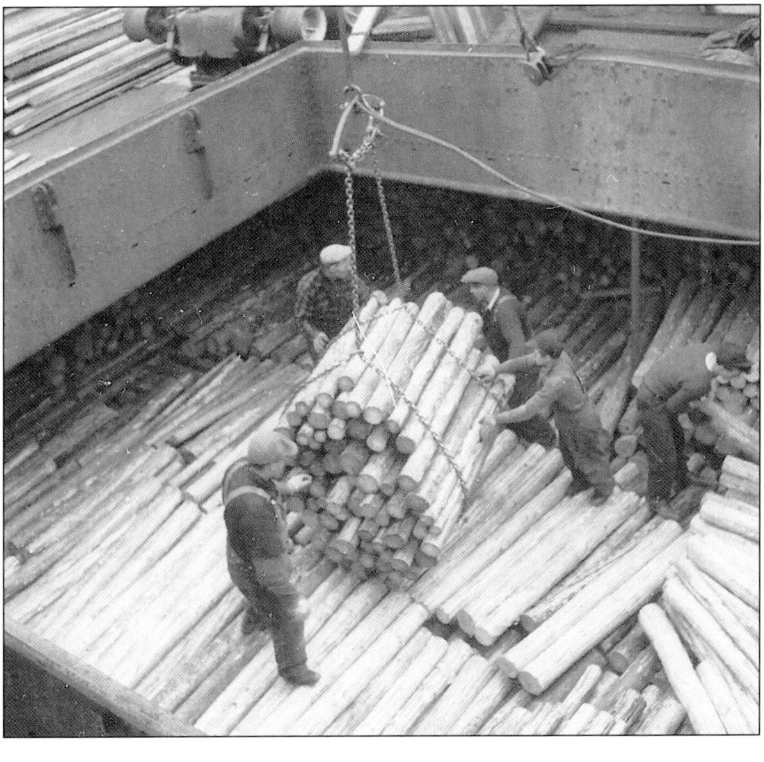

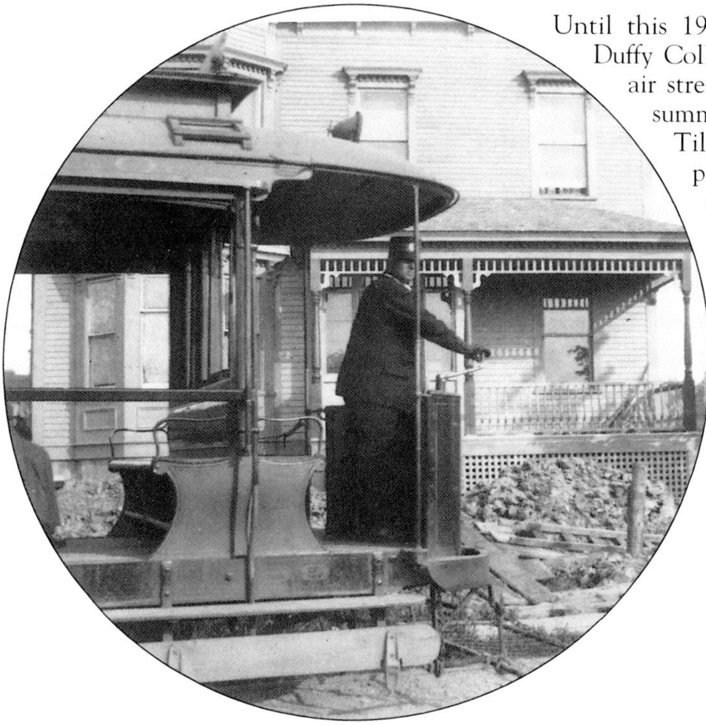

Until this 1911 photo was found in the Duffy Collection, it was believed open air streetcars were only used on the summer route to Seaside Park from Tilton's Corner, to the 13-acre park the company developed and ran from 1904 to 1920. However, John Vincent Kelly, pictured here, guiding his car up Tower Street, shows that this was not the case. (Courtesy A.V.F. Duffy.)

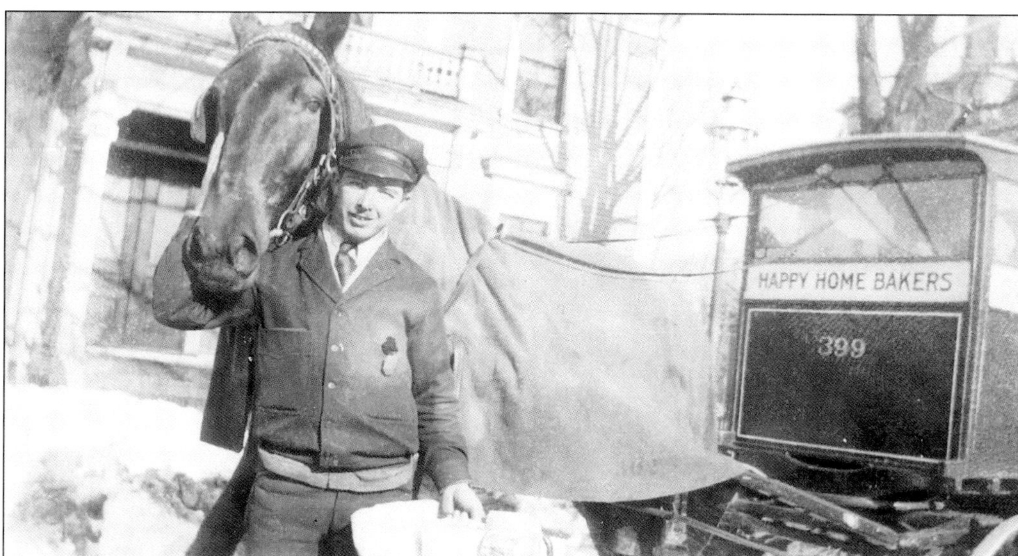

Gerry Maxwell found this photo among many other Saint John images, although no record of this bakery and no home exactly duplicating the background in this picture can be found. It is assumed it is in the West Side, but if not, it still accurately portrays those whose jobs were in the field of delivering goods, such as baked goods, milk products, ice, and wood, or who carried off junk, ashes, or garbage. (Courtesy Gerry Maxwell.)

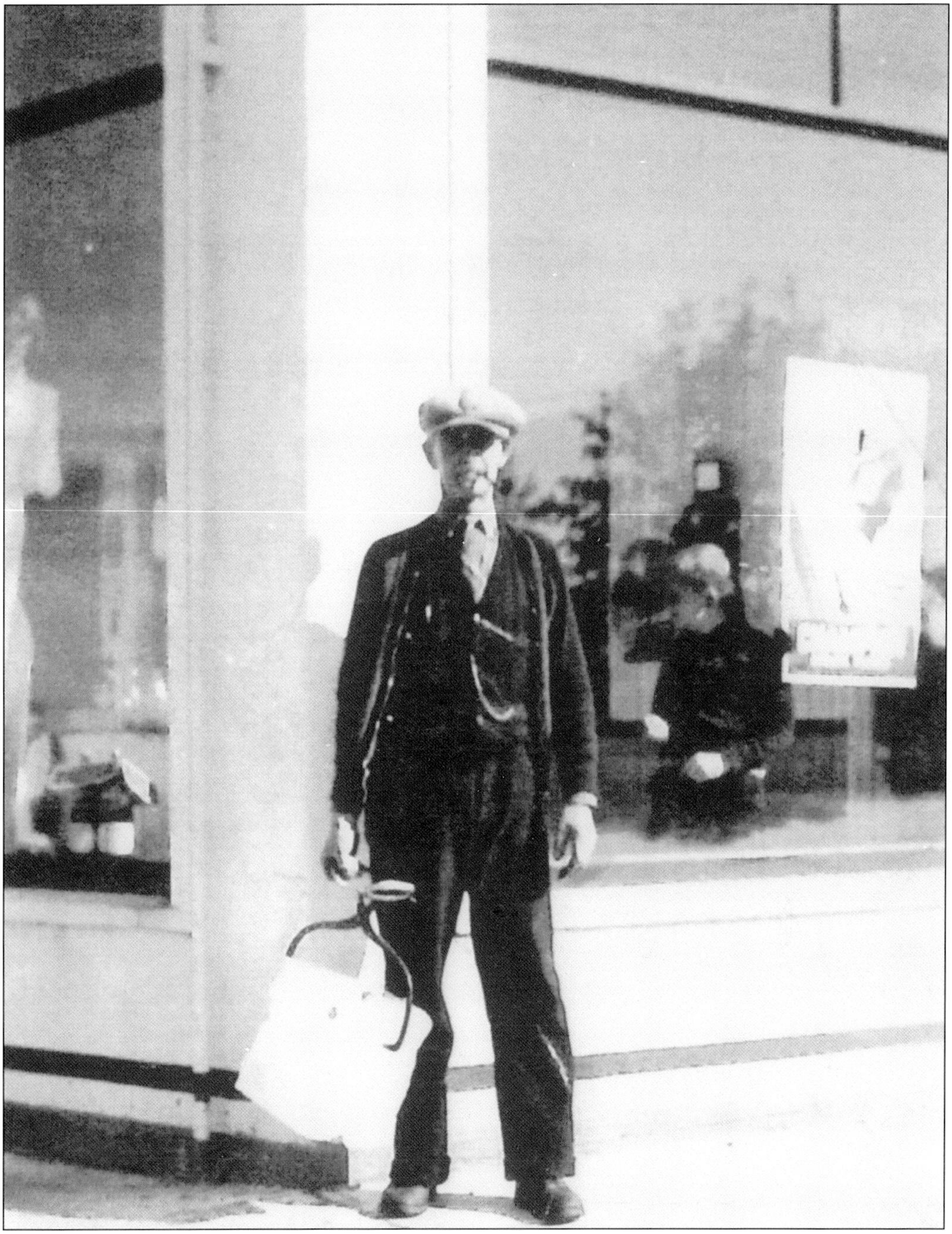

Samuel McAllister, the iceman, has his ice tongs firmly entrenched in what seems to be a 50-pound block of ice outside Stout's Store, on the corner of King and Ludlow Streets. Ice came in three sizes—home, store (as shown), or business, and cost 25 to 50¢ a block. Prior to the 1950s most of the ice for Saint John West was harvested and then stored in sheds at Spruce Lake, 6 miles from the city. The railway used tons of ice, which they crushed and dumped in reefer cars in order to keep meat and vegetables fresh when they left the refrigerated ships and moved across the country to western markets.

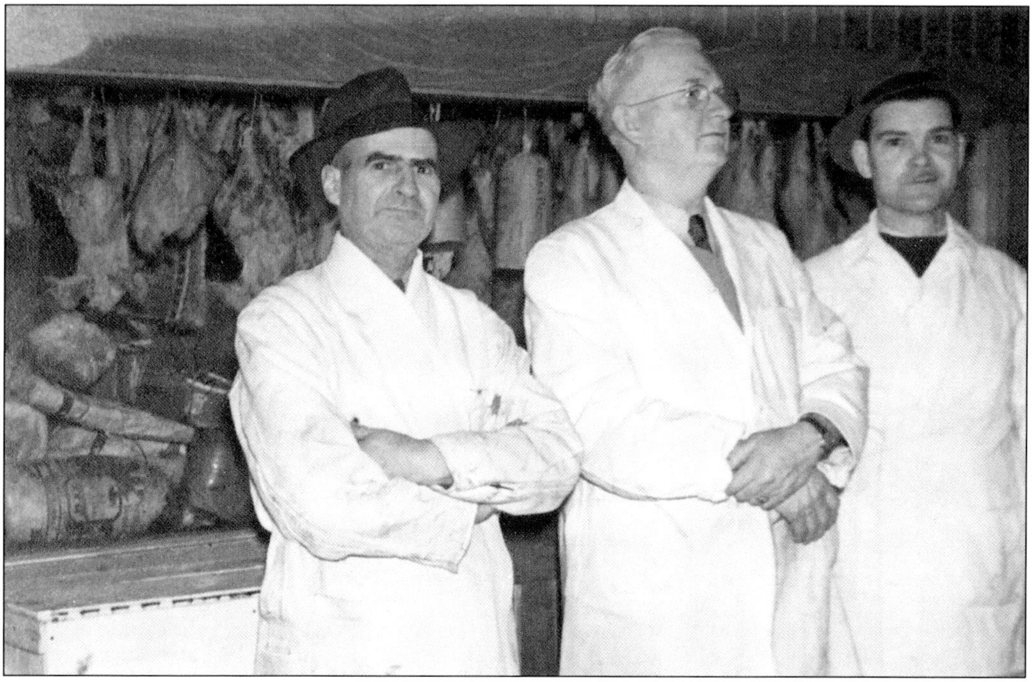

Above we have three meat-cutters at T. Donovan and Son's Store at 203 Queen Street. From left to right are, Tommy McCarthy, Leo McGiggan, and Bill McCaully. Donovan's did a large trade in provisioning ships at the port and was so well known that this photo appeared as a postcard. Barb Huskins loaned it to us. Below is Lillian and George Geary, who operated a grocery and meat store on the corner of St. John and Ludlow Streets. Typical of many families, they worked long hours only to see shopping patterns change and erode their business. They retired in October 1980. (Courtesy Art Geary.)

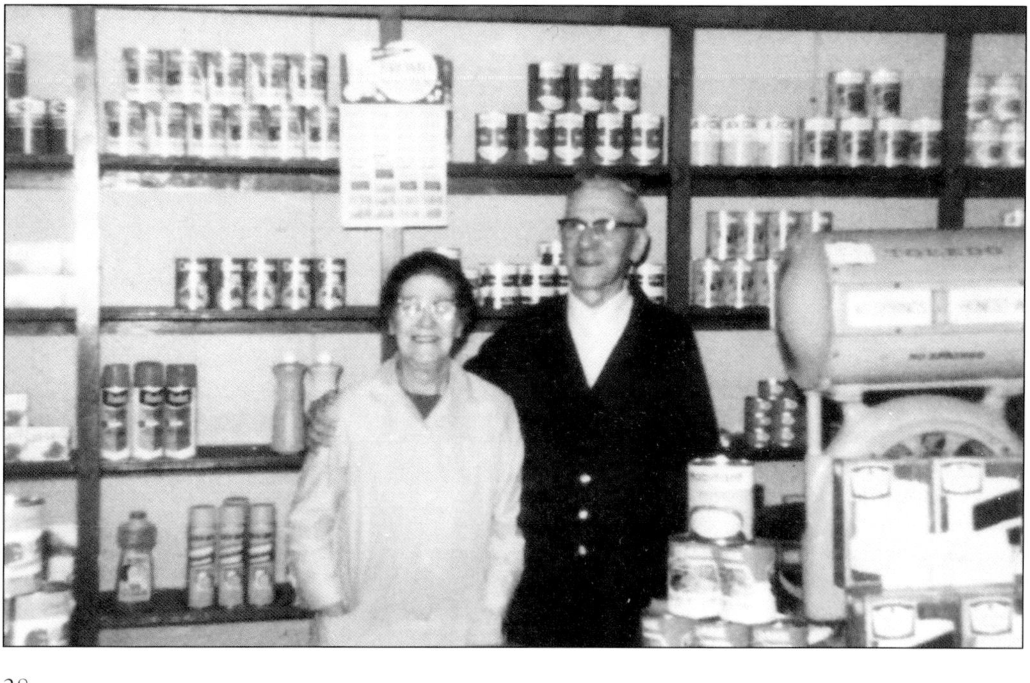

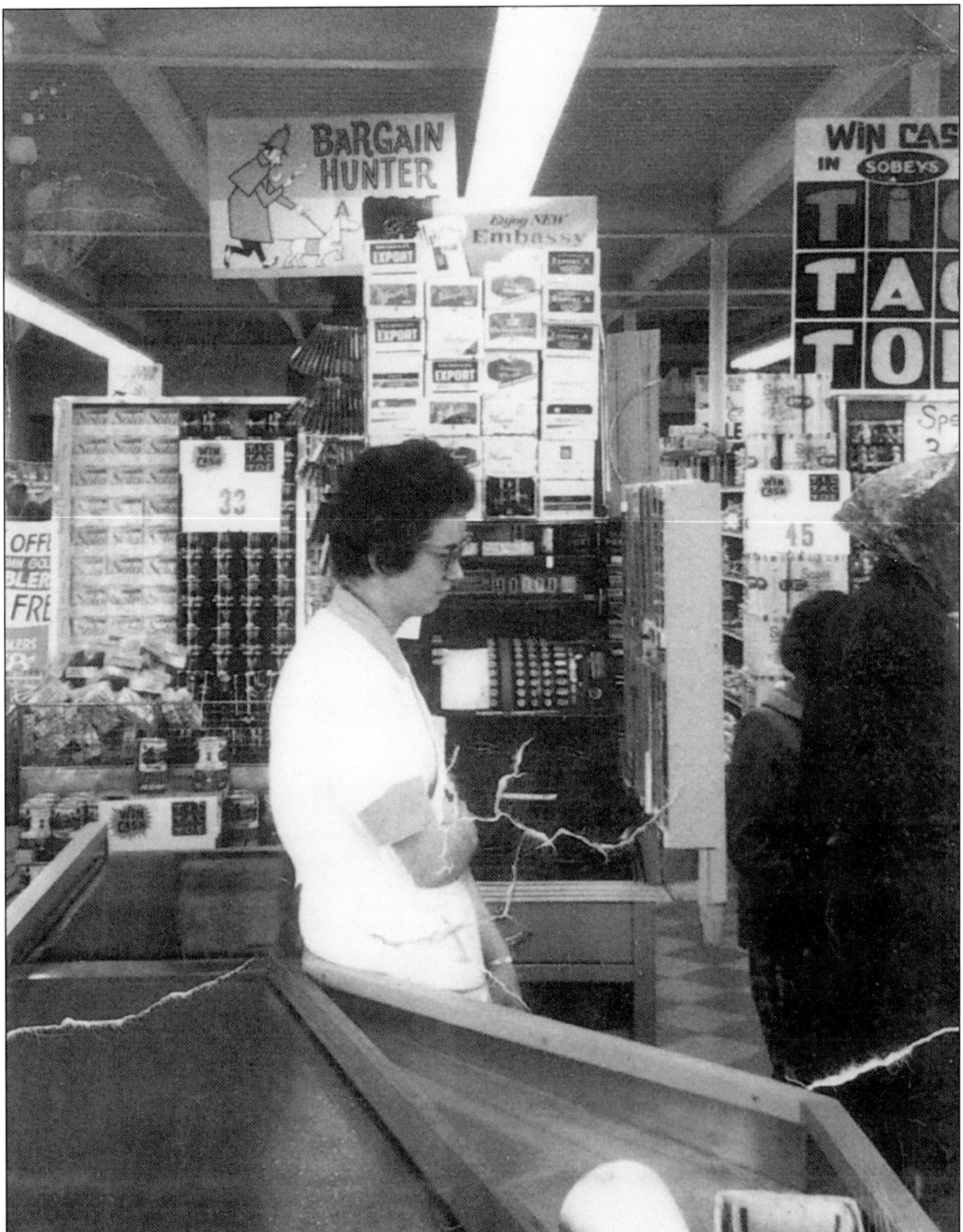

In 1962 the Sobeys chain opened the first modern supermarket on the site of the former Ludlow Street Baptist Church, corner of Duke and Ludlow. West Siders considered it a delight to be brought up to date and to be able to enjoy the latest in shopping methods. The clerks, like Paulette Adams, were delighted too, but jobs Sobeys provided were short-lived, as the evolving supermarket business soon made the relatively small store as uncompetitive as the corner stores it had driven out of business. This store closed in 1974; Paulette went to work at the newly opened K Mart which in turn closed—becoming a Zellers in 1998.

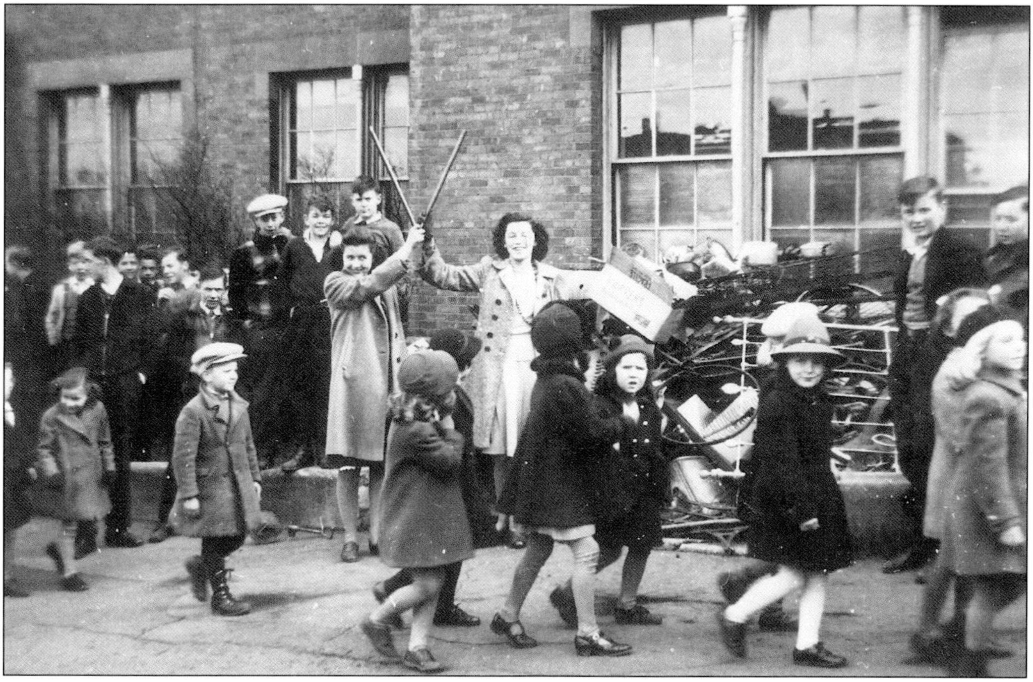

The teaching profession was one of the few steady jobs a woman could hope to attain in Saint John West in the early part of the century and through to the Second World War. When New Albert opened in 1922, 13 of the 14 teachers were female. In this World War II-era photo, two unnamed teachers are enthusiastically urging their pupils to contribute to the pile of scrap to assist the war effort. (Courtesy New Albert School Archives.)

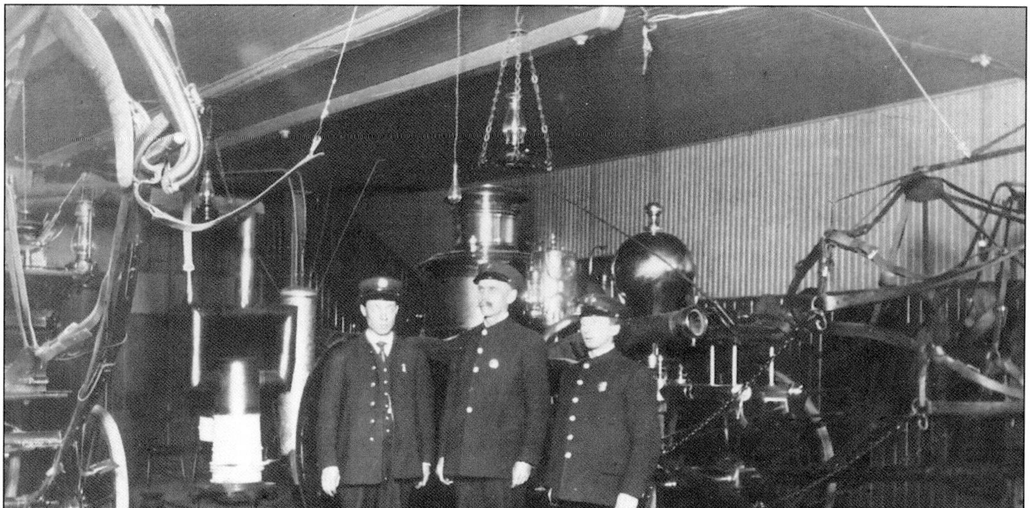

For the men of the community seasonal work was the norm. One exception was to attain a position with the fire department, which maintained a station at 286 King Street. In this 1927 photo, horses are still being used, and the unidentified trio are looking over the harness being suspended from the ceiling. It was designed to drop onto the horses, who were trained to come immediately into the correct position once they heard the fire alarm sound. (Courtesy Gerry Maxwell.)

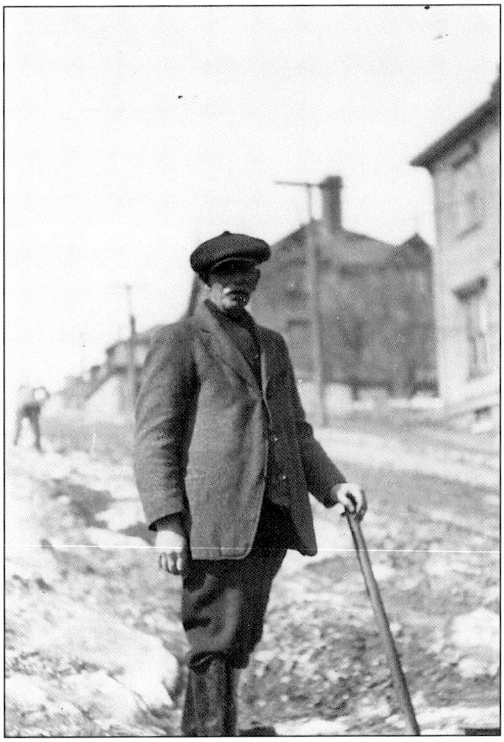

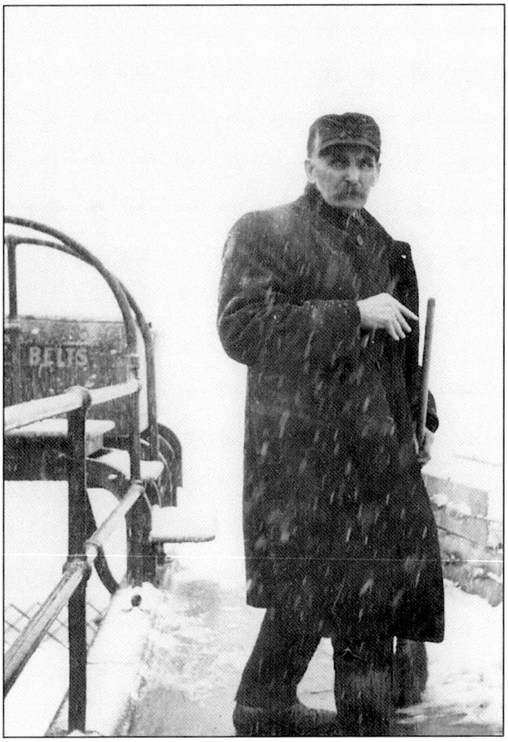

Top left: George Evans is shown digging a ditch on Miller Hill on Watson Street in 1920. At the hilltop (right) is the Peters' House, now the Hammond house, where the first successful Canadian use of ether as an anesthetic occurred on January 18, 1847. *Top right:* Captain Norwood on the ferry float is cleaning the way for his passengers in 1920. (Both courtesy A.V.F. Duffy.) *Bottom:* Three burly railway men, clad in heavy clothing, pose beside the 1914 grain elevator. The author's grandfather, who was section foreman of the Bayshore line, is pictured on the right.

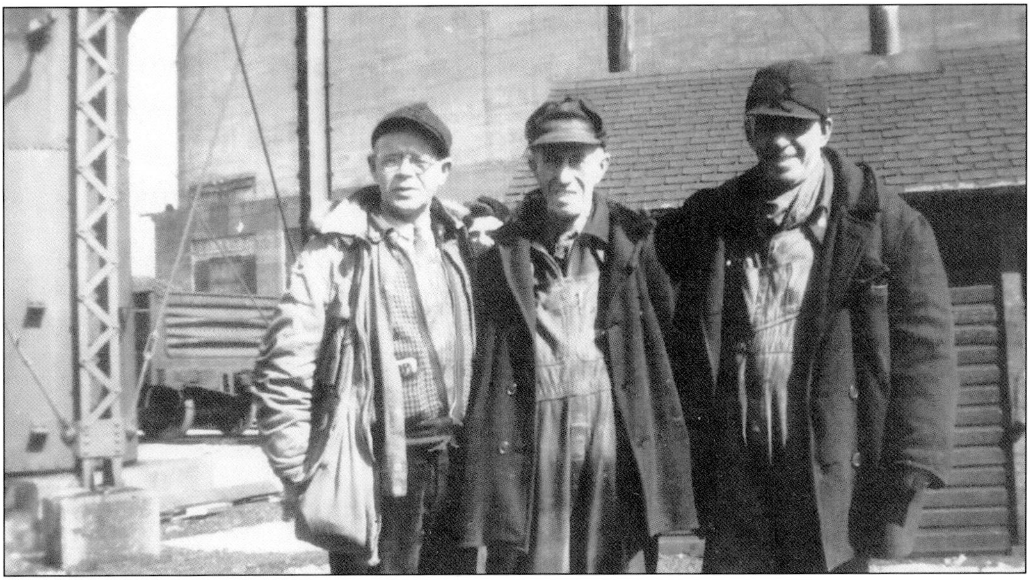

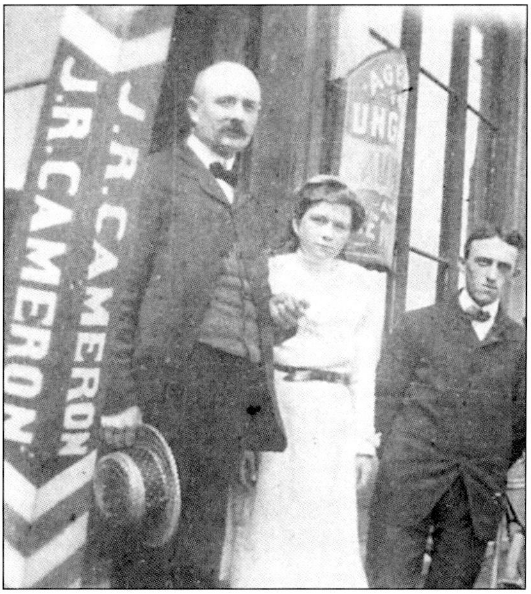

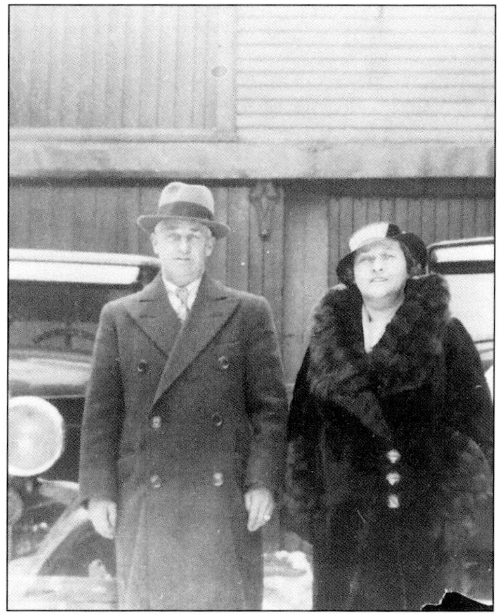

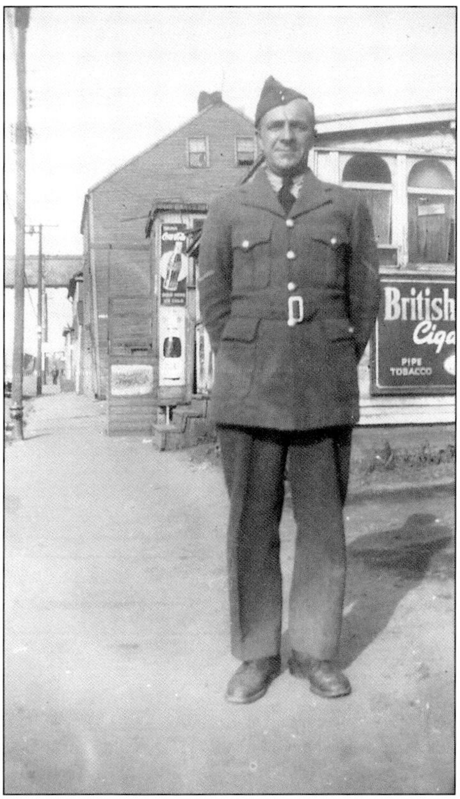

Top left: Jasper Cameron operated a barber shop for his livelihood on Union Street, then later on Market Place. *Top right:* In 1935, Al Kindred is pictured beside his Model A, which he used in taxi service for citizens of Carleton who had appointments "over town" as they called the city centre. *Bottom left:* Sailors and soldiers were a common sight on the streets of Saint John West due to the troop movements through the port and the layover of naval vessels and merchant ships. Many young boys were encouraged by the sight of these men to "join up". Note the "dogcart", the name for retired streetcars, which were refurbished and served as lunch counters in several places along the waterfront. This one is on St. John Street.

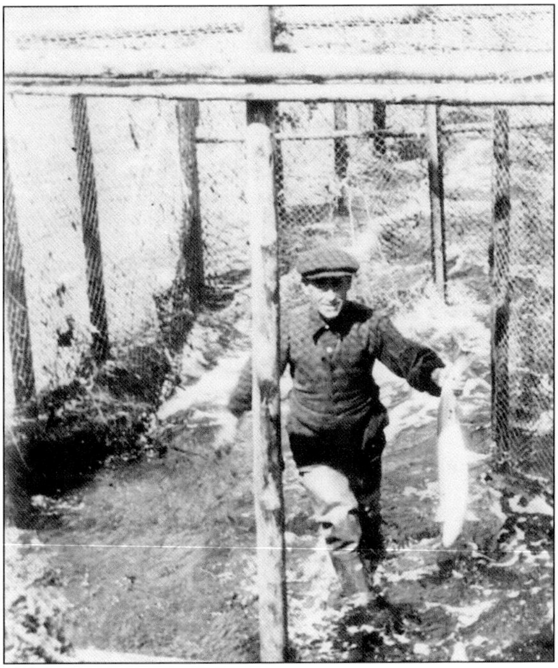 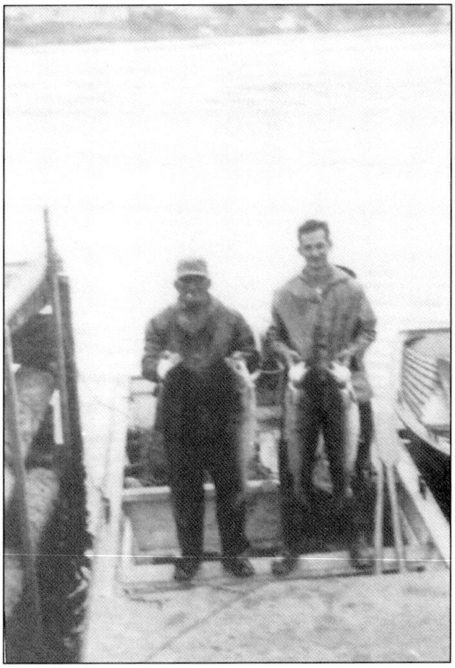

Large schools of spawning gaspereau, shad, and salmon were spring visitors to the waters around Saint John West, and long-term fishing rights were held by many residents. The top photo shows Kutch McCullum with a salmon taken by net in the St. John River below his Water Street home. To the left is Leo Doucette and Bill Miller holding the catch of the day, possibly their reward for helping a licensed fisherman. Since the days of the natives, weirs or fish traps were built out from the shore to catch the fish in the Bay. The four weirs pictured in this photo (below) of Beatteay's Beach were photographed by Cecil Strange around 1910. As with all 400 weirs along the Fundy coast, they were named, these being the Dolly Watters, Paul McDade, Jake McDade, and Leonard & Jack Ward. Later, they were owned and fished by Bernie and Harry Walsh. (Courtesy Robert Taylor.)

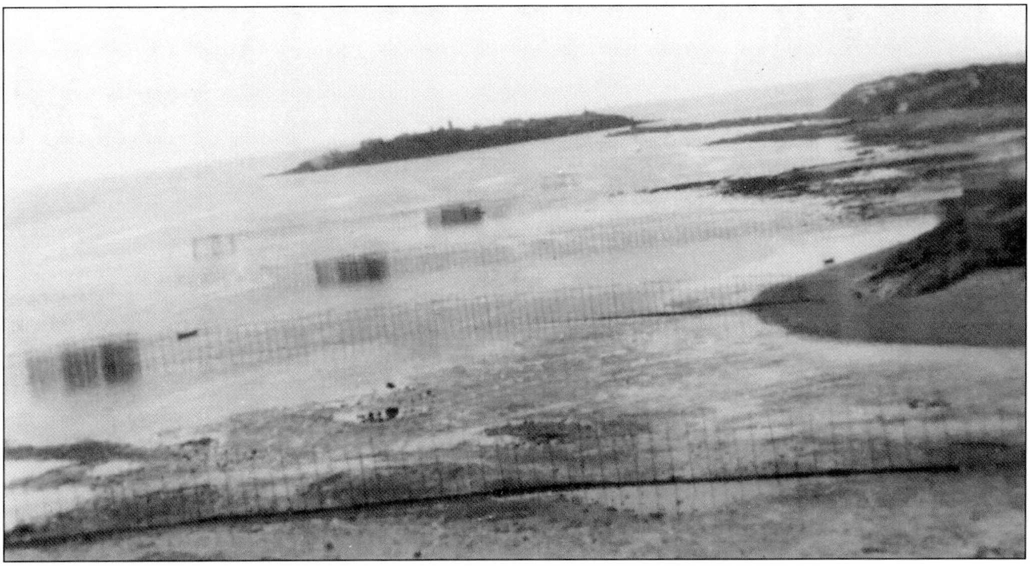

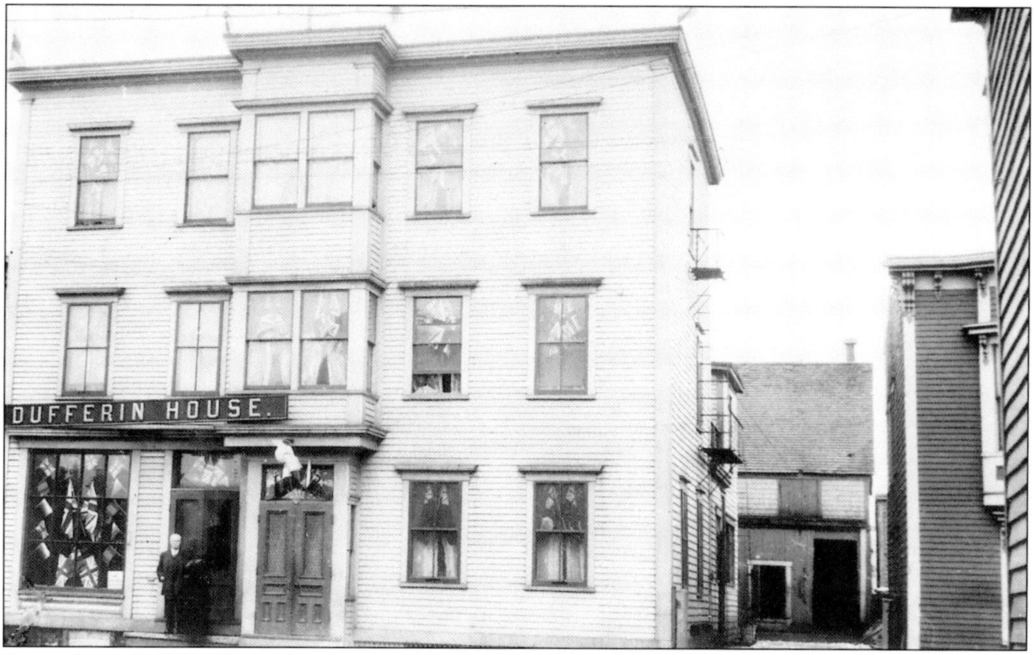

From the A.V.F. Duffy Collection we conclude this look at work in Saint John West with a view of Dufferin House (1877–1931), which was owned by the Duffy family. This is thought to be Isaac Duffy leaving the premises, which have been decorated for a special occasion, most likely the Coronation of George V in June 1911 or Old Home Week of July 1912. The Dufferin house was one of several hotels in the area. These included Blue Rock House 1872–1887, Western House 1874–1931, Tema House 1877–1899, Alexandra Hotel (also known as Martello Hotel) 1903–1908, Carleton House 1907–1932, and, lastly, The Maple Leaf Hotel 1933–1969. The lady shown below is Lydia Duffy, who was well known for her cinnamon twists. She was the widow of Isaac Duffy and, upon his death in 1916, took the business over.

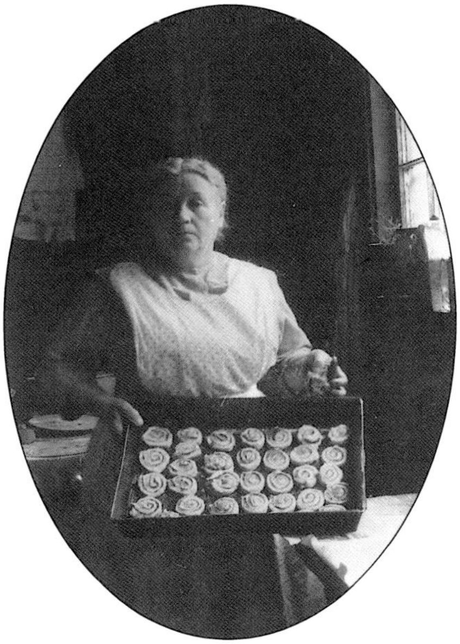

Three

Where They Played

There were few official playgrounds in Saint John West until the 1950s, yet there were many unofficial places where leisure time activities occurred. For the most part West Siders found ways of using the streets, the Harbour, the various vacant fields, and tangles of alders for their play areas. In addition, they made excursions to beaches and parks outside Saint John West for their enjoyment.

As you will see in this chapter they loved to climb the hills at Blue Rock, to the heights at Tower Hill, up the knoll of Courtenay Hill, and to the lava rock outcrop on Winslow Street. They worked pathways through the alders in Nellie Jones' woods on Woodville Road, and in a fringe of forest along Prince Street overlooking the Reversing Falls. They played informal games of road hockey on deserted streets and ball in the public squares and vacant lumber, coal, and pulpyards. They flocked to informal competitions in the harbour and fraternal parades that wound through the streets of Carleton led by their own Carleton Coronet Band, or by the men of the Salvation Army Band. Through Cochrane's field they biked to Duck Cove; via Fairville, they hiked to Dominion Park, Greenhead, and by the Falls bridge, walked to town, visited historic sites, shopped in the old city market,or perhaps hiked in Rockwood Park, then returned to the comfort of their West Side home via the harbour ferry. On such outings, they created lifetime memories, a few of which were captured on film and are shown in this chapter.

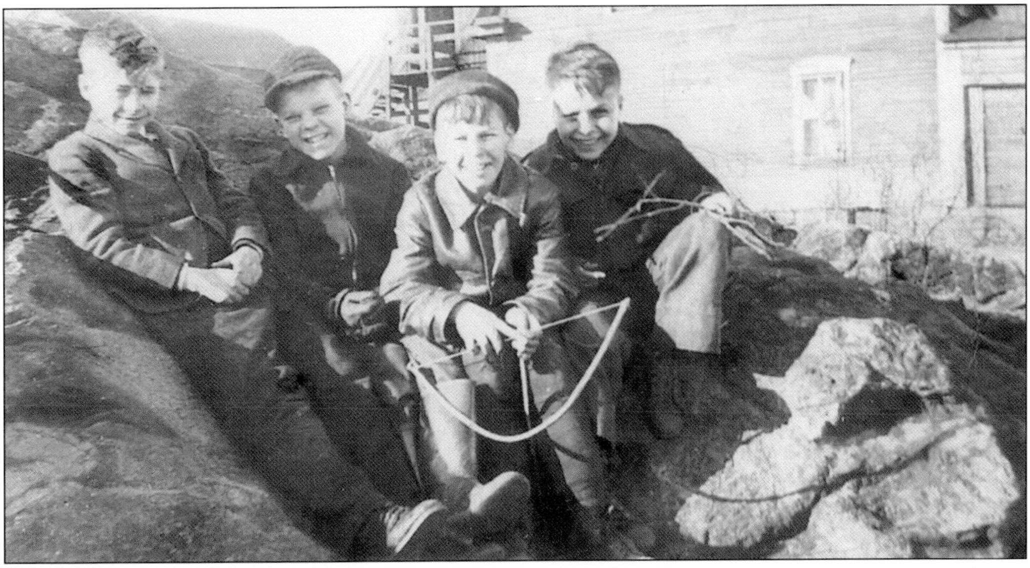

Pictured here are four "big game hunters" on Blue Rock Hill in 1946. From left, in back are Gerry Wills, Herbie Shewbridge, and Bill Boyd. Holding the bow and arrow is George Irvine, who, through his sister Betty Thibodeau, made this photo available.

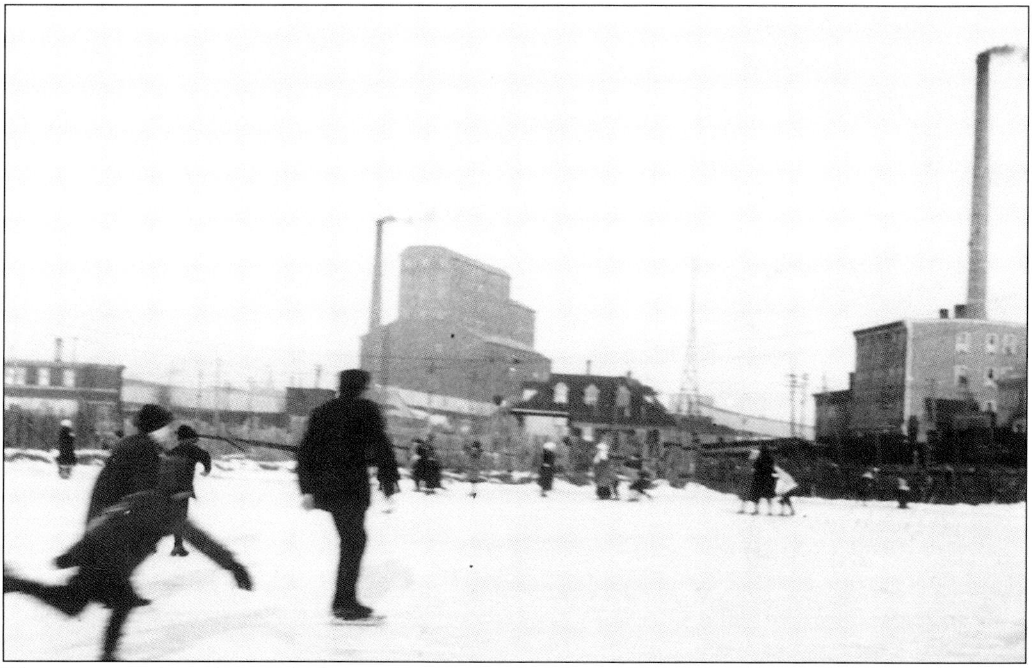

There were at least four rinks located in the Carleton area that were open to the public. Above, the Millpond area was a natural rink, which also had a private, fenced rink that was operated by Hilton Belyea as shown here. It survived to the 1930s when the Millpond was filled in.Then the Market Place rink was operated on the filled-in Millpond and is shown (left bottom) during a winter carnival for the Carleton club. It served until the mid-1960s. Tower Pond was a small pool of water that froze over near Martello Tower. It was more generally known as the Beaconsfield Rink and was used from earliest times till the late 1970s when it was filled in and became a football field.

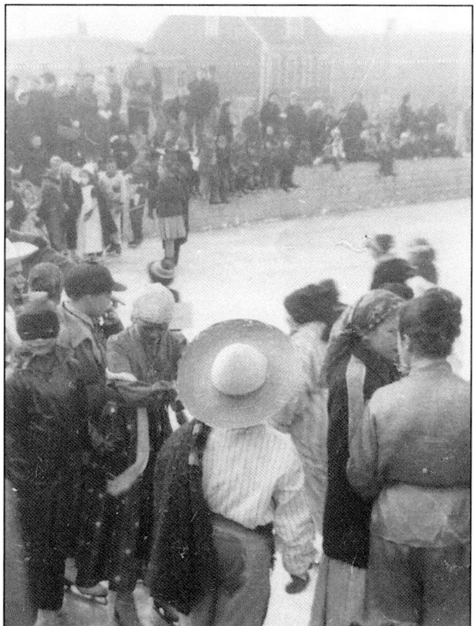

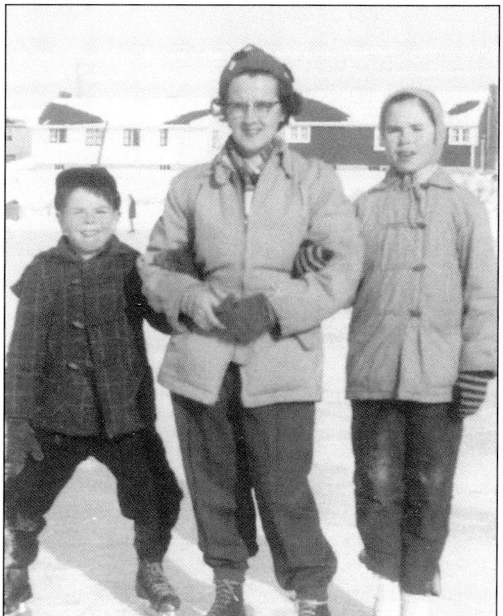

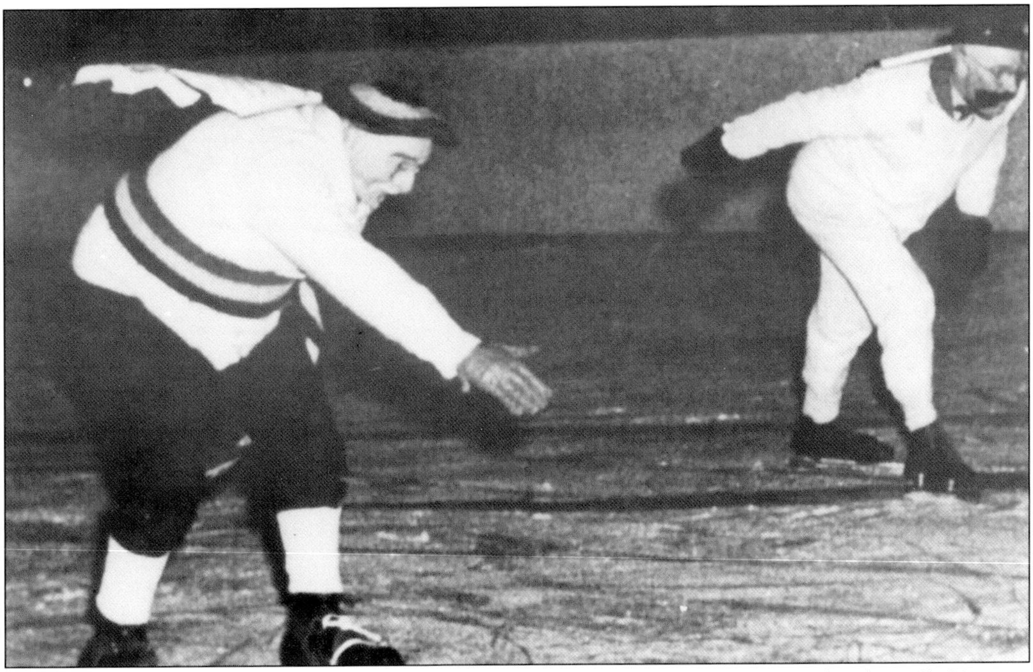

On the back of this picture in his own hand is written ". . . Alderman J. Fred Belyea (left) races Councillor Arthur Doherty who had challenged him . . ." Belyea stipulated the race was to be on long reacher skates. The race was held at the Policeman's Sports night in the Forum in 1951. Belyea added, ". . . I won by 60 feet and was 78 years old at the time . . ." He lived to be 95, and died in 1968.

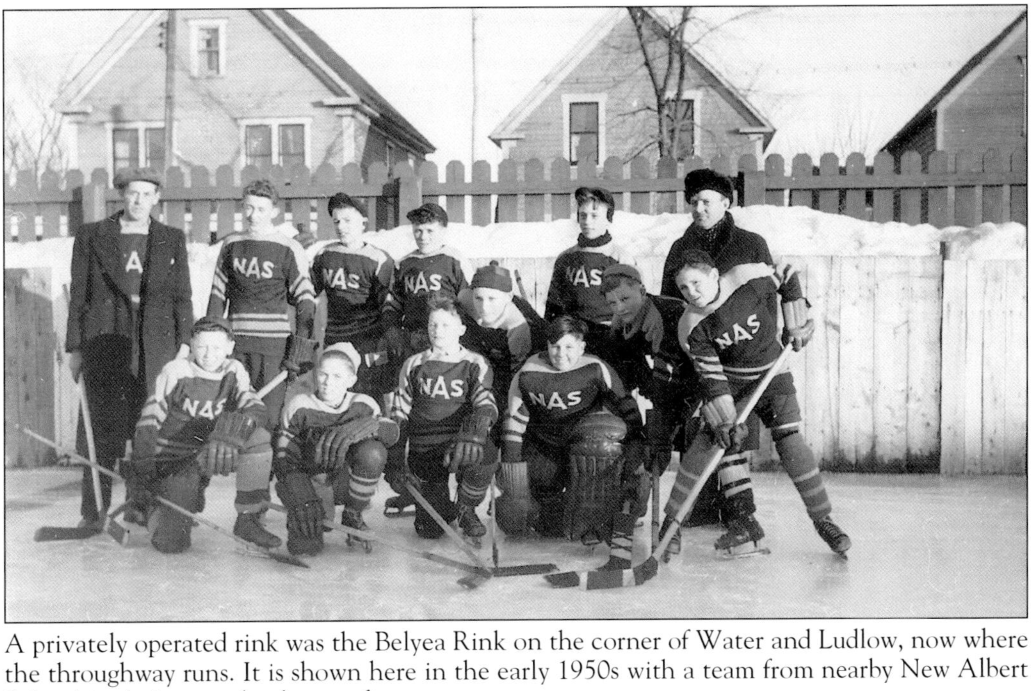

A privately operated rink was the Belyea Rink on the corner of Water and Ludlow, now where the throughway runs. It is shown here in the early 1950s with a team from nearby New Albert School in their smart hockey outfits.

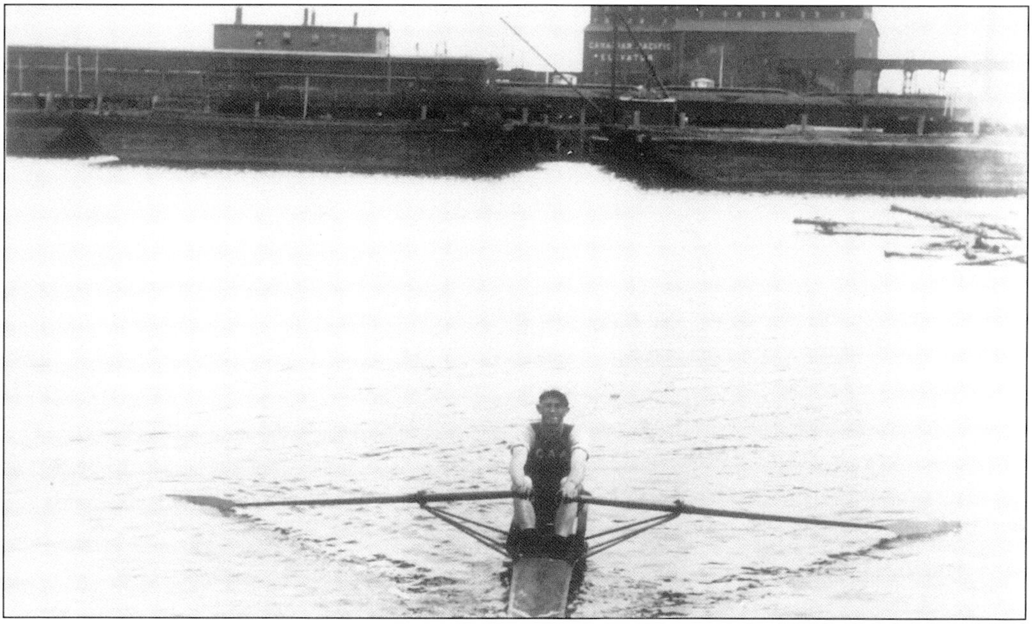

The sculler pictured in Saint John Harbour, just off the 1896 Canadian Pacific grain elevator, is Harry Walter (Bud) Nice, who died on September 15, 1914, at the age of 29. His daughter provided the picture, though she never knew him, as she was conceived in the weeks before he died. She has been given clippings, which show he was a champion sculler and rowed with the Belyea crew of Carleton. She was also told he had a great capacity for holding his breath. He would dive off the Rodney Slip and when all thought he had drowned he would surface mid-harbour. (Courtesy Connie Cunningham.)

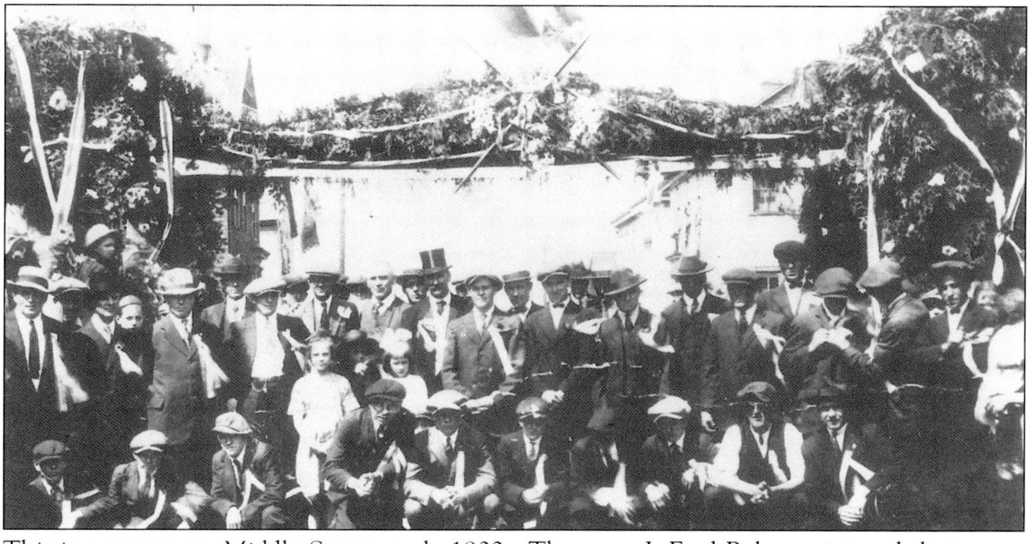

This is a regatta on Middle Street, early 1900s. The same J. Fred Belyea, pictured skating on page 37, is the man pictured in the top hat in this picture. An evergreen archway has been strung over Middle Street for this regatta. It was a Saint John West crew of Elijah Ross, George Price, Samuel Hutton, and Robert Fulton, who went to Paris in 1867 and stole the sculling championship away from the Europeans. It was an unbelievable feat and the highlight of a long history of rowing and sculling competition between fishermen in the harbour.

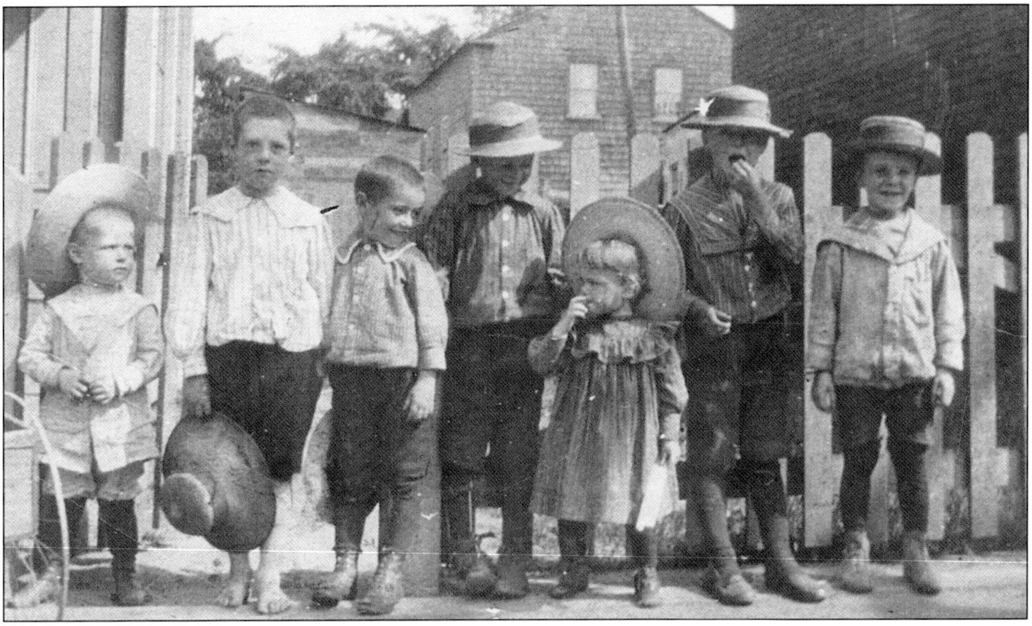

Here is a nice contrast of youngsters in Saint John West about 50 years apart. The top photo is an unknown group whose clothing is in sharp contrast to the group standing outside the King Street Zanzibar Restaurant. It operated from 1957 to 1960 at 202 King Street. Fred identified 11 of the 15 in the photo: Elaine Murphy, Barb Ralston, Fay Anne McGuigan, Myrna Tracey, Barb Bonnee, Rose Mae Blanchard, Betty Perry, Perry Wilson, Lillian Arsenault, Thelma Chamberlain, and Polly Lord. (Below, courtesy of Ellen Burke.)

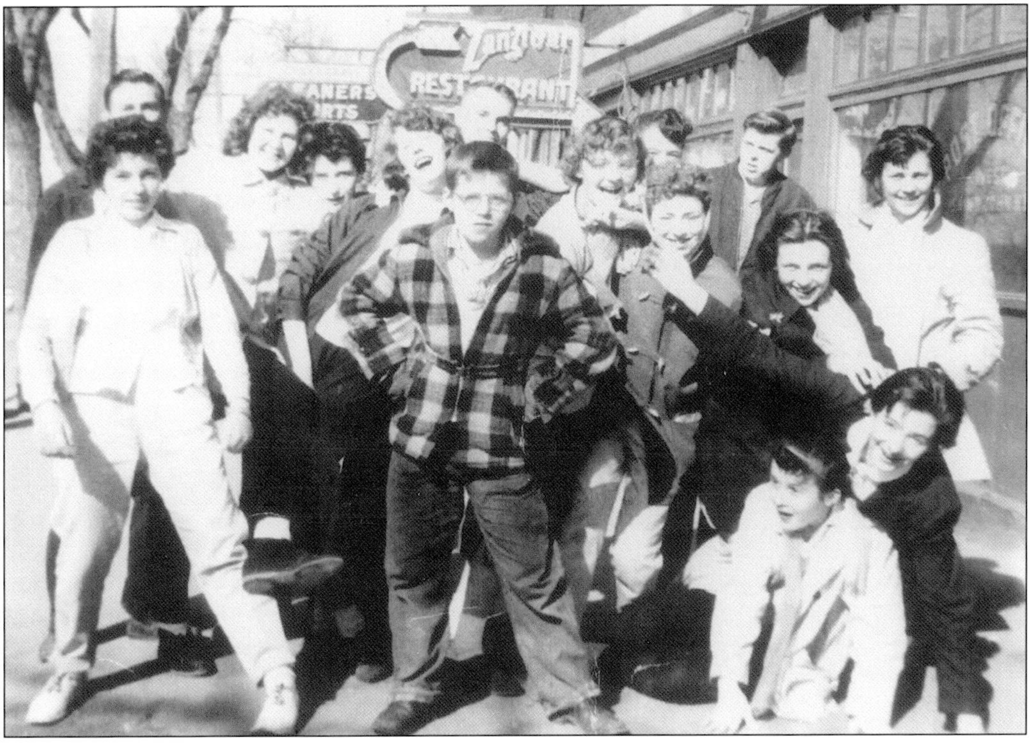

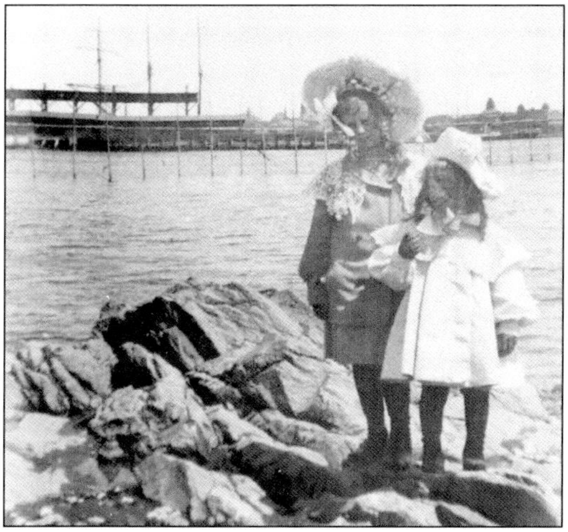

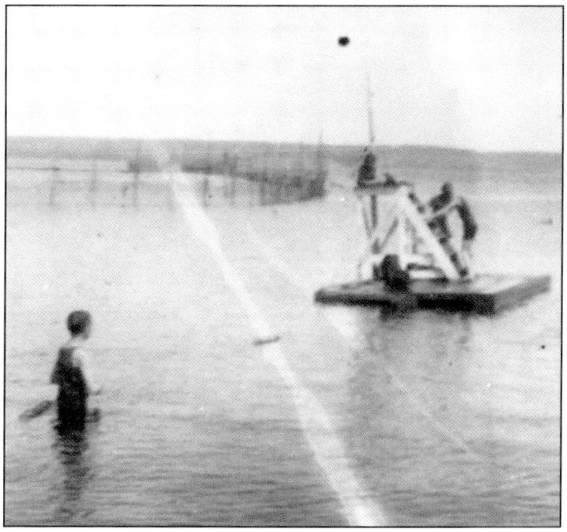

Left: These youngsters are more likely out for a Sunday stroll than out for a dip in the waters of Blue Rock or Beatteay's Beach behind them. In the background is the Dolly Watter's weir. See page 33, which shows the rocks on which the children are standing. In the background is the very end of Sand Point Wharf, and across the harbour the South End Barrack Grounds are visible with the Exhibition buildings just over their heads. (Courtesy Jack McIntyre.) *Right:* If the young ladies above had chosen to swim beside the pier they might have enjoyed a swim out to the raft anchored offshore. Photographer A.V.F. Duffy called this area Nice's Beach in his 1915 photo. Other photos of the area identify it as Blue Rock Beach, Beatteay's Beach, Beatteay's Rocks, and occasionally Beacon Beach because of the offshore Beacon light.

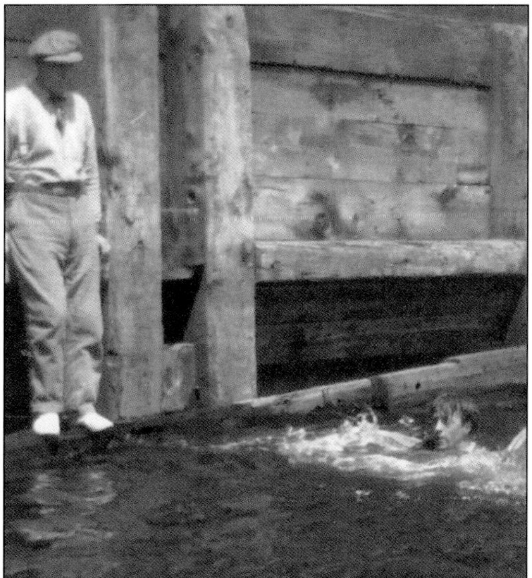

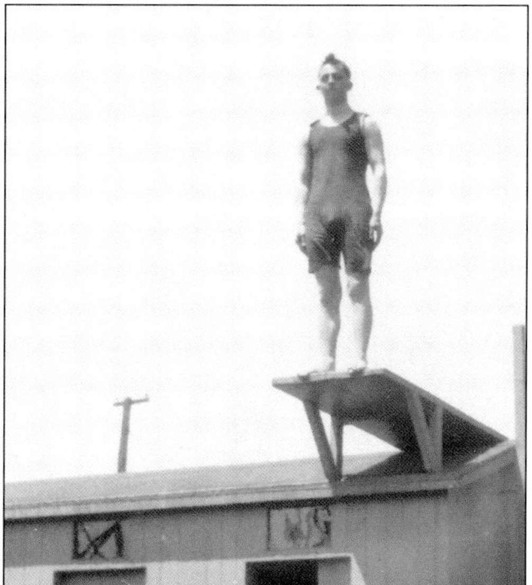

Left: Before the days of chlorinated swimming pools, the boys and girls of Saint John West learned to swim in a scow, which was anchored, then partially sunk off Rodney Slip. (Courtesy A.V.F. Duffy.) *Right:* A.V.F. Duffy also caught William Owens about to dive off the board adjacent to the swimming scow in 1914. Owens would have had a cool dip into the five degree water in the Harbour. In addition, he would have had to contend with debris, even raw sewage, floating from the Millpond, which was generally used as a dumping ground in that era. This would have made it a dive only a few would have been interested in doing.

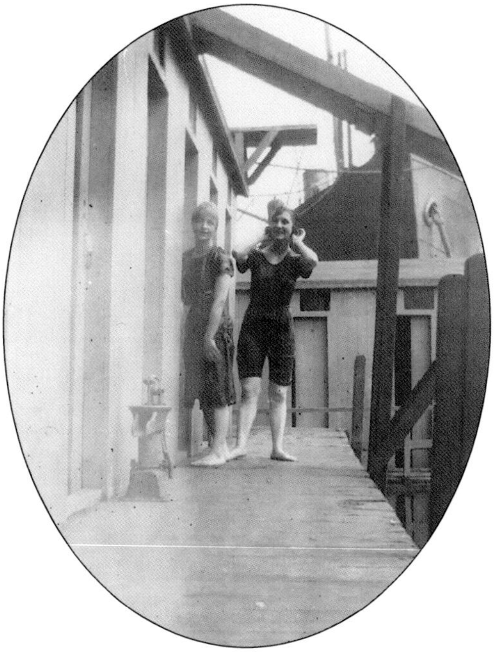

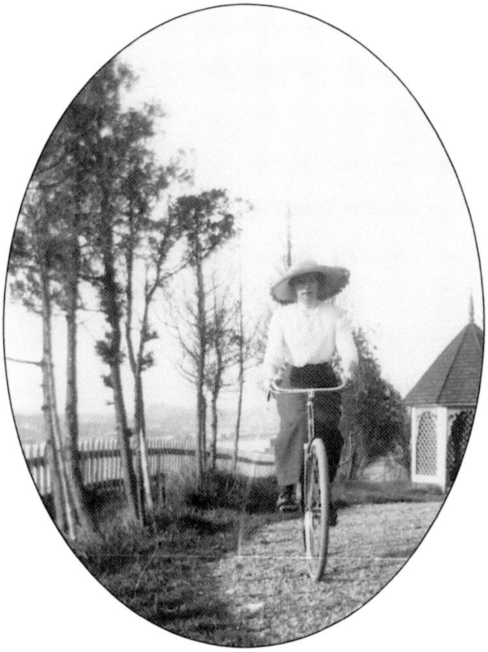

Left: Young ladies also swam at the scow. In this photo taken by A.V.F. Duffy in 1915, Dorothy Laynon is putting on a bathing cap prior to a swim. *Right:* Young ladies also adapted to Emilia Bloomer's riding habits, i.e. wearing bloomers for decorum, and enjoyed peddling along a pathway on Prince Street. This pathway has long since disappeared, and were it not for A.V.F. Duffy's 1915 photo we'd know nothing of these Prince Street grounds and gardens.

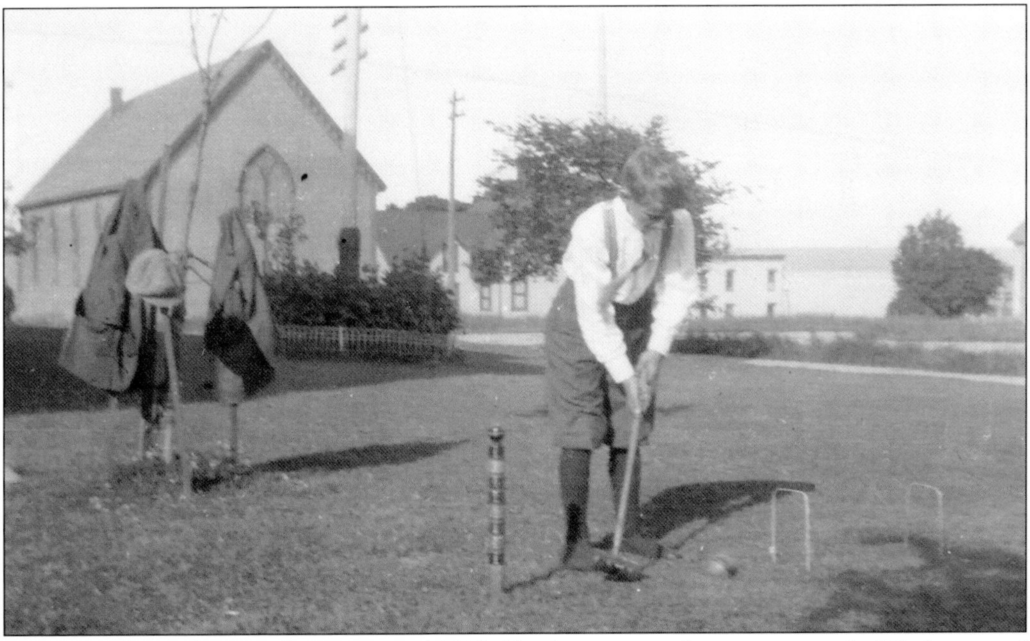

A.V.F. Duffy was busy in the summer of 1915. He also went to the opposite end of Carleton and took this picture of a young man playing croquet behind St. Jude's Church, overlooking Saint John Harbour with the hills Redhead in the distance.

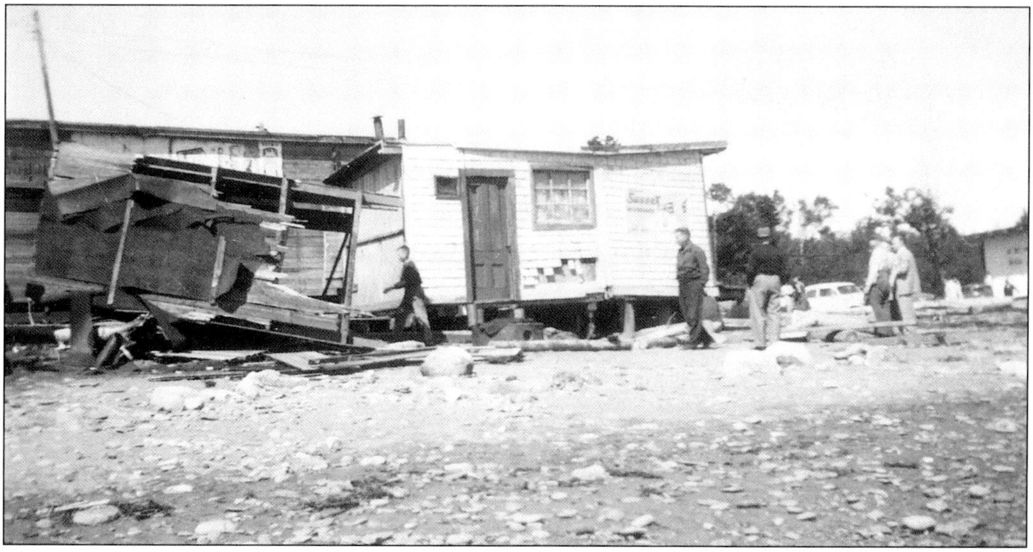

This picture is captioned, "1954, McLaren's Beach after Hurricane Edna." This was the beginning of the end for the attractions on this beach. In the earliest times it had been a popular place for the Natural History Society's outings. Nan McAllister developed the first canteen in the 1920s. She had a dispute with the builder, who then built a second canteen on Holy Cross Cemetery land opposite hers. It was run by the Shannons for some years, and considered the "Catholic" canteen while Nan's served the "Protestant" visitors. Or so it is said! There were also some bathhouses and cottages on the beach. The last of them were swept away in the Groundhog Gale of 1976.

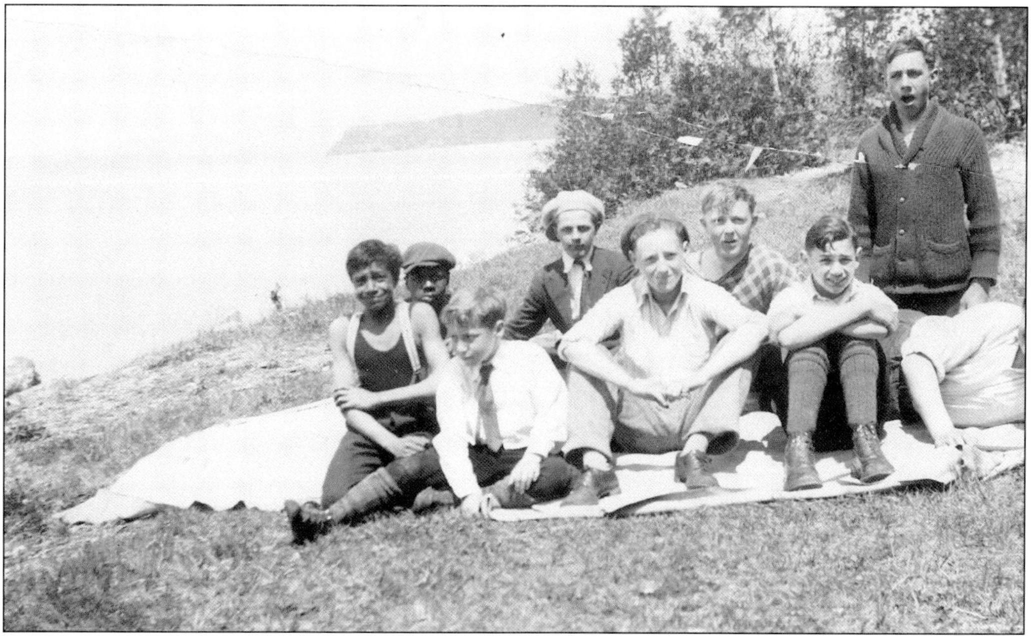

Tuxis boys at Greenhead are pictured here in 1932. The walk to the Greenhead area, via Main Street in Fairville, was about an hour from Saint John West. The reward was the chance to explore the quarries, old caves, abandoned lime kilns, and take a fresh water dip while in the area.

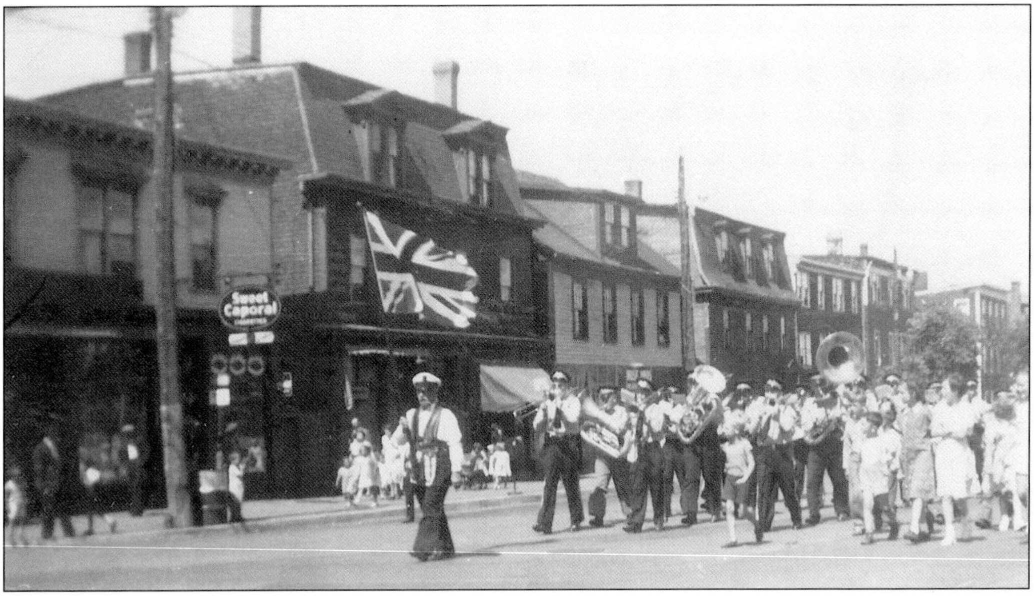

The Prentice Ladies (Rolston Chapter #5 L.A.P.B.) were one of many fraternal organizations in Saint John West. Normally they carried on their benevolent work from their halls or meeting rooms, in this case the 1893 I.O.O.F. Hall on Market and Duke Streets. Annually they would hold public events and parades as seen here on King Street in 1960 in the top photo. Following the parade that day, they went to the Cedar Hill Extension Cemetery and unveiled a plaque to former members as shown in the lower photo.

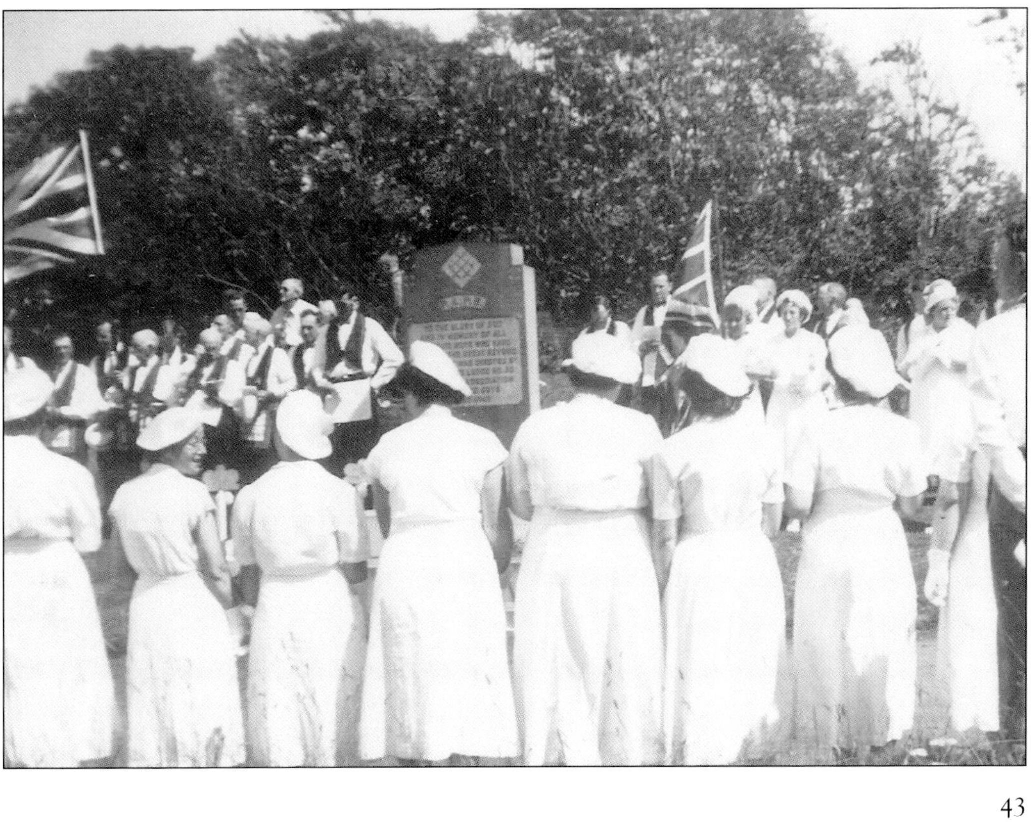

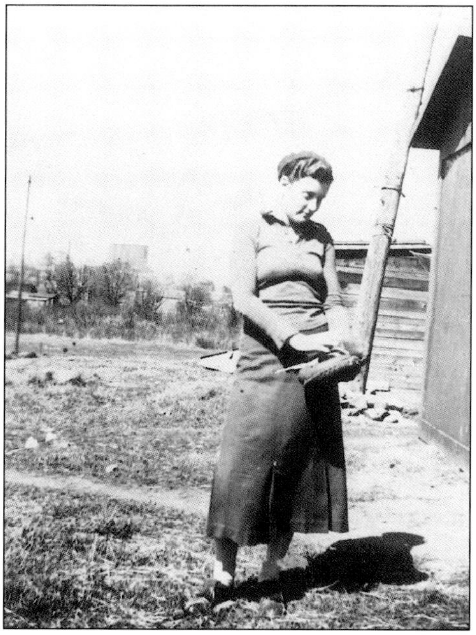 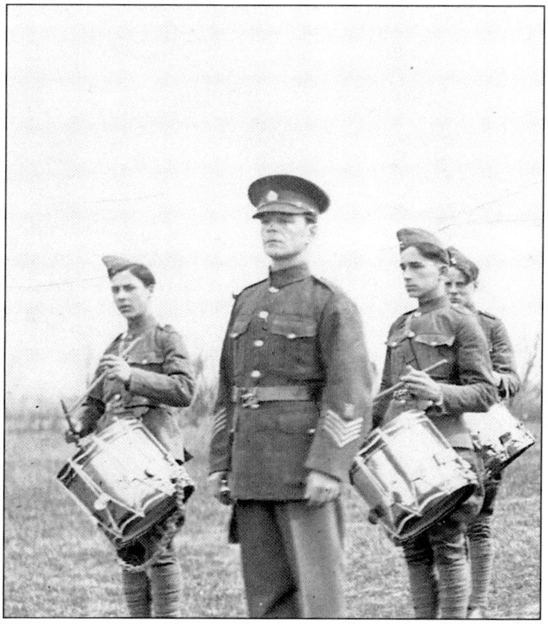

Left: In times past, Carleton ladies played ball too, as this photo from the 1930s shows. She's holding a huge, old days catcher's mitt at the ball field, which was built on Lancaster Street at Winslow. It was created as the ashes hauled from local homes were deposited in a gully below the rocky hillside, which was a popular sliding spot until the "Mountain Estates" were established in the late 1980s. *Right:* In 1932 the members of the New Albert Cadet Corps Band marched to Cochrane's Field, now in the Dunn Avenue area of Fundy Heights, to hold the practices. (Courtesy Gordon Chase.)

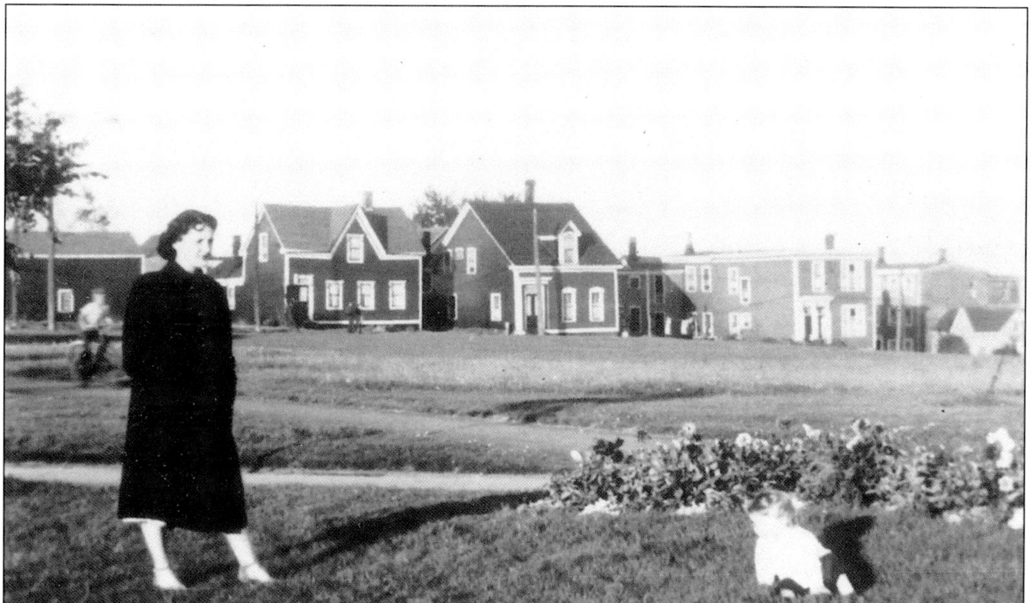

Queen Square, with its beds of dahlias, which Johnny Duncan planted in colourful clusters in the center triangles, was a popular place for Saint John West mothers to take their children on a sunny afternoon.

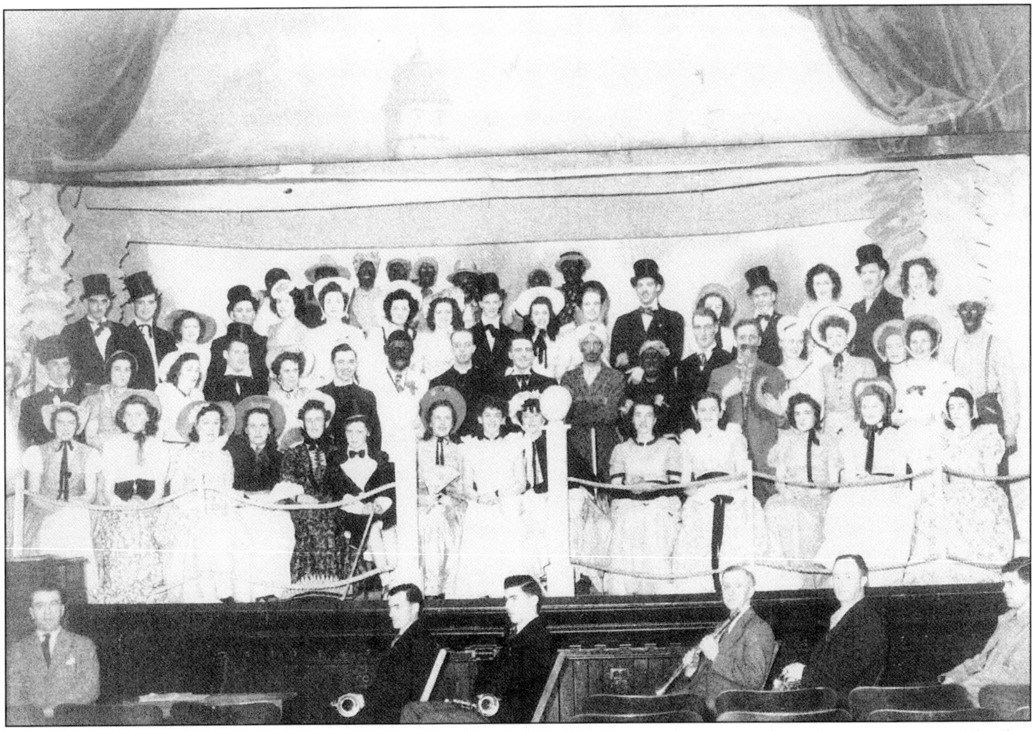

Shown here is a minstrel show at St. Patrick's School. This is the sort of performance—with the black faces—that would not be repeated in 1999.

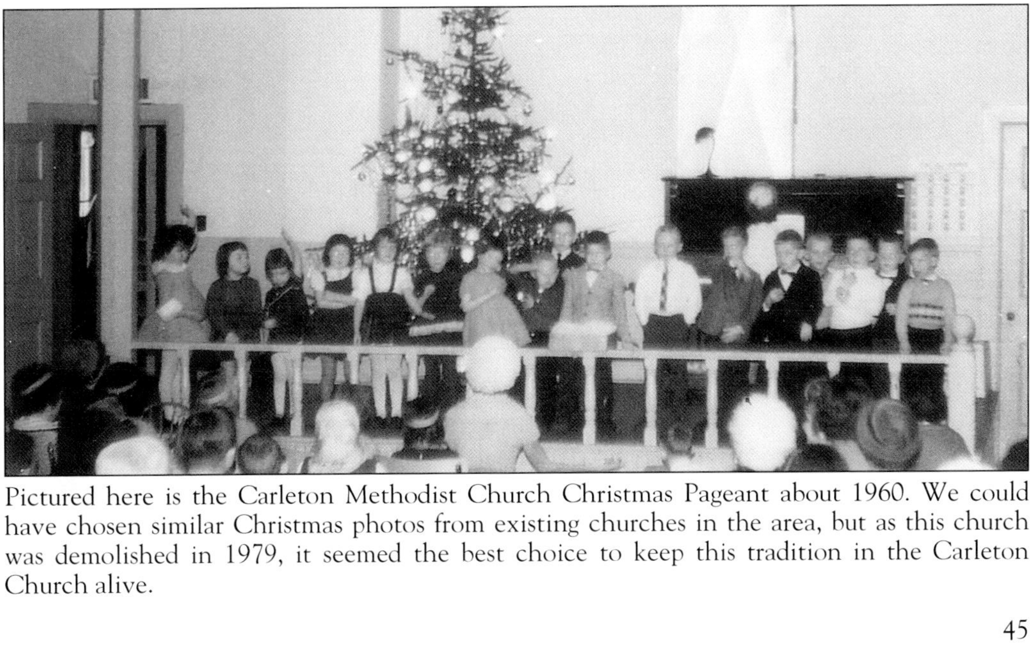

Pictured here is the Carleton Methodist Church Christmas Pageant about 1960. We could have chosen similar Christmas photos from existing churches in the area, but as this church was demolished in 1979, it seemed the best choice to keep this tradition in the Carleton Church alive.

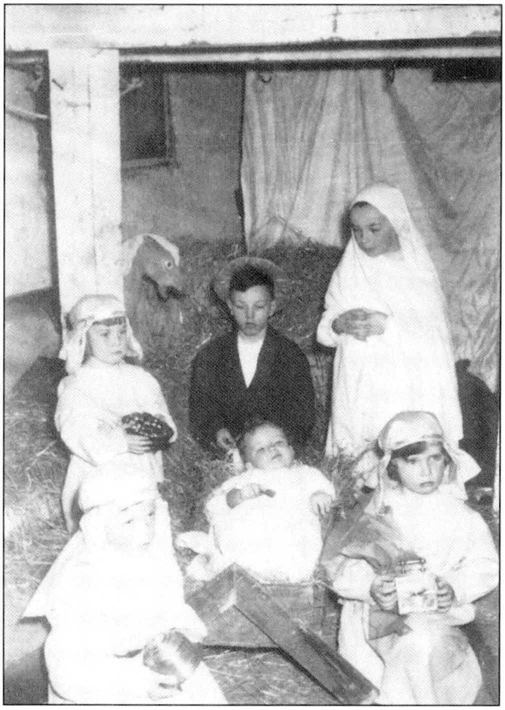

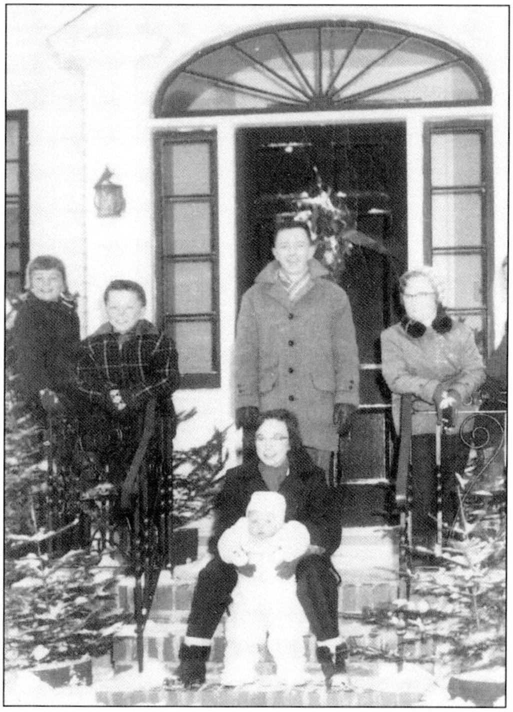

Harry Burley took the first Christmas picture of the family of Dr. Harry and Margaret Peters, of 440 Champlain Street in their annual "Children's Photo" taken from 1948 to 1959. The manger scene shown in 1952 was in their basement, with Tom in the left front, Jane just behind him, and Monte holding "Jesus", a.k.a. Dick. Mary is to Monte's left, and Ann is on the far right. In front of their home, in 1956, Hope is the new addition being held by Mary—and Mary arranged the sleigh in the 1959 photo at the Ashburn Lake Riding Club—but photographer Lou Wilson, who grew impatient with the delays in shooting, eventually got fed up, and superimposed another horse and background, which none of the family recognized. Thanks to Mary Burchill for the details and Gerry Maxwell for the photos.

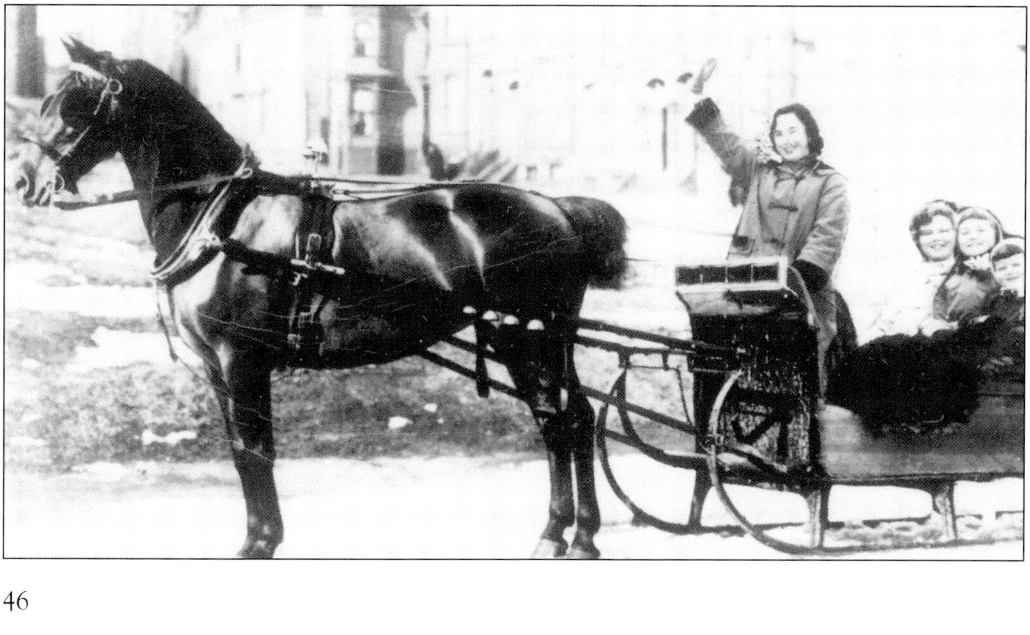

Four

WHERE THEY SHOPPED

Among the pictures we accumulated following the success of *Saint John West and its Neighbours*, were many of the family-owned shops and stores of Carleton. Many came to us with no background information, but the scenes in the photos were recognizable as shops of the area, and we tried to add details as we could.

We are indebted to Alice and Charlie O'Brien for a great deal of the background information in this section. They often knew the stores pictured, sometimes even the unnamed people, or were able to refer us to someone who did. Charlie, who lived on Germain Street, estimates there were at least 42 stores in the area in the '40s when he was a lad, and he worked for several, delivering groceries from 8 to 6 daily for $3 a week. Until they married, Alice worked at Harned's, next door to where she had been born on King Street. Living on opposite ends of the West Side likely helped them to fill in many gaps in the information we had.

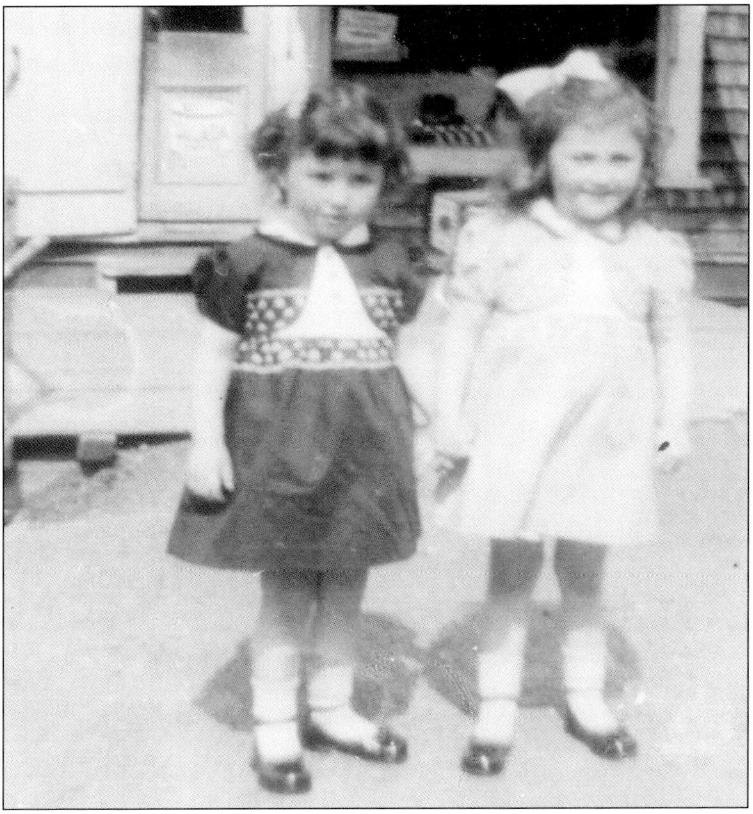

Lynda and Elaine Thibodeau, decked out in fashionable pinafore-style dresses, are posed in front of their grandparents' bakery at 370 Lancaster Street in 1951. This was the second bakery Eddie and Grace Trecartin ran, the original having been "down Carleton" on Rodney Street from 1941 till 1949. Such family-run operations were typical of the area and era and somehow supported large families, but not many as large as that of Eddie and Grace, who had 15 mouths to feed.

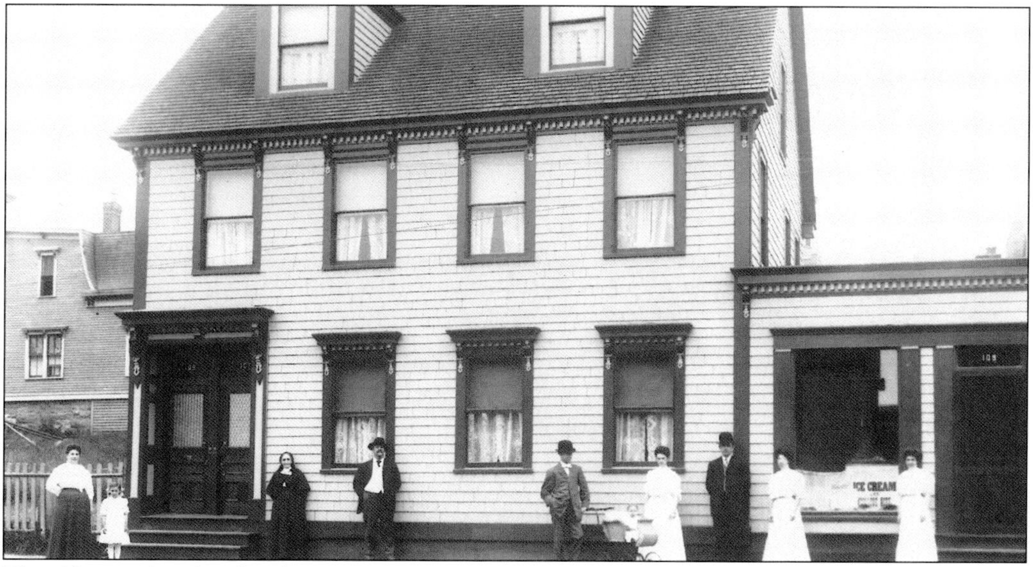

The Christopher family of 105-109 Ludlow Street, where the Bank of Nova Scotia now stands, is pictured above in a 1910-era Isaac Erb photo that has proved to be very interesting. Third from the left is Grandmother Christopher, who would have known some of the earliest Loyalist settlers of Carleton. In the carriage is her great-granddaughter, Marjorie Sutton, who was 90 in 1997. The others, from left to right, are her granddaughter Amelia Christopher, her great-granddaughter Madolin, and left of grandmother is her son and Amelia's husband, Charles Wilbur Christopher. To his left is his son-in-law Sutton and his wife Emily (Christopher) Roxborough, separated by Marjorie in the carriage. Charles and Amelia's remaining children, Edgar, Maud (McKim), and Luta stand by the store Maud first ran. (Courtesy Vintage Photo and Frame and Ruth Harris.)

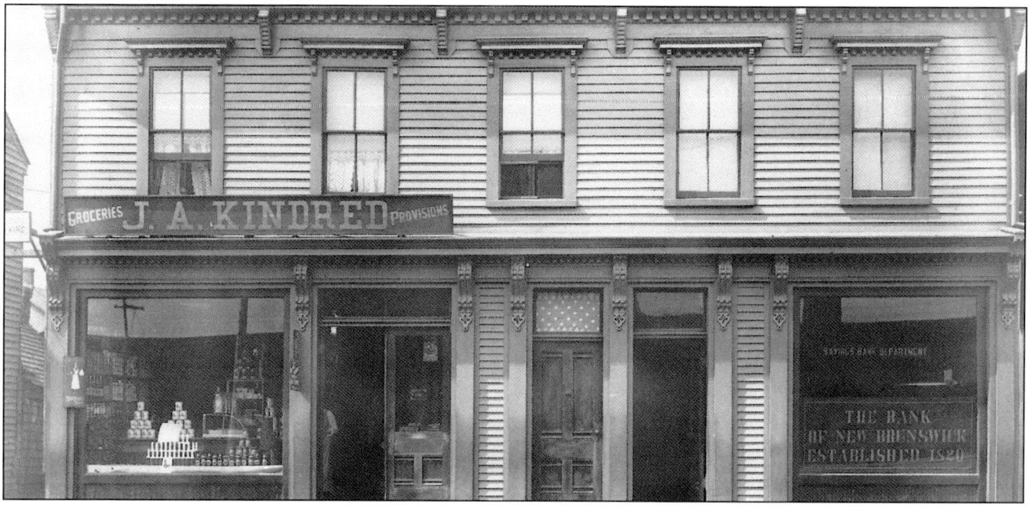

The J.A. Kindred store stood at 111 Union Street, and its next-door neighbour, the Bank of New Brunswick, had yet to move into the imposing building shown on page 55 when this Erb photo was taken in 1906. Besides his grocery business, John Amos Kindred also ran a livery stable and was collector of the mails for some time in Carleton. He was a faithful member of the Charlotte Street Baptist Church. He was born in 1847, and died in his 87th year in August of 1934. (Courtesy Vintage Photo and Frame.)

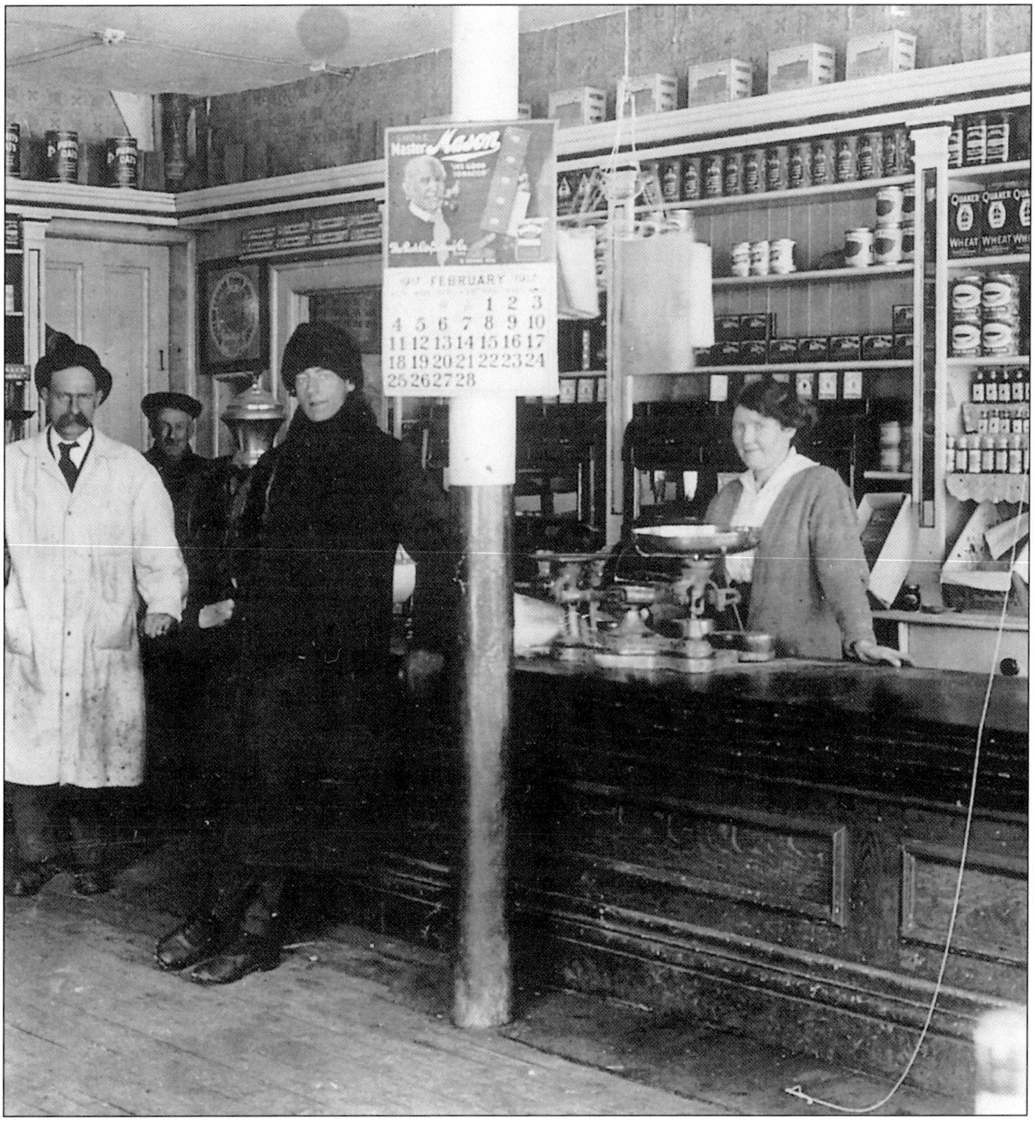

These folks, gathered in February 1917 in a Saint John West store, may have been discussing the imminent paving of Union Street, a $4,600 project, or wondering where in New Brunswick the new post office would be built, a $5,000 project. They could have been discussing the dry dock project in Courtenay Bay, wondering if it would ever be completed or if the government would finally come to their senses and move it to the Millpond in Carleton where it was planned to be built in the first place. These were all topics of interest when this photo was taken.

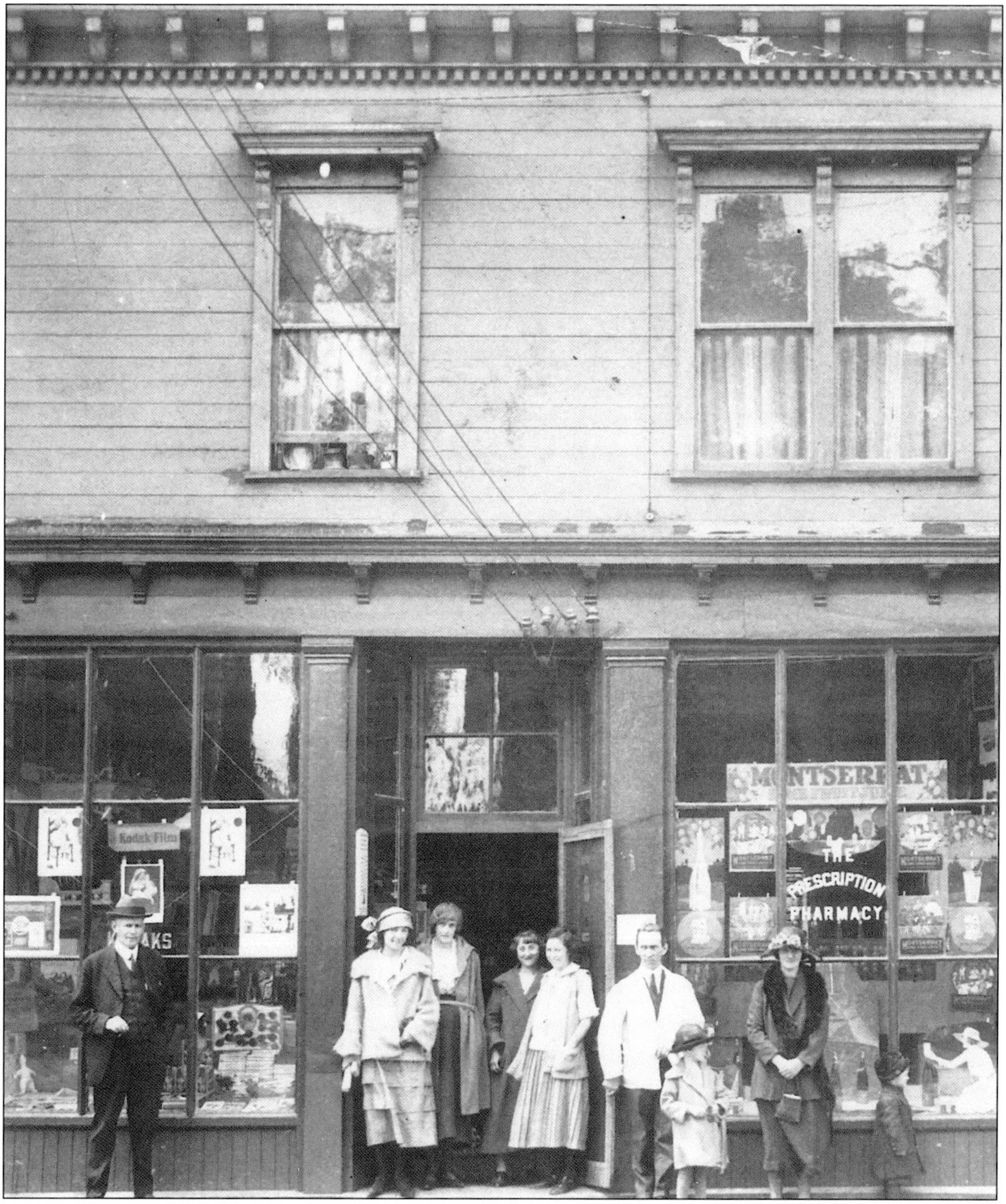

The Ingraham's Drugstore name shows up as early as 1901 at 127 Union Street. In 1933, it shows up at 269 King Street, where this photo was taken. Though the name lasted till 1973, Jean Brown actually ran the store in the early 1950s, and Frank Trecartin took over the business in 1956 and operated it until 1973. In the adjacent building, Ingraham tried a restaurant business for a short time, then Atkinson's took it over and ran it successfully for ten years or so, till the early 1950s. Then West Side Radio and TV, Boudreau's, and Child's Bakery also found it a convenient spot for business.

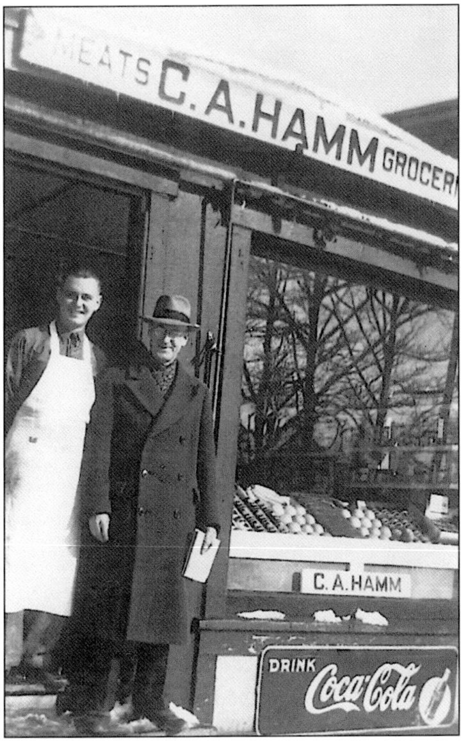

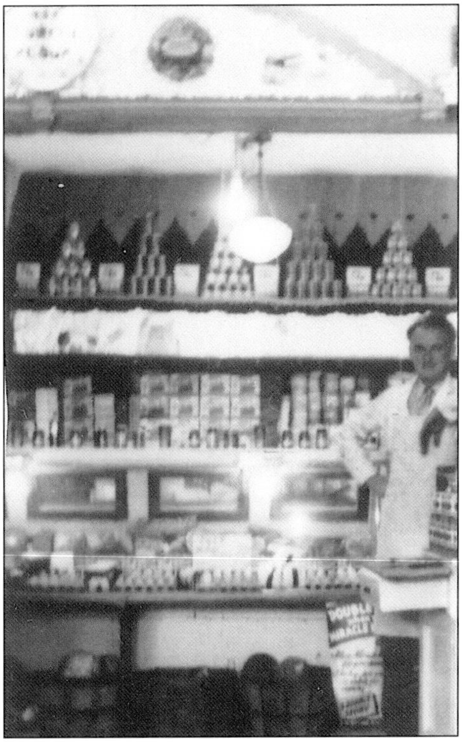

Left: The C. Albert Hamm and Charles P. Hamm Grocery stood at 264 Watson Street. It opened in 1946, and Charles P. closed it in 1959 and then ran a grocery store at 371 Fundy Drive. *Right:* Meisner's Store at 79 Ludlow Street was in operation from 1940 to 1972. Like most other stores, they employed boys for delivery. Charlie O'Brien remembers being sent from a similar store with a 4¢ yeast cake, arriving back at the store to find a neighbour wanting a 10¢ loaf of bread. They both got them delivered and somehow the store still made a profit.

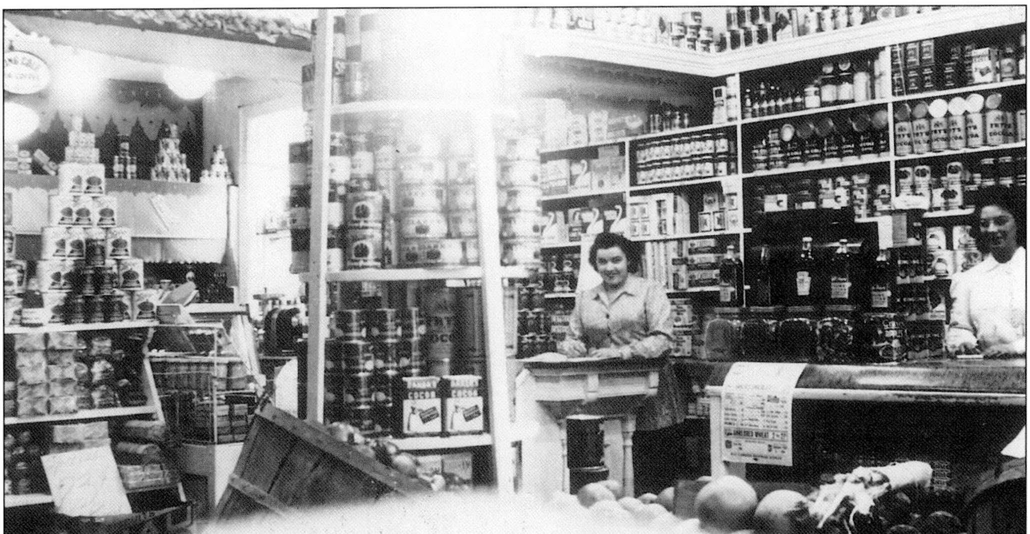

This closeup of a typical interior of a Saint John West Store, self decorated by the owner, is thought to be a predecessor of the Meisner's store at 79 Ludlow street.

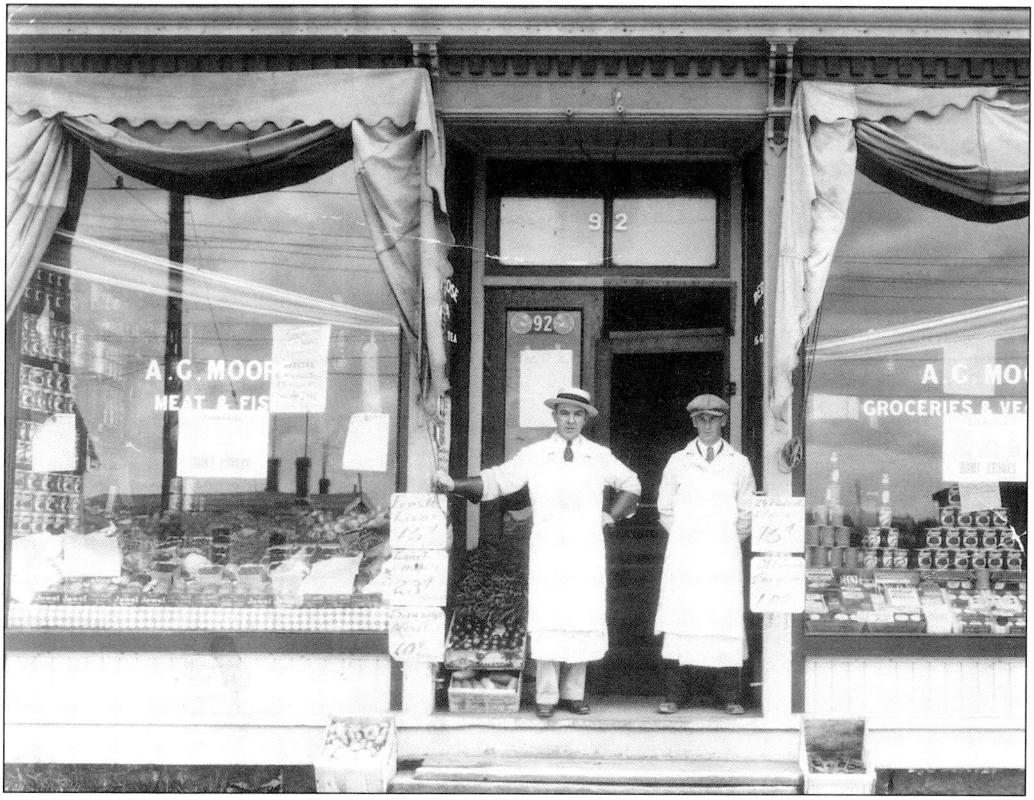

A.G. Moore ran a meat, fish, and grocery operation at 92 Prince Street from 1931 to 1958. His brother Willard ran a similar operation in Fairville. In this top photo is Albert Moore on the left and Alva French on the right. Alva's daughter, Doreen Gould, remembers her father worked there only four years as a meat cutter and then found wages at the port much better and moved there for his employment for 48 years.

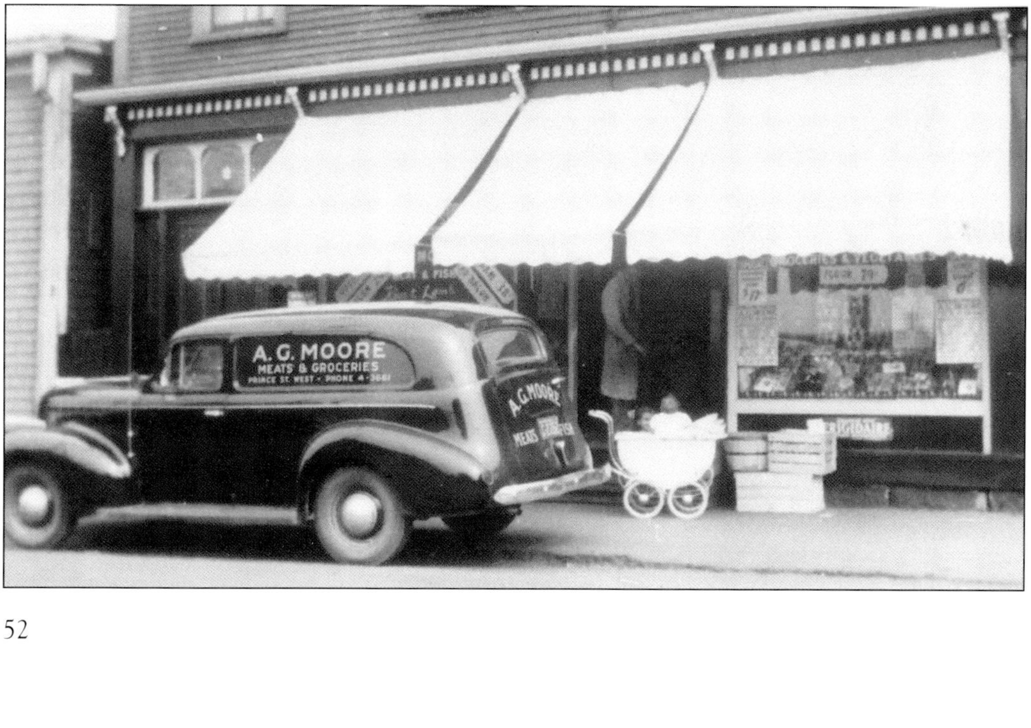

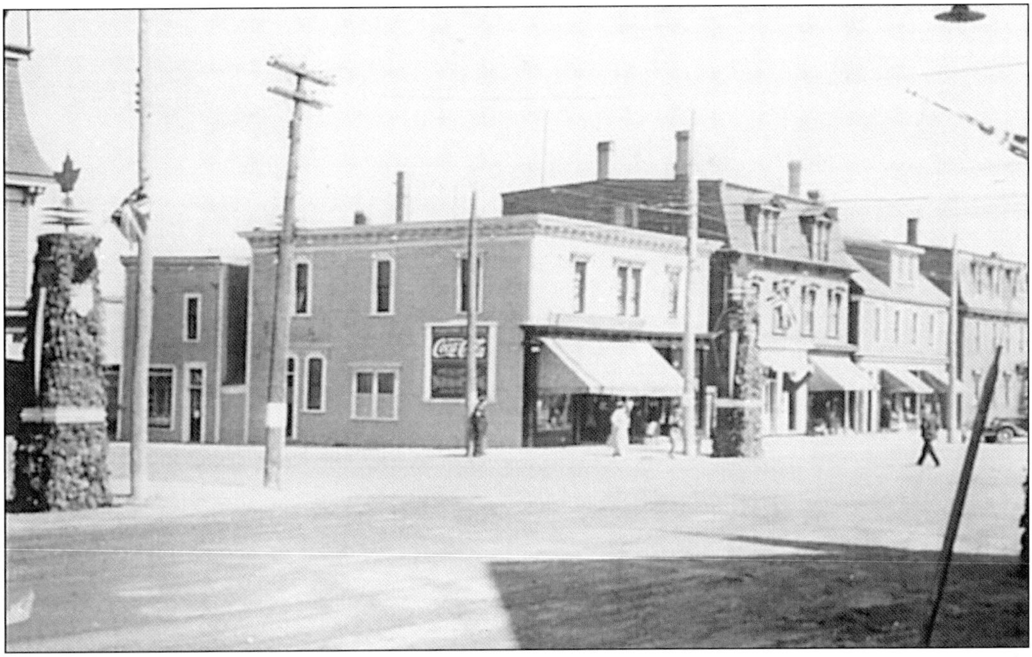

Alice O'Brien recalls the excitement of the King and Queen's visit to King Street on June 13, 1939. The corner of King and Ludlow, shown here, was lavishly decorated with greenery pillars, as were other important corners in the city. Buildings were well decked out too. (See page 125 in the closing chapter for a few.) Alice watched the royal couple pass by from the dormer window of the fourth house on the corner of King Street in an apartment of friends Charlie and Manie Doyle.

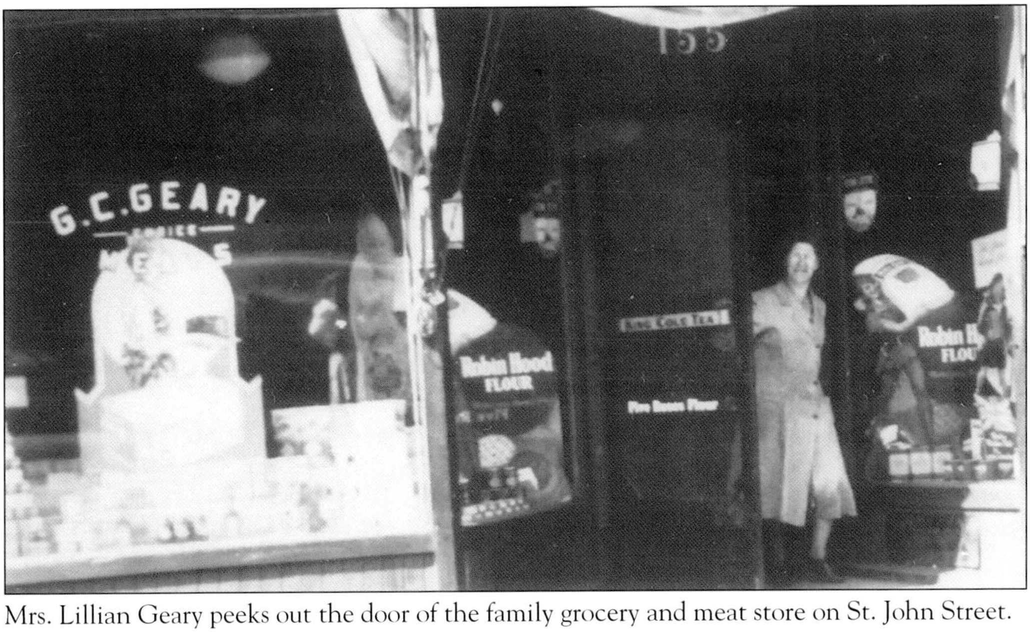

Mrs. Lillian Geary peeks out the door of the family grocery and meat store on St. John Street.

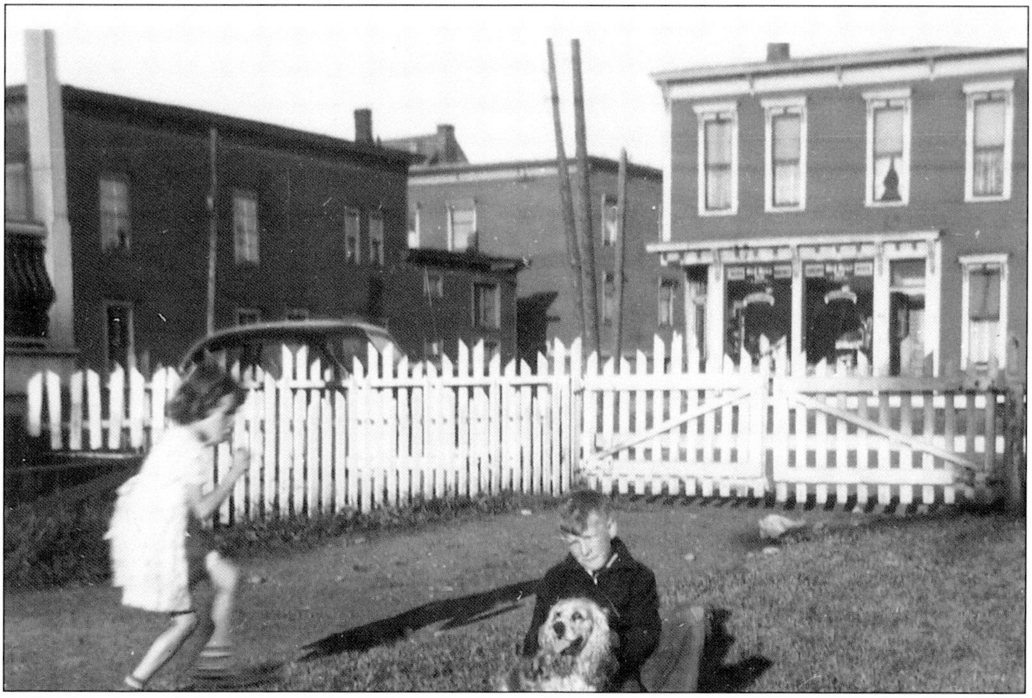

Ask who owned this store and you'll be told it was (George) Alston's Grocery by those who remember it in the '30s, or (Archie) Dryden's Grocery by those of the '50s, or Bert's Grocery (Bert McFarlane was Archie Dryden's daughter) when this picture was taken in the '60s.

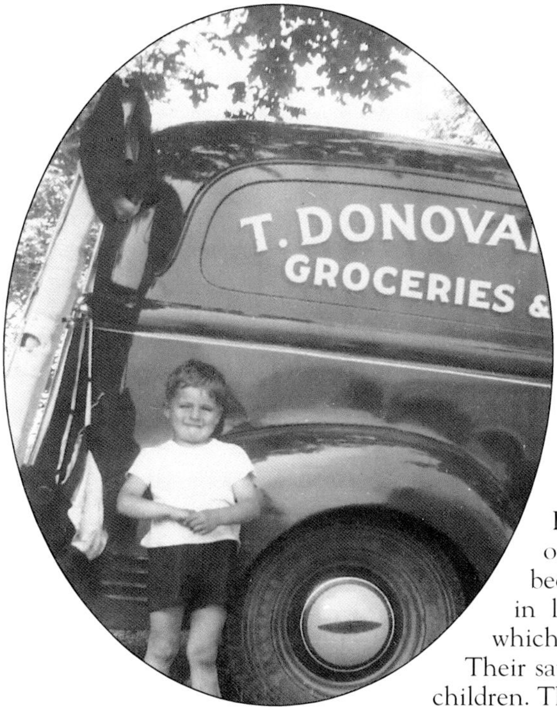

Pictured here is Donovan's Delivery wagon on Queen Square. The young boy may have been tagging along helping an older brother in loading groceries, or meats for the port, which was a large part of Donovan's business. Their sawdust floor was a great attraction for local children. The business closed in 1956.

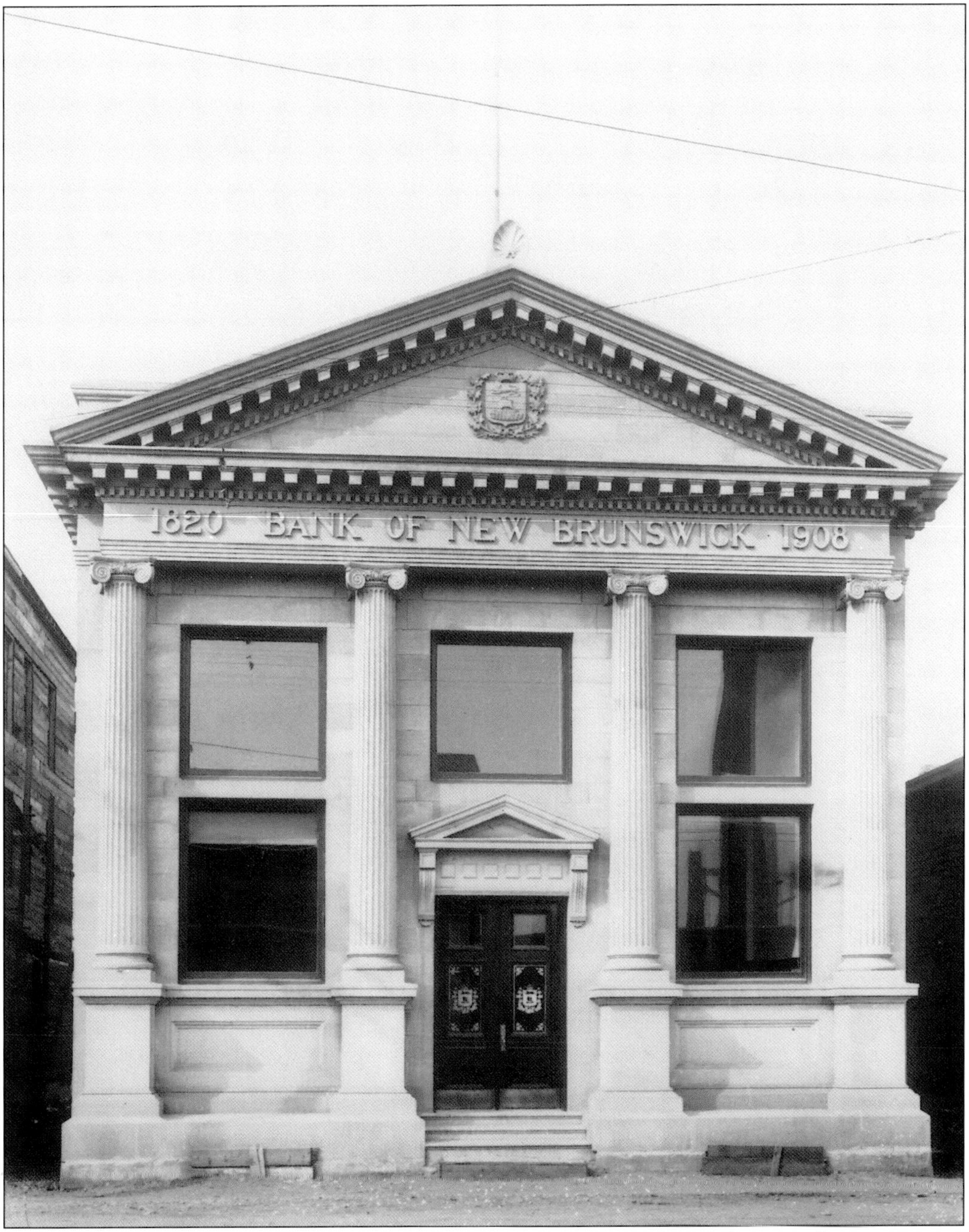

The decorative Bank of New Brunswick on Union Street West replaced the store-front operation shown on page 48. This photo was taken by Isaac Erb in 1909. The Bank of New Brunswick was later swallowed up by the Bank of Nova Scotia. A larger but similar-styled building still stands on Prince William Street in downtown Saint John. (Courtesy Vintage Photo and Frame.)

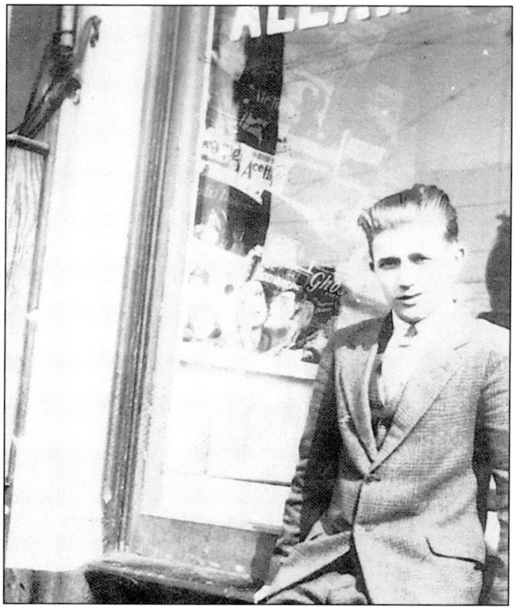

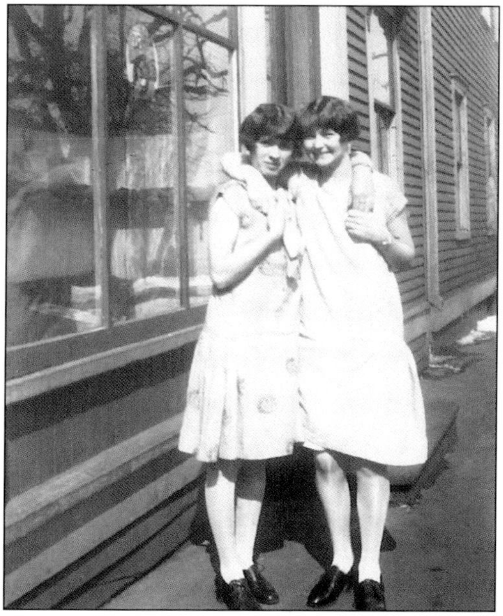

Left: Pictured here is Rudman Allan's lower King Street Store prior to 1932. Hazen Walton is standing in front, perhaps planning to sneak in for a look at the "True Romances" and other pulp periodicals that can be faintly seen in the window. *Right:* Shown in this 1950s photo is Iliffe's Shoe Repair on King Street, which was one of several such shoemaker shops in Saint John West that could be counted on to keep shoes going for another season.

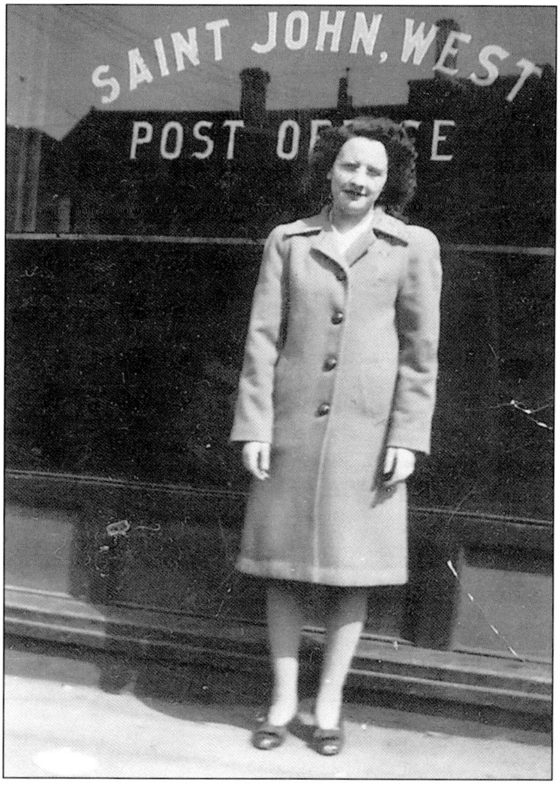

Lois Watters recalls she was going home from Sunday school at nearby St. George's Church in the early 1950s when she stopped on King Street to have this photo taken at the Saint John West Post Office. She's not sure if she went into the adjacent Star Restaurant for a sundae on that occasion, though it was a popular stop for her and her gang. (Courtesy Lois Guthrie.)

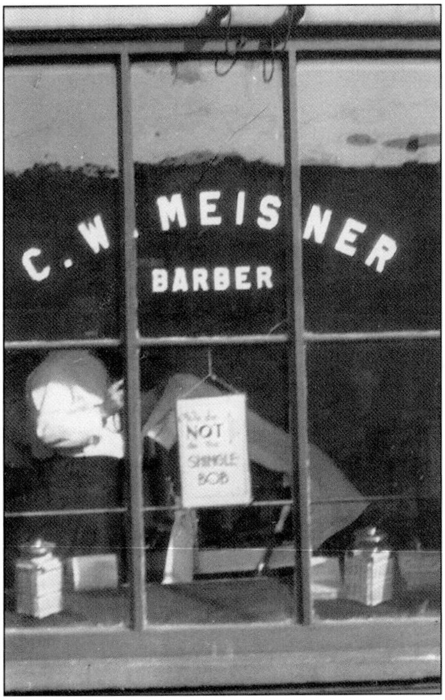

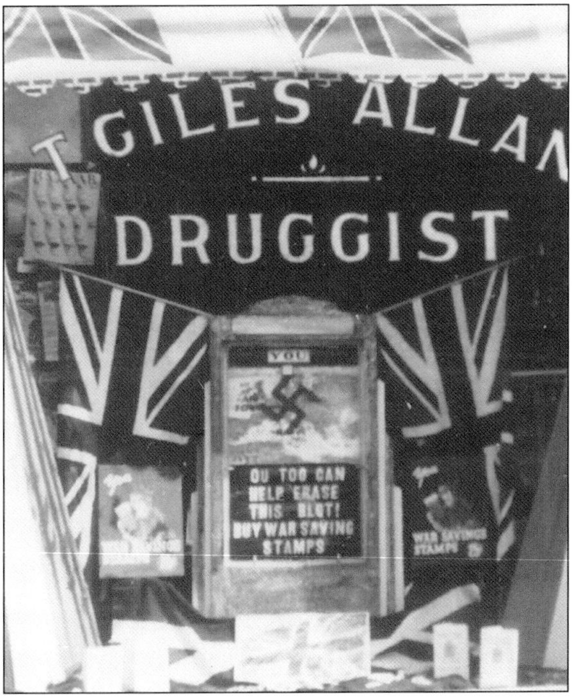

Pictured are two interesting 1940s signs on King Street stores, which are self explanatory, except, who knows what a "Shingle Bob" style was, or why Charlie Meisner would not do this cut?

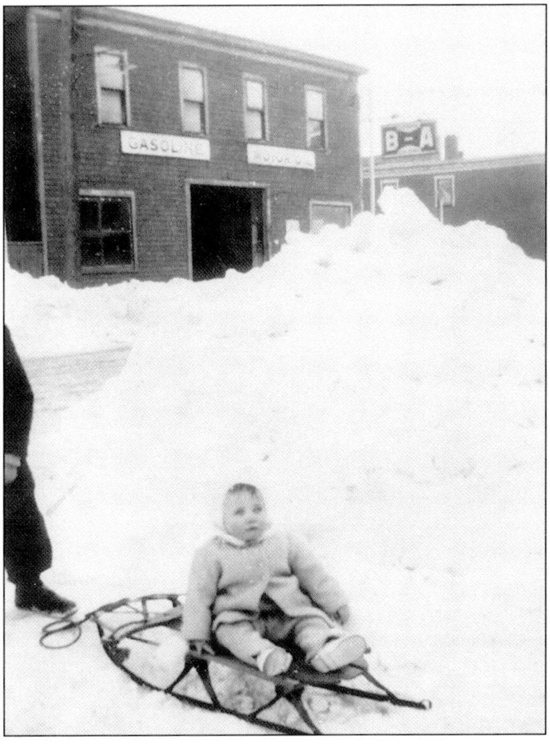

The Maritime Garage on Rodney Street was one of only three local spots to buy gas as cars became popular. The other two were W.E. Emerson on King Street and the Olive Street Garage just over the border from West Saint John in what was known as Beaconsfield.

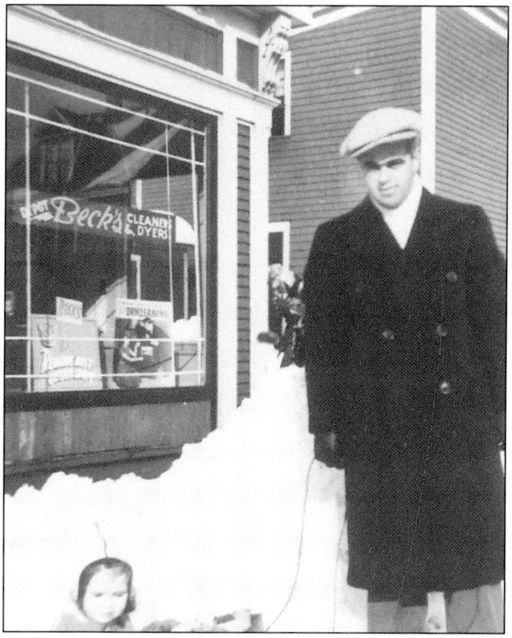

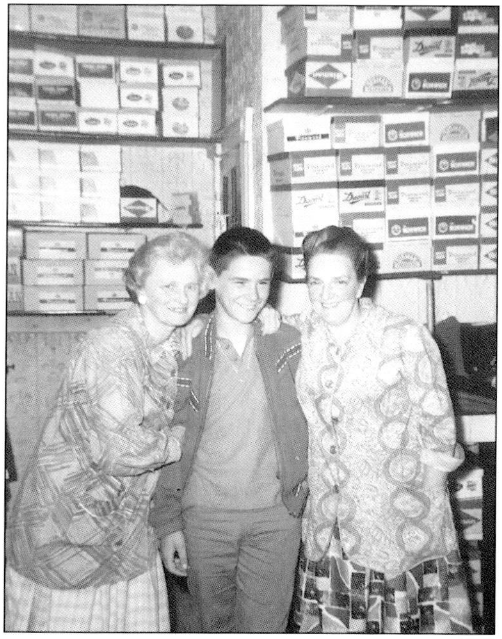

Left: Beck's Dry Cleaners on Rodney Street kept area residents' clothes spiffy, including this stylish coat being worn by Gerry Driscoll in 1950. (Courtesy of Betty Walsh.) *Right:* George Harned's daughter Vivian (Sweeney) and her co-worker, Pat Campbell, give their delivery boy, remembered only as a Daigle family member, a bit of a hug just before the store closed in 1956. (Courtesy Vivian Sweeney.)

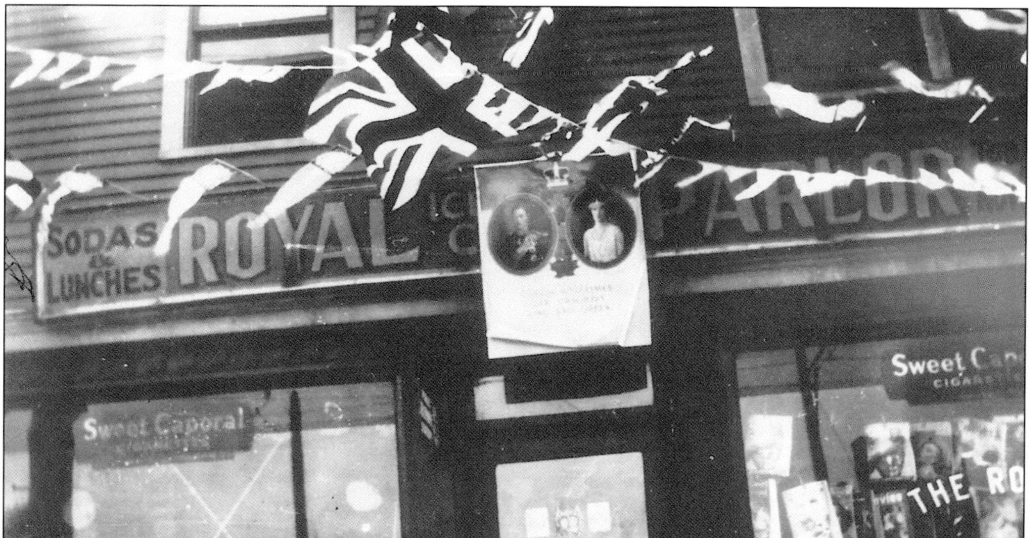

Lanes operated a lunch counter business that became generally known as "Peck's" on Market Place, but was officially known as "The Royal Ice Cream Parlour", seen here when decorated for the King and Queen's visit in 1939.

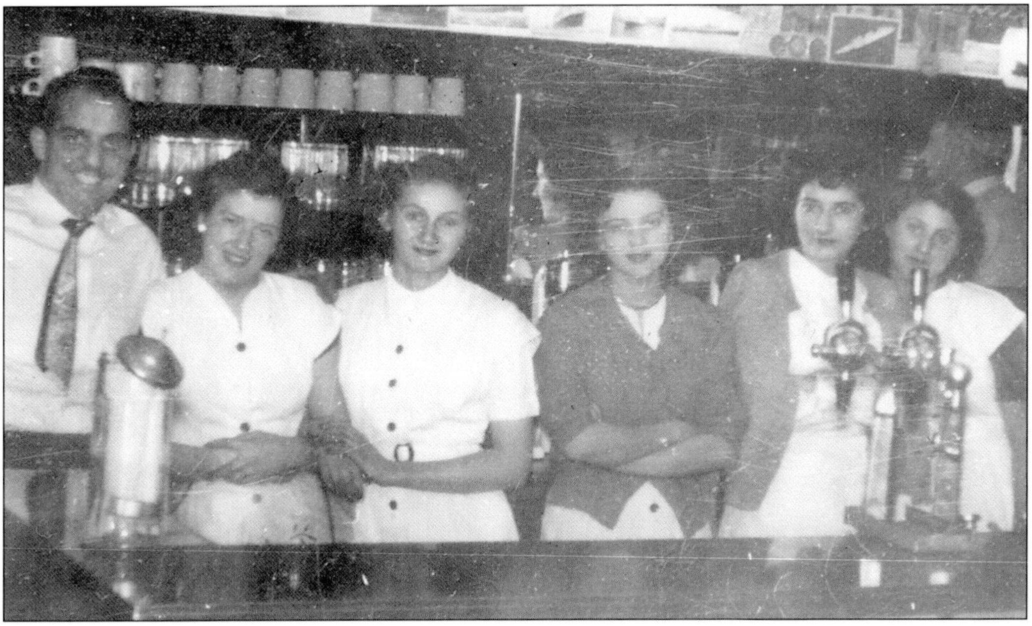

This is the interior of Gar's Restaurant, with owner Gar Meltzer on the extreme left. Sailors who came into port were Gar's steady customers. They could easily walk over the over-track bridge, known locally as the "cage" or "birdcage", and many left behind postcards (see over Gar's head) of the ships they served on as a memento of the good times at Gar's.

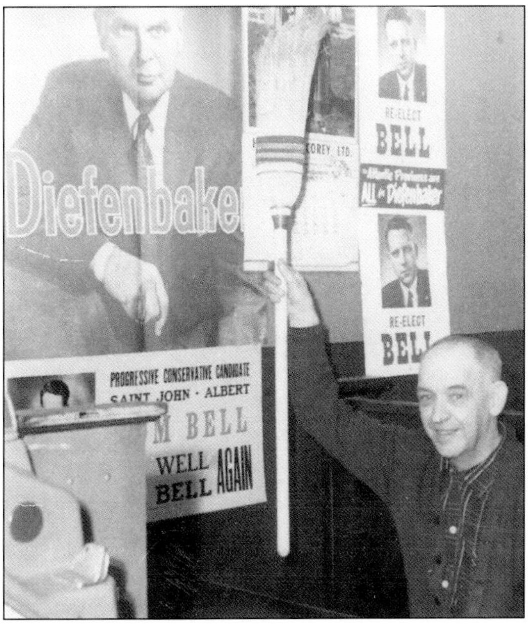

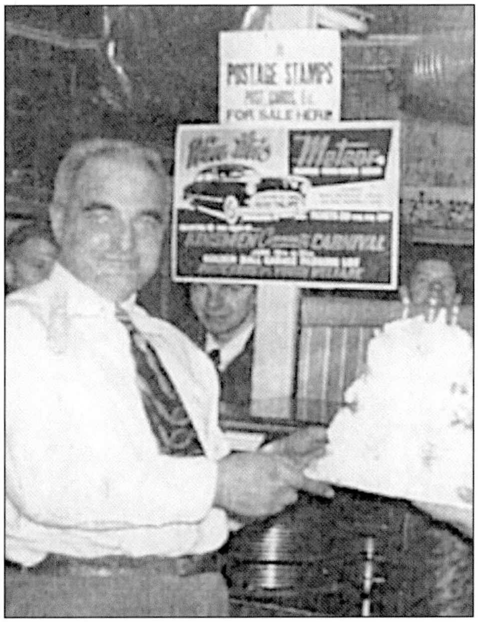

Left: Shown here is Peck Joyce's Store, with "Peck" himself acknowledging his strong support for Diefenbaker, affectionately known as "Dief the chief". Dief won the election in 1957 and became Prime Minister. If he had visited Peck's, he would have been treated to the longshoreman's special of two dogs and a coffee for a quarter, just like anyone else. *Right:* Gar Meltzer is pictured on the right. He was about to present his brother and partner Bill with a birthday cake at their restaurant at the foot of Rodney Street.

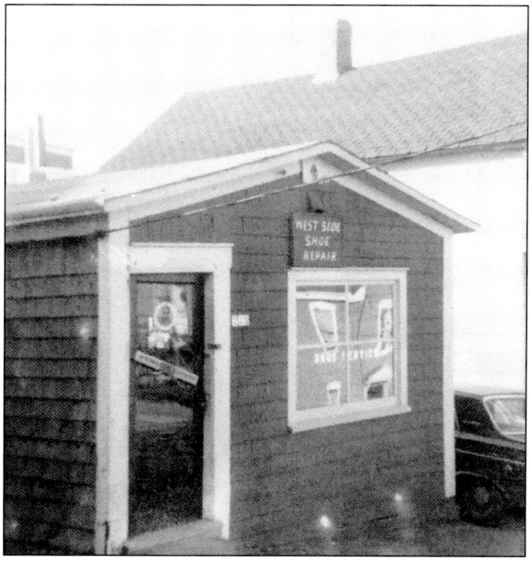

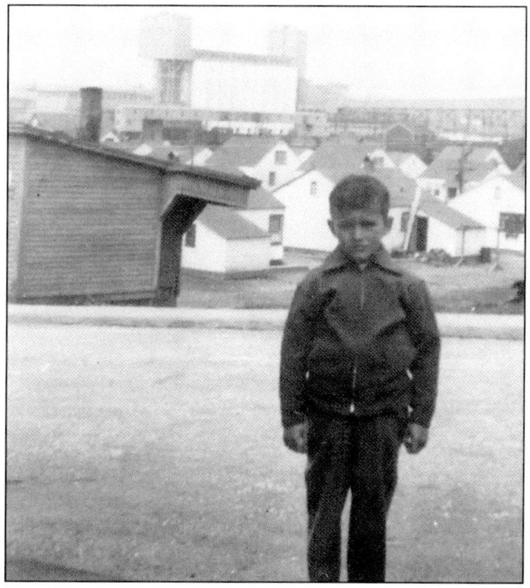

Left: Fillmore's Shoe Repair, in the former Herrington Store at 215 Watson Street, replaced a smaller shop attached to a home that Fillmore had run on Rodney Street. *Right:* This is the Carleton Coal Yard at the edge of the Millpond on the corner of St. John and Ludlow. It looks like the late 1950s when it was being run by the Aldermans from St. James Street. Since 1970 it has been the site of the Royal Canadian Legion, Branch #2.

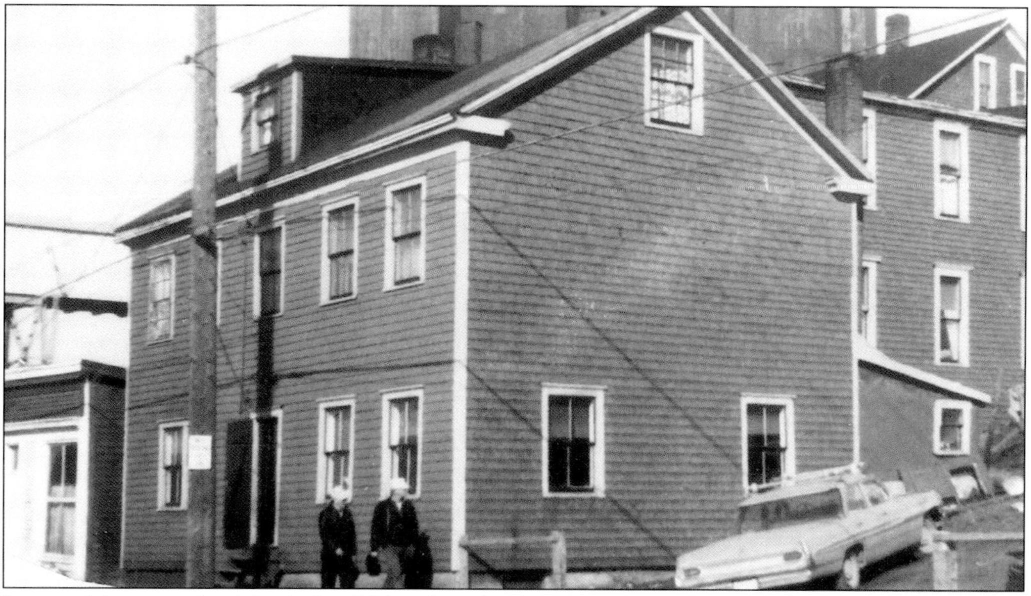

Pictured here is the Maple Leaf Hotel and Al's Restaurant on St. John Street. The hotel accommodated longshoremen from the north shore of New Brunswick, and some from Quebec who found work at the port from November till April. They were often called "highbooters" by locals (but not likely to their faces). Some say they shared beds and slept in shifts to keep costs down. Of course, this kept occupancy and profits up for owners Frederick J. Manning (1933–1943) and Vital Richard (1947–1969).

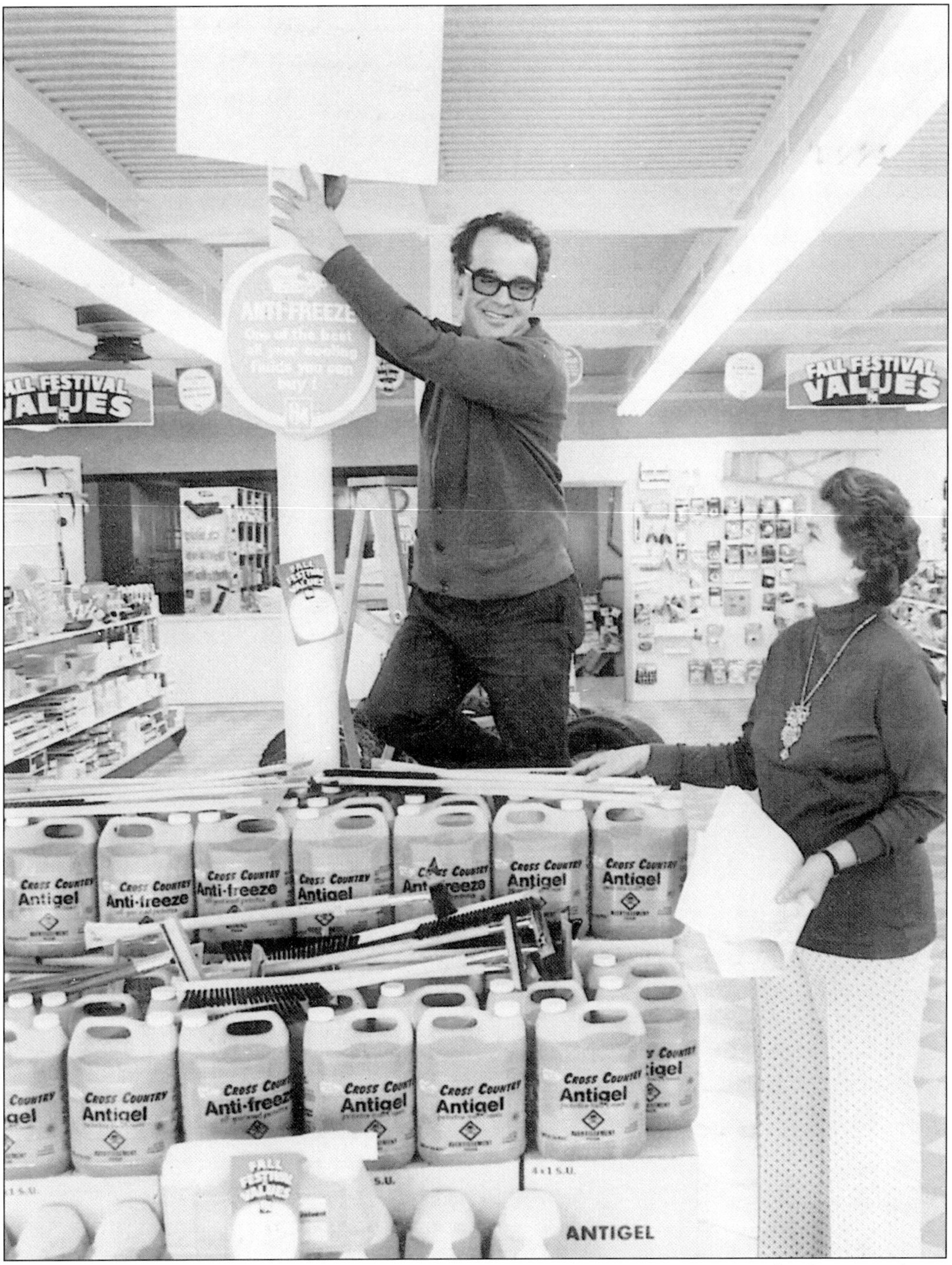

This is the grand opening of the Handy Andy Store on November 5, 1975, in the former Sobeys' building listed as 115 Ludlow Street. The business was owned by Gordon Boyd. In the opening publicity, his partners are listed as Vice President Jasper Cameron and Secretary-Treasurer Eileen Campbell. His associate in the photo is Bonnie Gillespie. The store lasted only three years, then for a time it housed an auction centre run by Charles Palk. Today it is a popular Frenchy's used clothing outlet.

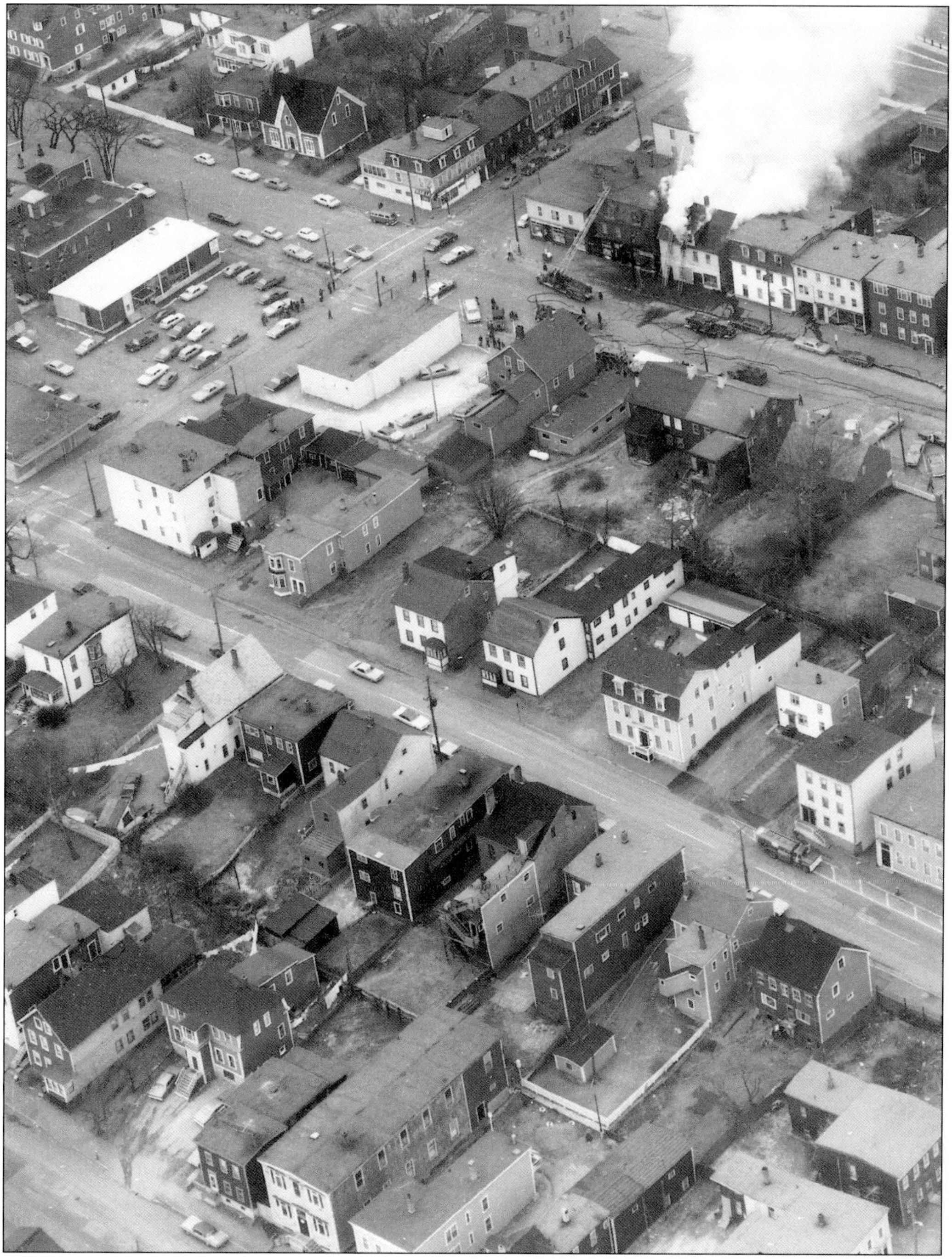

Fire destroys the Rose Brother building on King Street West in the late 1970s. It would have made sense for those displaced by the throughway to move to the King Street area, but many of the buildings were old, had been used as commercial space, and then sat vacant for some time. Thus, they were a target for vandalism and fire, as was the case here. As one was destroyed, it seemed to speed up the process, and soon another would be burnt or torn down, till the street was largely vacant lots by the early 1980s.

Five

The Club

When the Community Theatre closed in 1958, community activists Dr. Harry Peters and Ron Lynch felt it could be turned into a community centre for children of the area. At that time there were more than a thousand children in St. Patrick's and New Albert schools—the so-called baby boomers. Though the churches served them well with youth groups such as Scouts and Guides, there was a developing interest in wider athletic endeavours, and there really was no building that served exclusively for such recreational pursuits. Peters interested Kay Robertson in helping the cause, and she became the agitator at city hall. Many new programs got underway, primarily with volunteer help, though Mel Harned and Ken Estabrooks were hired to work in the athletic area.

Among the volunteers was Fred Miller, who became the first full-time director in 1970. Fred served in that capacity until his death in December 1997. A memorial plaque stands in Tilley Square outside the centre as a tribute to Fred and the work he did in the community. He was truly known as 'Mr. West Side'. As a result of the work of those named (and many others it must be noted), the centre appears healthy and should continue to serve West Siders for years to come.

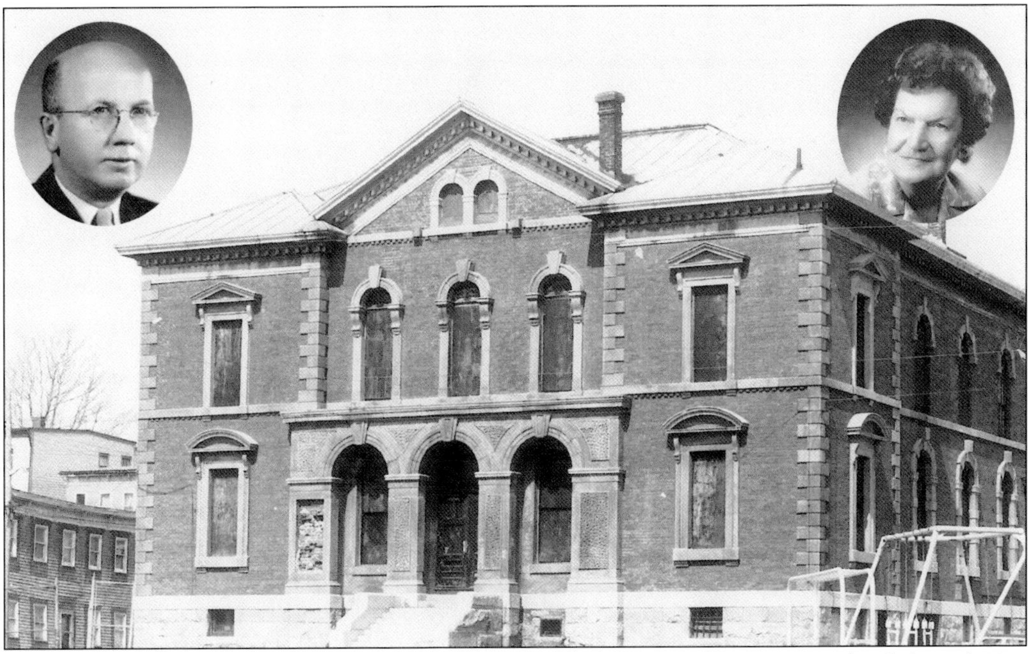

Shown here is the Carleton Community Centre, with Harry Peters on the left and Kay Robertson on the right.

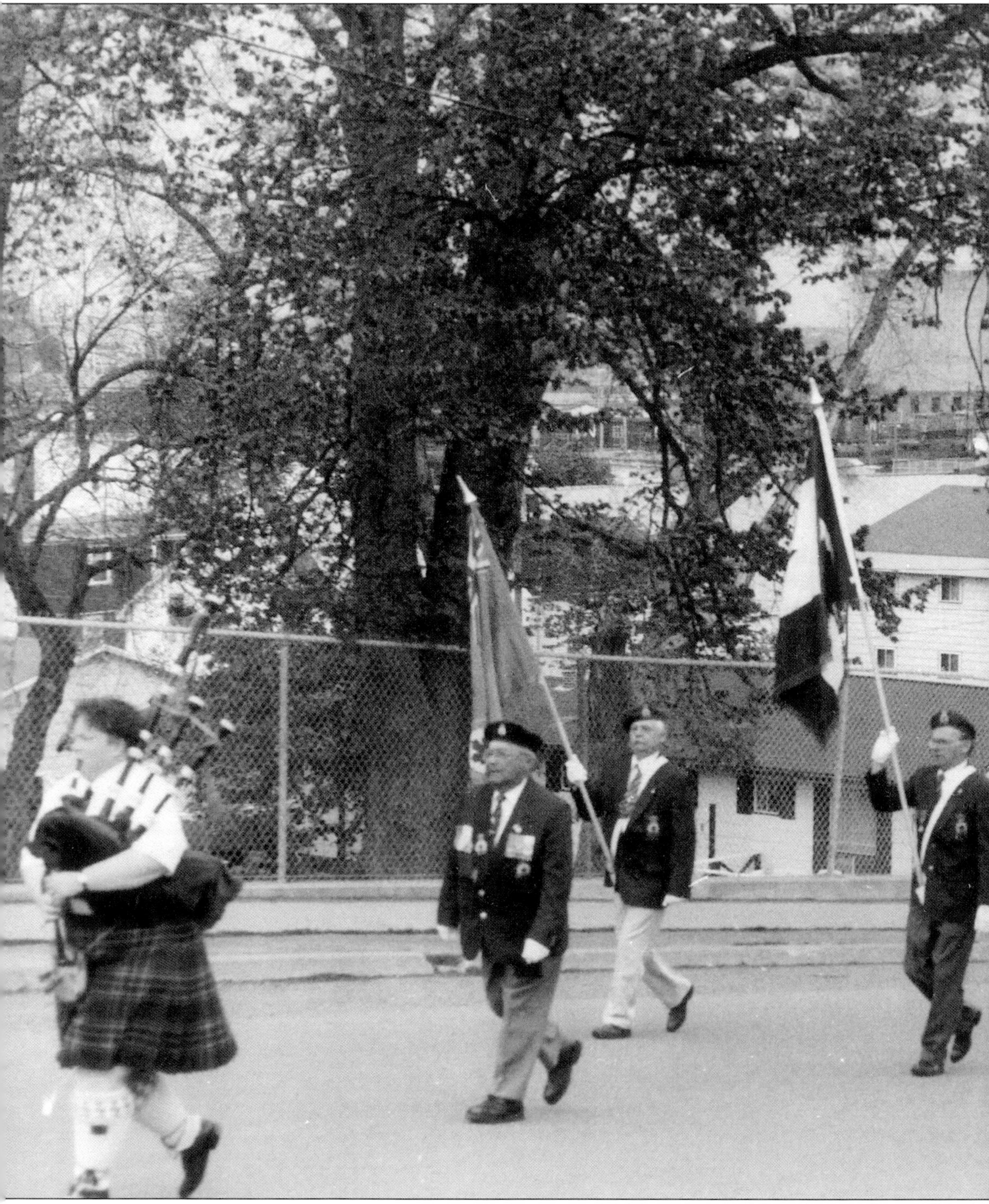

On June 6, 1997, the last parade for West Side Days in which Fred Miller was a participant was held. Fred is seen in the centre of the photo, marching up Ludlow Street hill near Guilford. West Side Days grew out of the Bicentennial celebration of 1984 when David Goss and Fred Miller worked to hold a day in tribute to the first mayor, Gabriel G. Ludlow, who lived on Duke

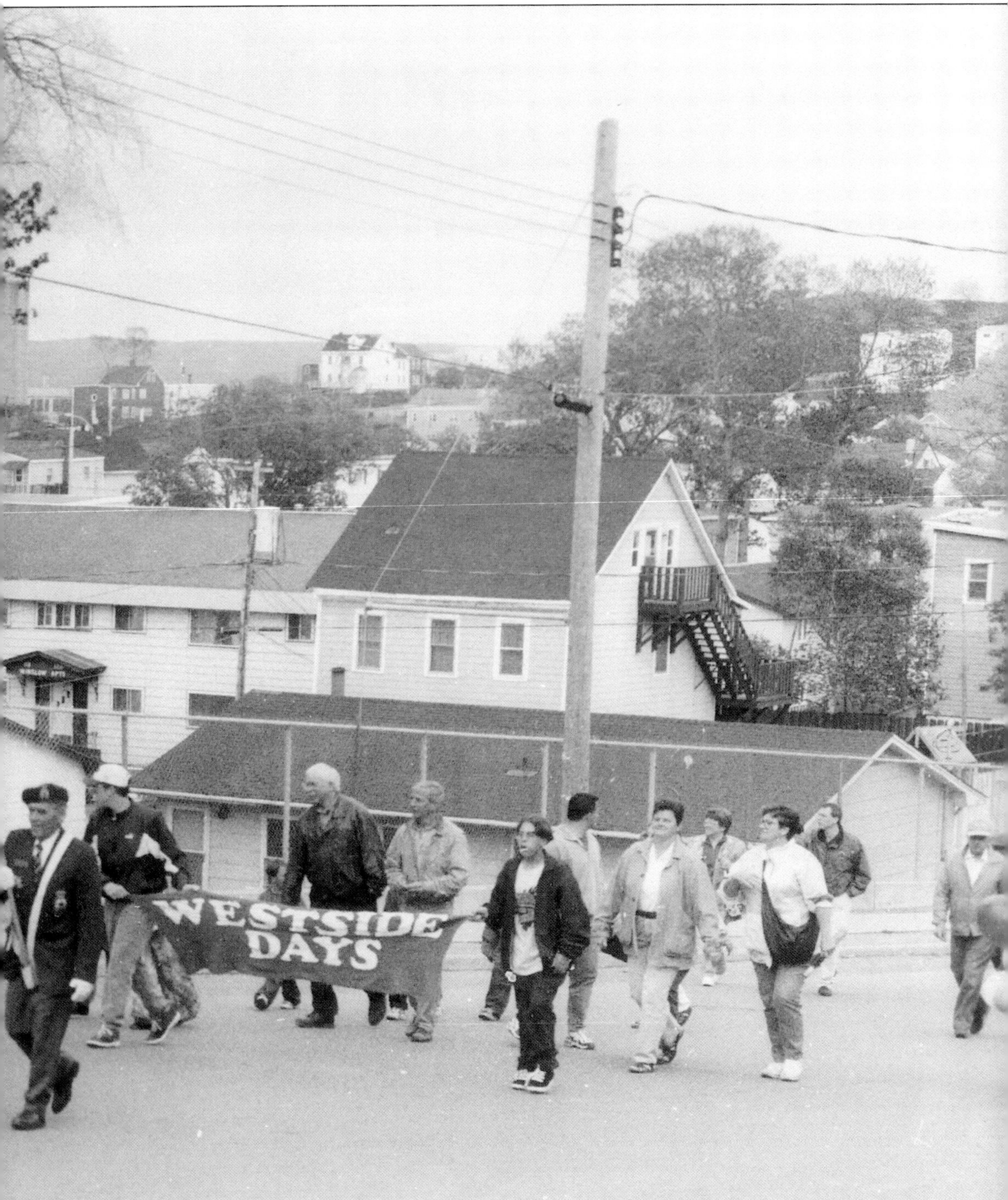

Street. Soon after that successful day, Fred formed a committee, and worked annually to see that the West Side Days were staged as a community builder and a part of the Carleton Community Centre program. The weekend has continued after Fred's death and should continue to be an important part of celebrating living in Saint John West.

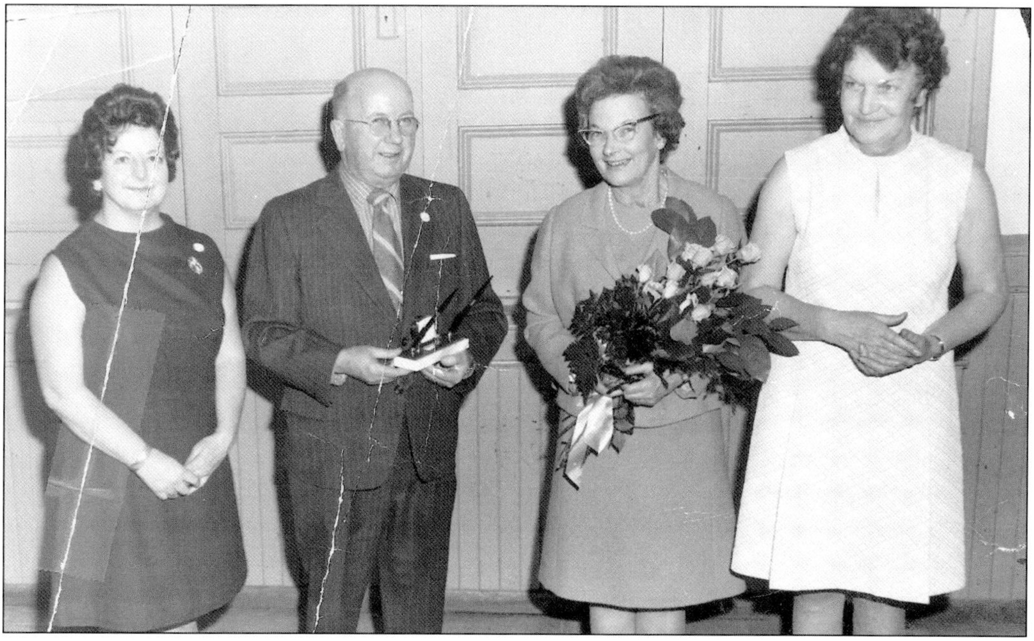

Inside the Carleton Community Centre, a presentation involving (left to right) Elizabeth (Libby) Parks, longtime volunteer worker at the club, Dr. Harry Peters, founder, his wife Margaret Peters, and co-founder Kay Robertson was photographed. Cy Oram took the photo about 1970.

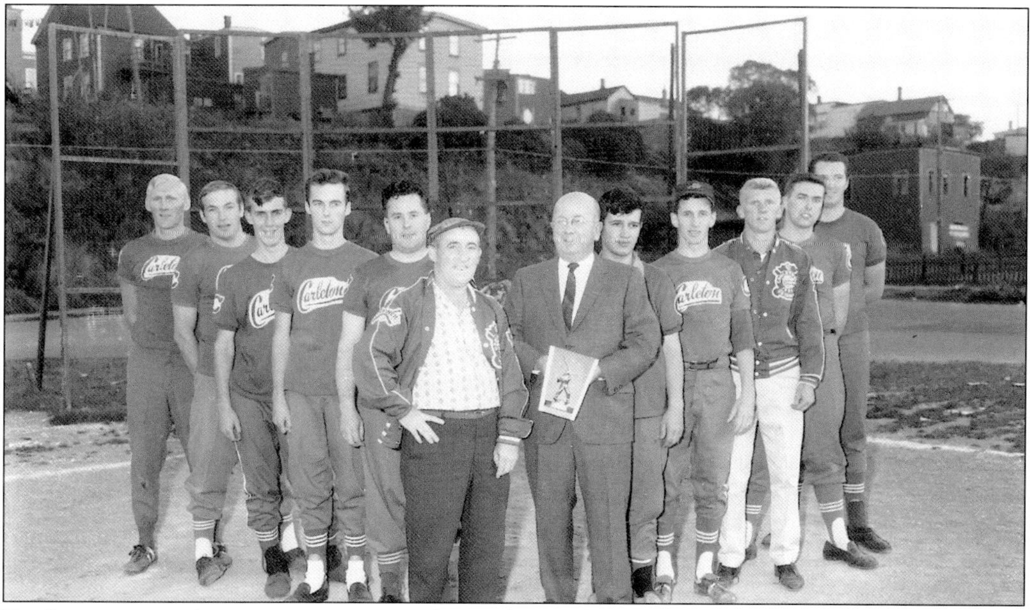

Dr. Peters is seen here presenting a trophy to the Carleton baseball team on what is known as the Millpond Field, located on the southeast corner of what was the Millpond. Fred Miller was the chief agitator for the development of this field where tidal waters had once flowed. Those identified left to right are: Brian Johnston, Gerald Bonnevier, Linsay Tracy, Mickey Tait, Mel Harned, Ben Donner, Dr. Harry Peters, Brian Vaughan, Fred Miller, Carl Johnston, David Orr, and Danny Keleher.

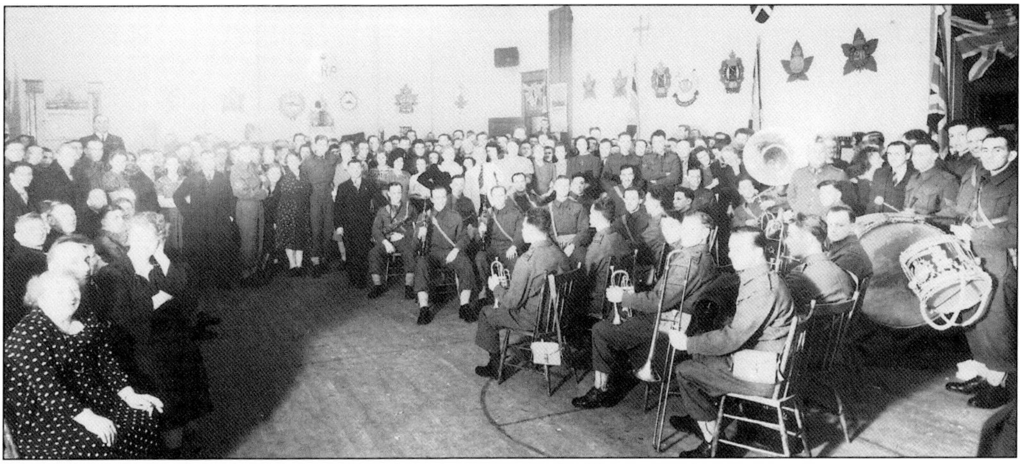

The Royal Canadian Legion, Branch #2, was established in 1926 and began to operate from the second floor of the Carleton Community Centre sometime during the Second World War. They remained there until they built their own building on the corner of St. John and Ludlow Streets in 1970. The Legion has retained a strong interest in the Carleton Community Centre. For some years they presented the Carleton Community Centre with a van, which was used to transport the children to events, and to this day they help the centre financially with needs not met by the City of Saint John, their prime sponsors.

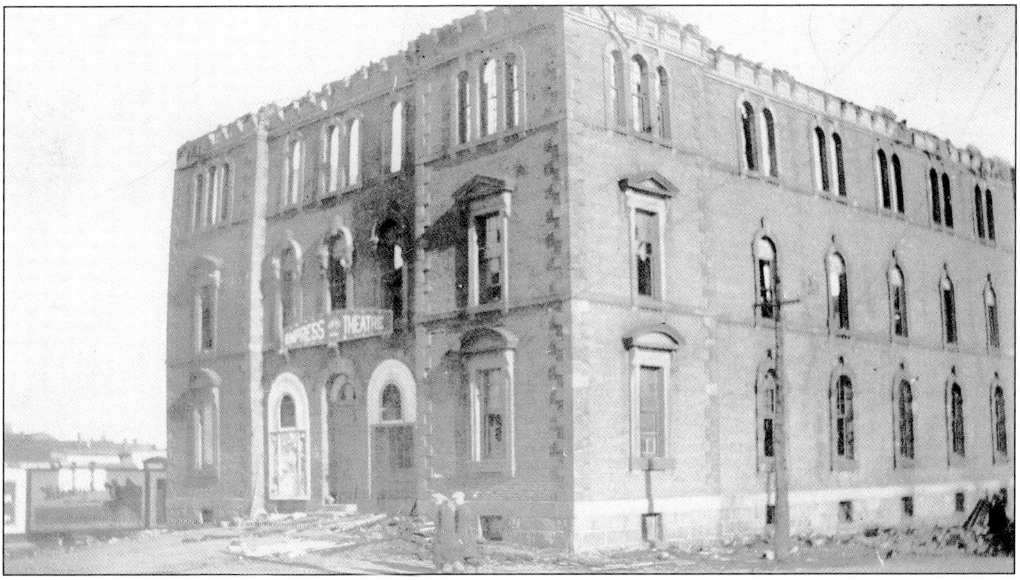

The date on this photo of the Empress Theatre, November 7, 1925, is perplexing. The fire that destroyed the building happened on October 14. The walls were supposed to have fallen that night, yet here is a picture with the walls intact a month later. The fire started in a projection booth and quickly burned through the walls. There were 150 in attendance and all escaped unhurt. After much controversy, a contract was let to the Stackhouse Brothers to board it up, and it sat unused and unheated through the winter of 1925. The following spring council decided to rebuild but without the third storey. The cost was $64,000, less $20,000 from insurance held.

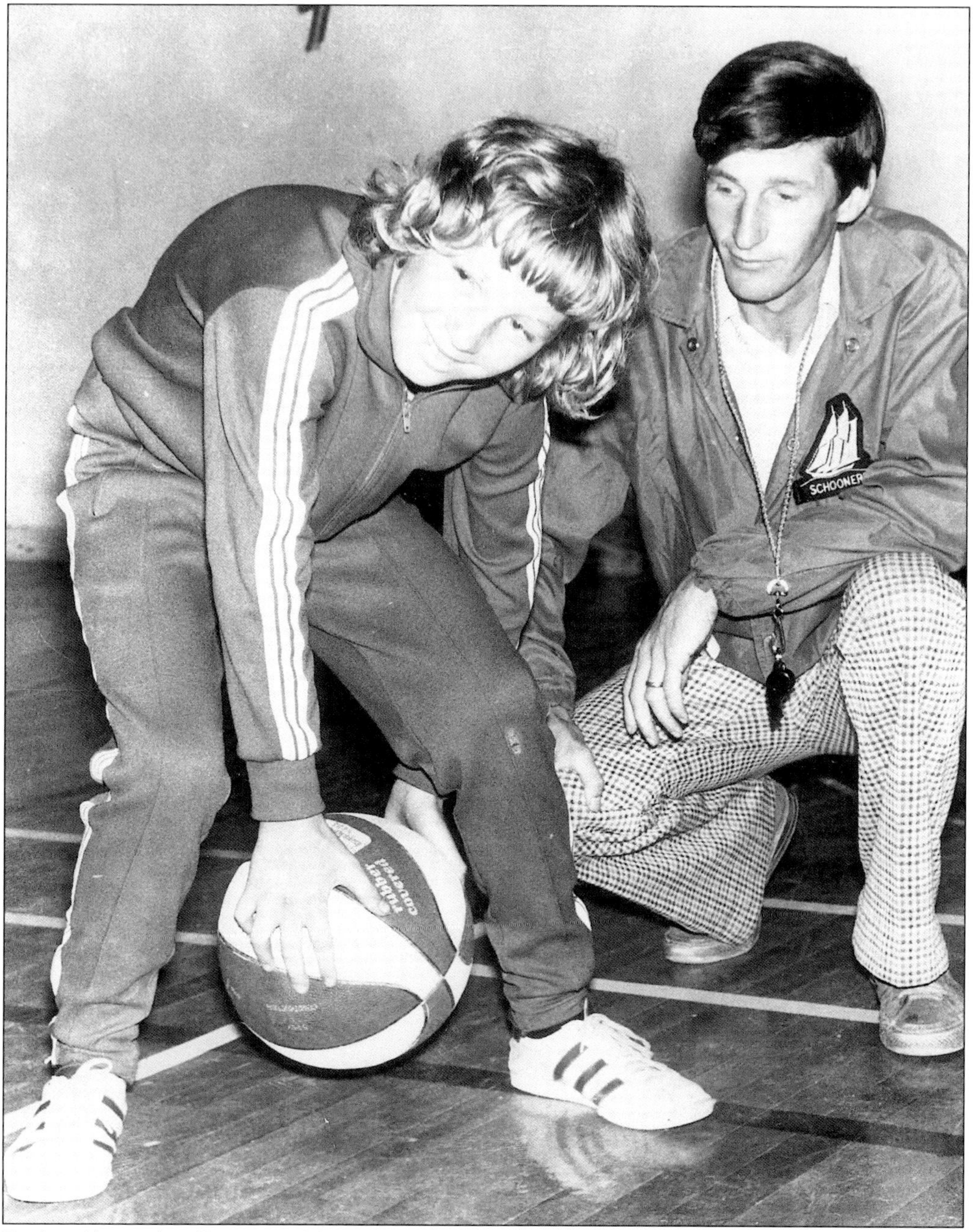

Fred Miller and Jeff McDonald are shown soon after Fred took employment with the club in 1970. Basketball teams from the club went as far as Boston to play teams.

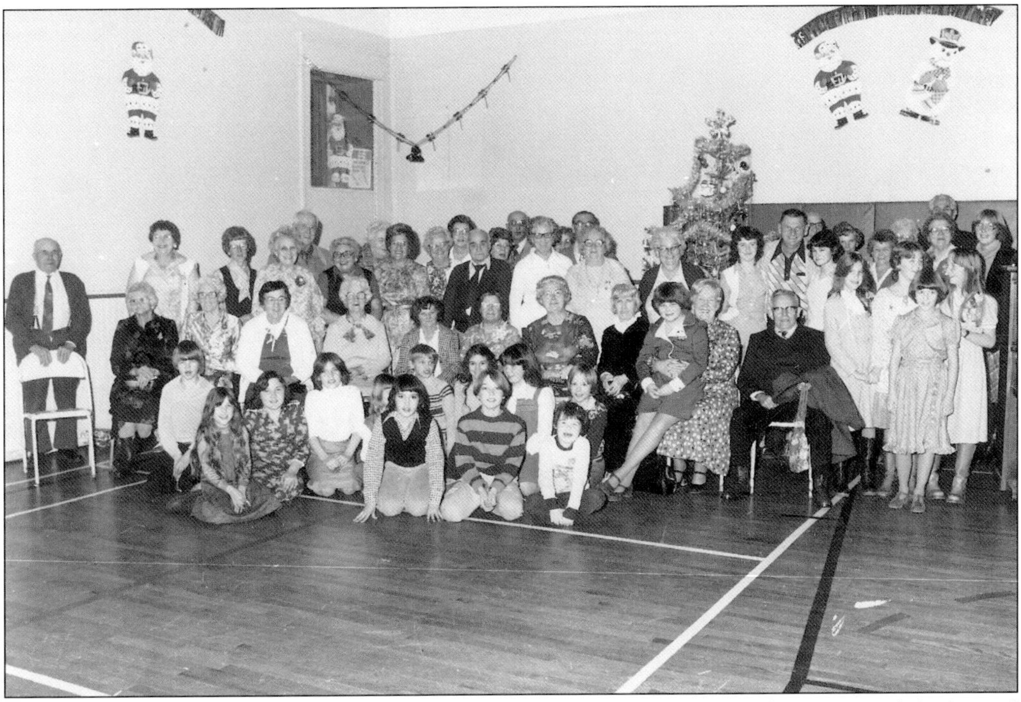

Seniors were an integral part of the work of the Community Centre, and a senior's club, formed there in the early 1970s, as shown here, was one of the first in Saint John. An active club continues to be a part of the program.

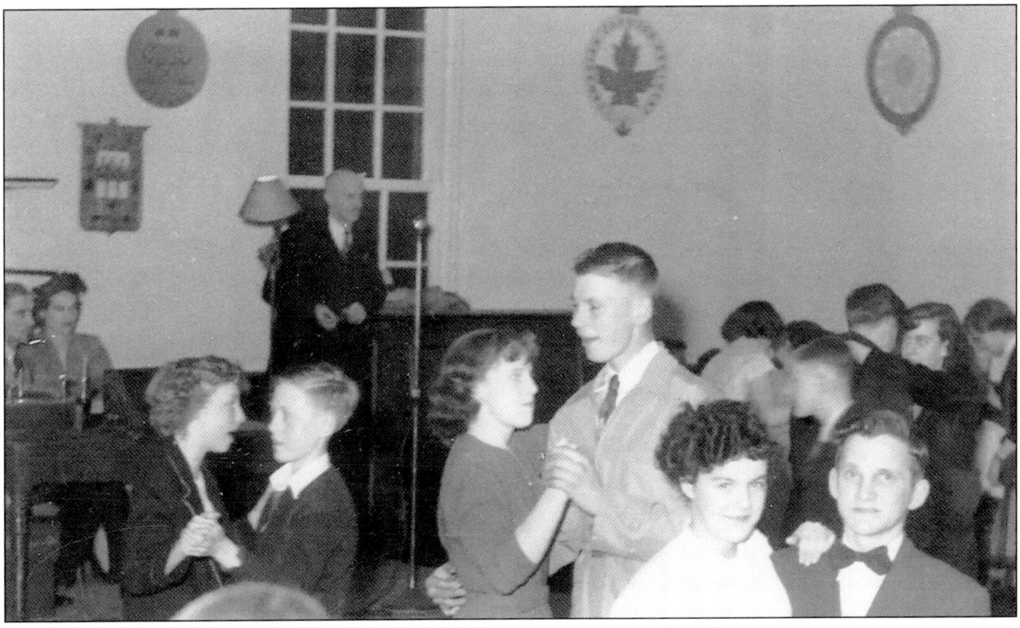

Teen dances have long been a part of the club's attractions, in fact, for some, the most important activity they offer. The participants in this 1950s dance are identified only as the Galbraiths. The teen dances continue to be a focus of the club and are held on Friday nights from September till May.

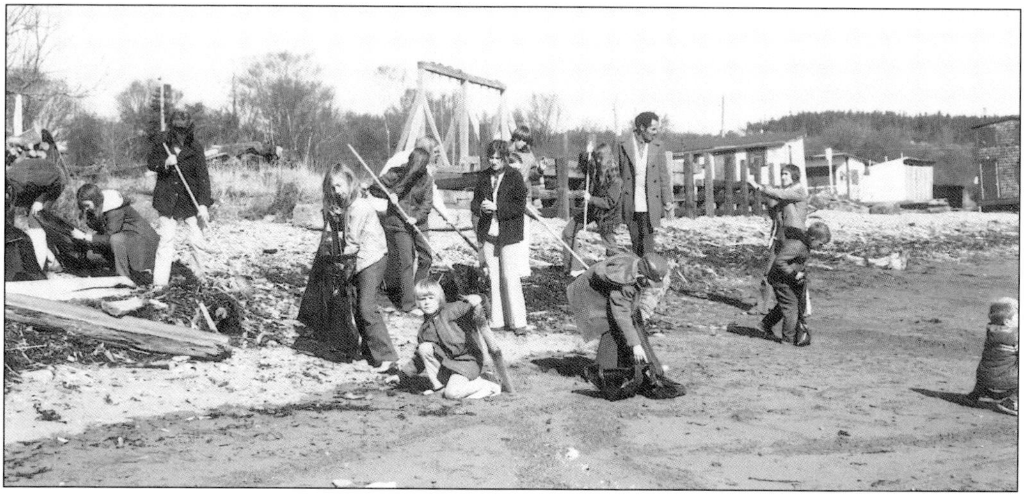

The club engages in various projects in the community, which are meant to help others, and this cleanup of McLarens Beach is one such activity. Though the beach is several miles from the club, the club still took on this shorefront cleanup project as a service to the community on several occasions.

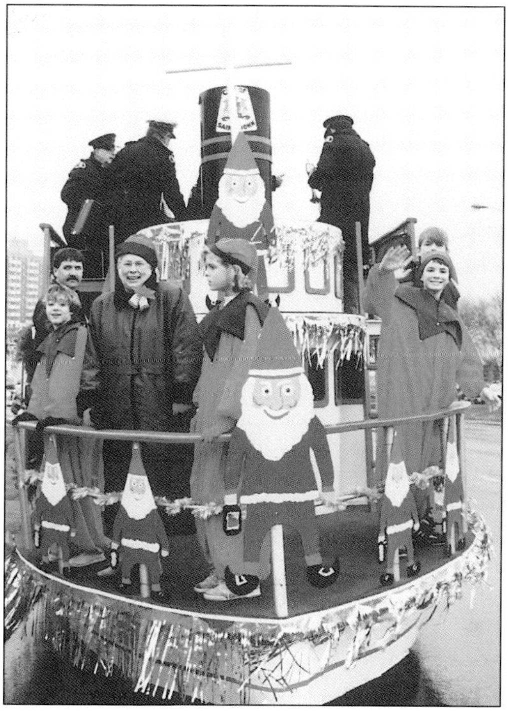

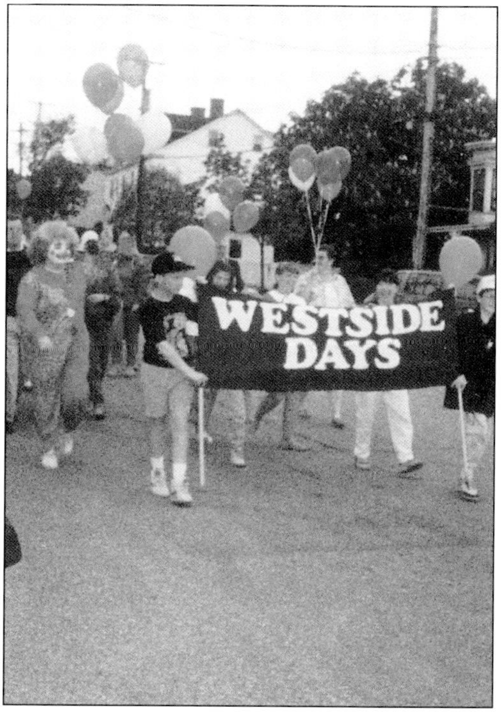

Left: Mayor Elsie Wayne (third from bottom left) honoured the Carleton Community Majorette group by inviting them to be the elves on her Christmas Float in the Saint John Santa Claus Parade in 1991. *Right:* The West Side Days "people" parade always winds through the streets of the lower West Side to let residents know that there is a wide range of activities underway to celebrate life in the area on the first weekend in June. One of the most popular was always the display of Fred's 600 plus photos, some of which have since appeared in "Saint John West and its Neighbours," and others that are included in this latest book.

Six

How They Got Around

Next to images of West Siders posed by the stores that they patronized, we found pictures of residents posing by cars (which they either owned or borrowed) as the type of picture that showed up most frequently.

Initially, Fred would view the cars as foreground clutter, something just blocking a building he would be interested in having a picture of in the background. Eventually, though, we came to realize that West Siders were passionate about their modes of travel as we are about the places they lived and played, and in this chapter, we try to honour that love.

So we will step back to the days of horse and wagon and the era of the streetcar, bicycle, and then to the early motor vehicles.

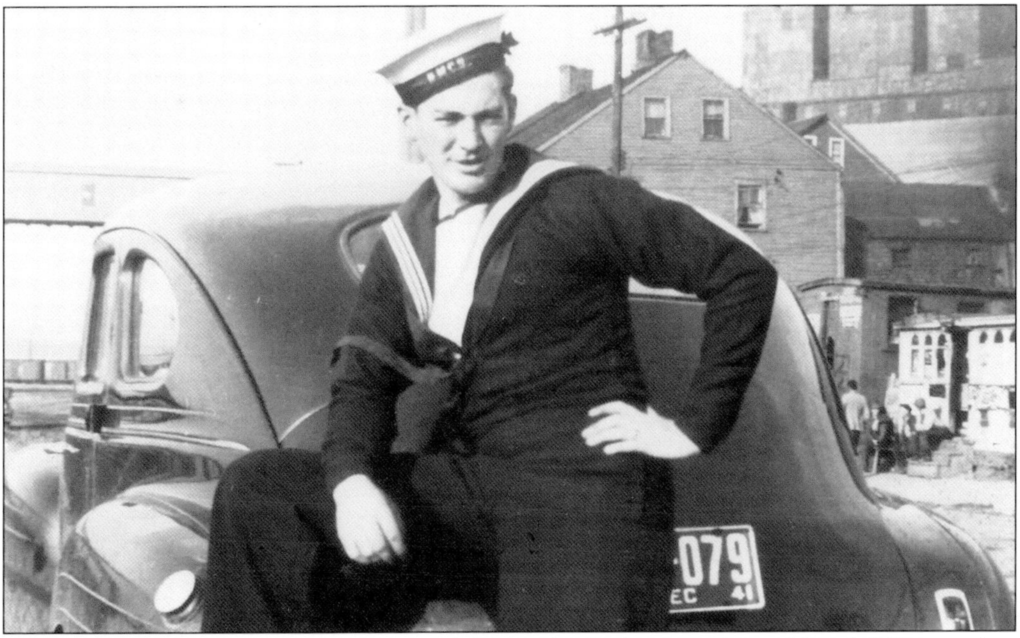

The picture above will take us only part of the way back, for it is a Second World War-era shot of an unidentified sailor proudly posed by his car, which the Tobin family gave Fred, on St. John Street. There were no other details attached to the picture, but it looks like there might have been a good story to tell from the look on his face and the beam in his eye. One wonders how many girls were just out of camera range waiting for a ride!

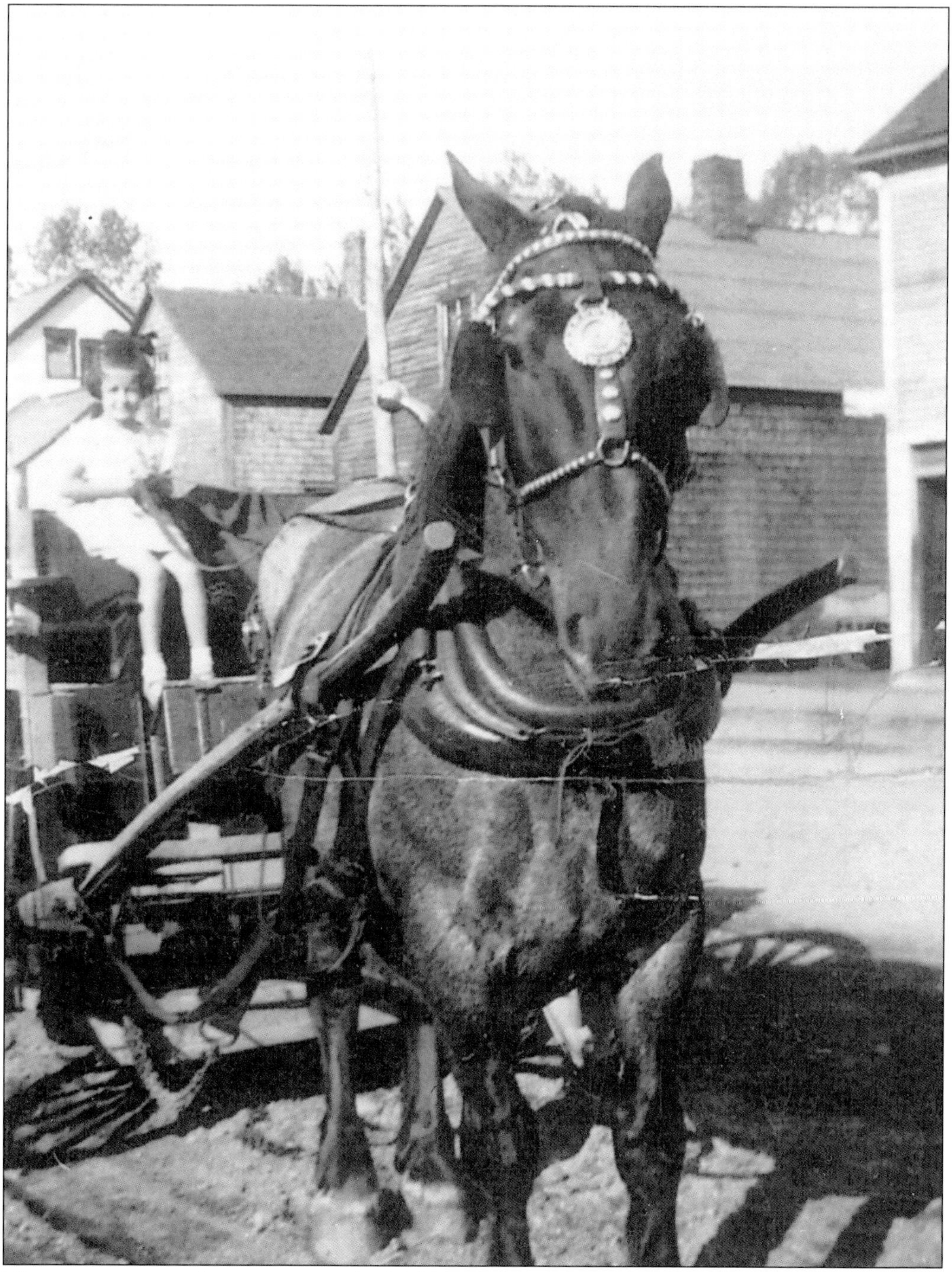

The inscription on this portrait reads, "Velma on the Crystal Ice Wagon on Rodney St." Velma has been identified as Velma McAllister. It is likely from the early 1920s, and the horse pictured is one of many who probably had a great deal of difficulty on December 1, 1922, when the law required New Brunswickers to switch to the right side of the road. The horses never quite figured this out and when left alone during a delivery the animals would often wander over to the left side of the road where they were originally trained to operate.

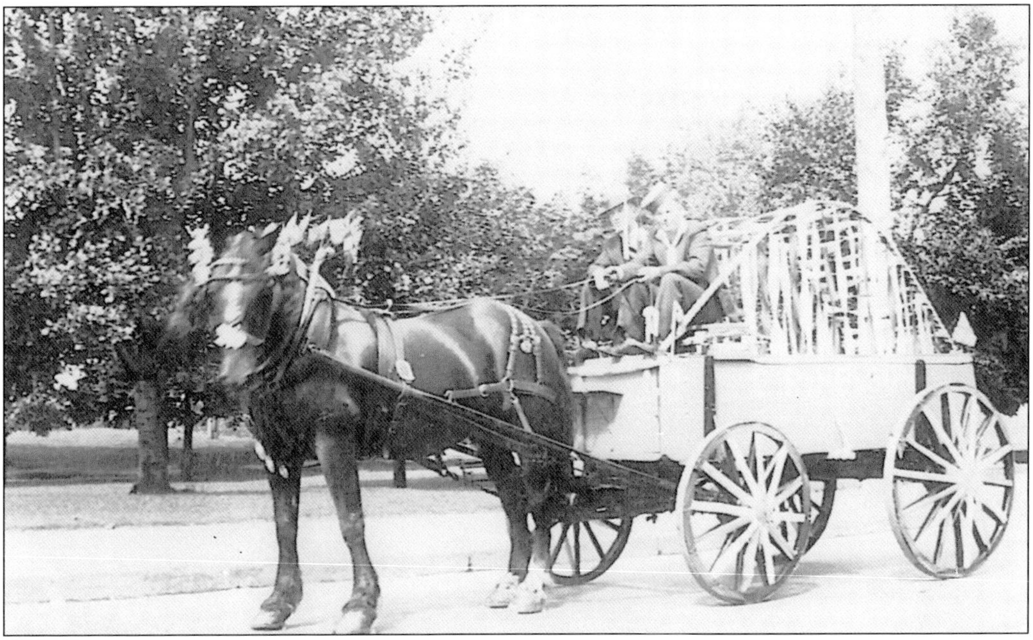

Hauling tons of dusty coal (26 bags to the ton meant you got a full load) one day, and then, the next day, being all decked out to participate in a parade (which the firemen may have sponsored or the sponsors of the sculling tournament may have arranged), was part of the life of the horse in Saint John West.

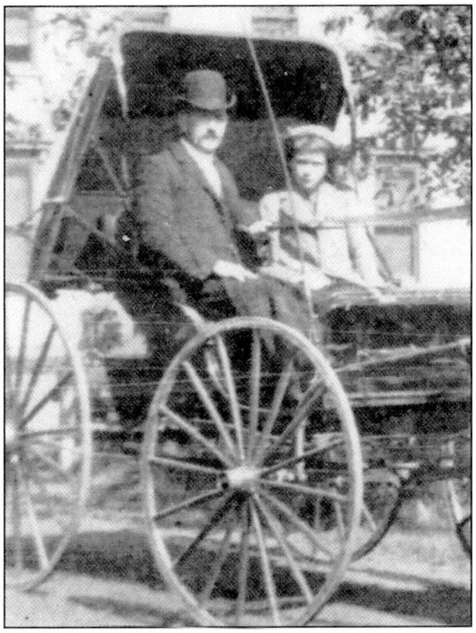

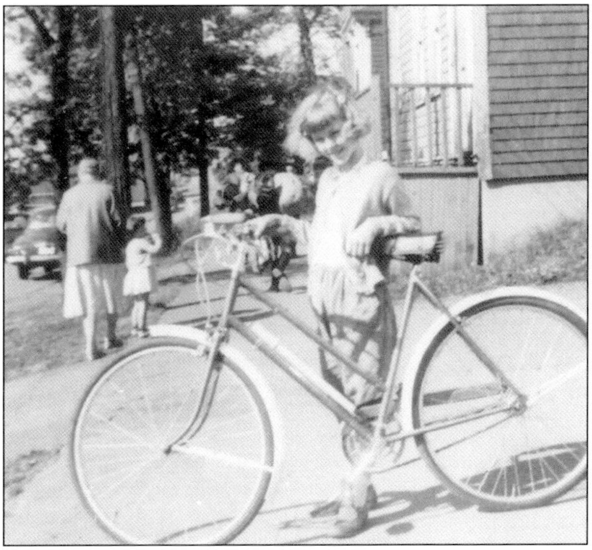

Left: Jasper Cameron Sr. returns to his home following a wagon ride. This may have taken him as far as Spruce Lake, a popular destination for West Side horsemen, or he may have taken the Reversing Falls bridge and gone out Douglas Avenue and up to Rockwood Park, where he could enjoy the circuitous trails developed there by the Saint John Horticultural Society to a plan by landscape architect Downing Vaux in 1894. Cameron can also be seen in his barber shop on page 32. *Right:* Betty Ann Carter, around 1958, proudly shows off her bike, which was basic transportation for most children from the late 1800s to the era of skateboards. Before the era of malls, most West Siders bought their bikes at W.E. Emerson's on King Street.

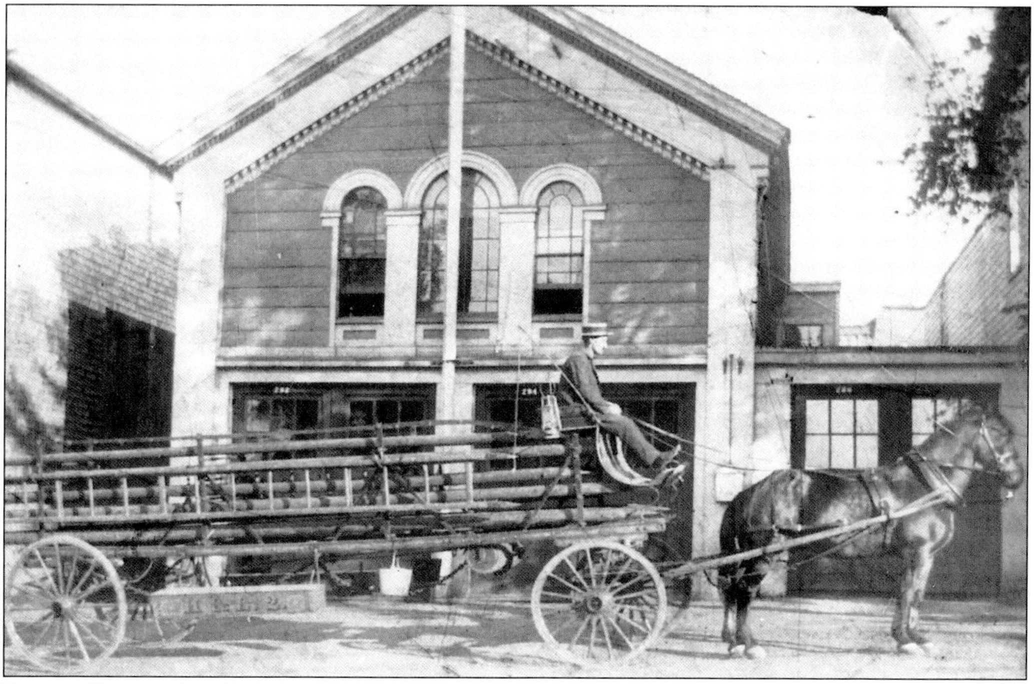

Pictured here is the No. 2 Hook and Ladder on King Street West. The building in the background was incorporated into the present brick structure in 1936. The current building is recognized in the Canadian Inventory of Historic Buildings as a Heritage Fire Station. It is the last of the old-time stations in continuous use, and has been threatened with closure a number of times in recent years.

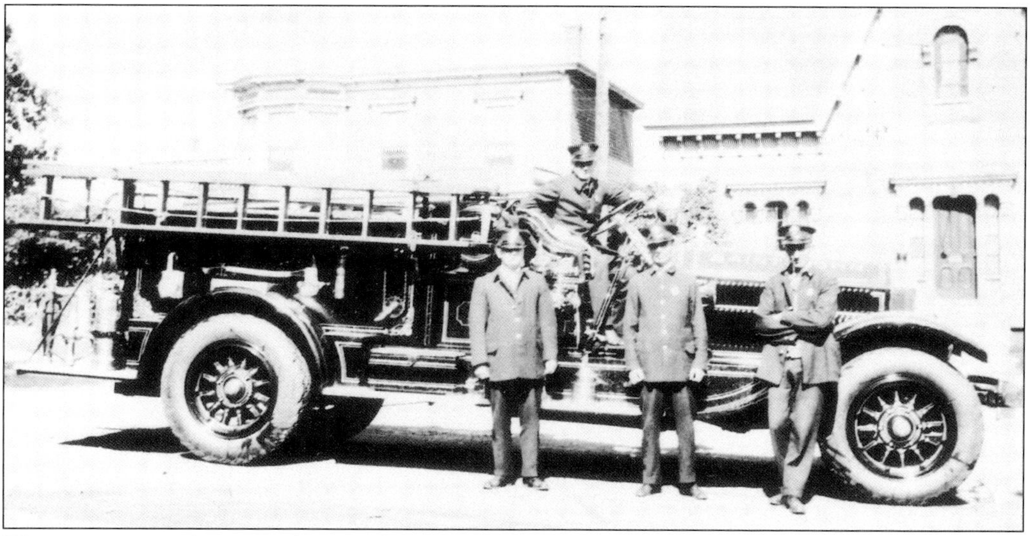

This pumper truck pictured around 1940 is probably very similar to one received at the King Street station in 1931. It reported to a grain elevator and pier fire, which raged through the Port on June 22 of that year. The new truck was taken out onto the floor of Shed #2 to fight the flames. It was soon obvious it was a losing battle. The firemen fled, leaving their new vehicle behind where it soon broke through the weakened floor. The vehicle remains on the harbour bottom to this day.

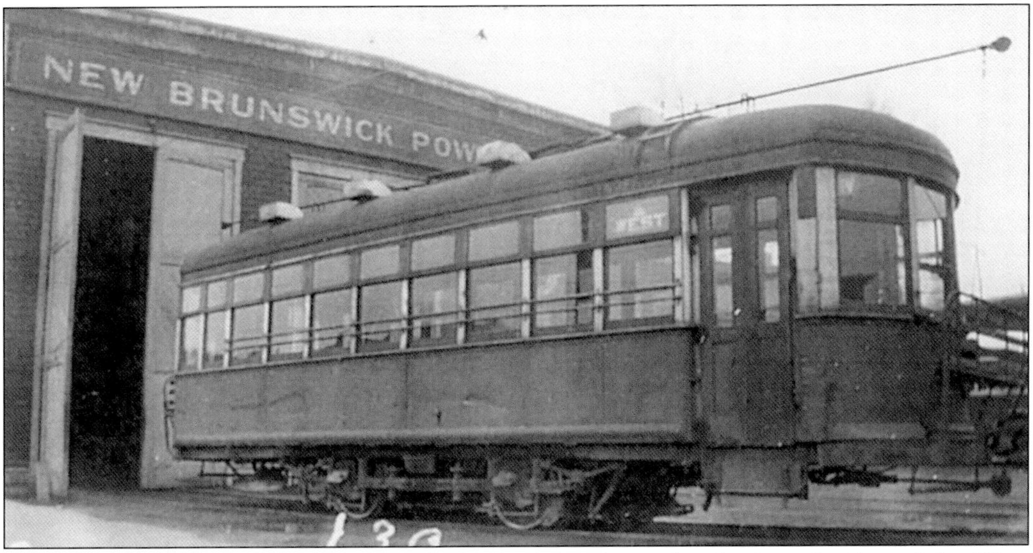

New Brunswick Power Company's car barn, the second one they built in the Saint John West area, was constructed on Tower Street after Union Street was levelled in 1932. From this barn the car went on what was called the "West loop", and this served those going to catch the ferry to town. It moved up Tower Street, turned south along Queen Square on Lancaster Street, and turned left through Queen Square itself. Then it went down Queen Street, along Minette Street, and over to the ferry floats. As Queen Square Park was not designed for such use, eventually, after much protest, the tracks were torn up in the square. Bus service replaced the streetcar loop in the early 1930s.

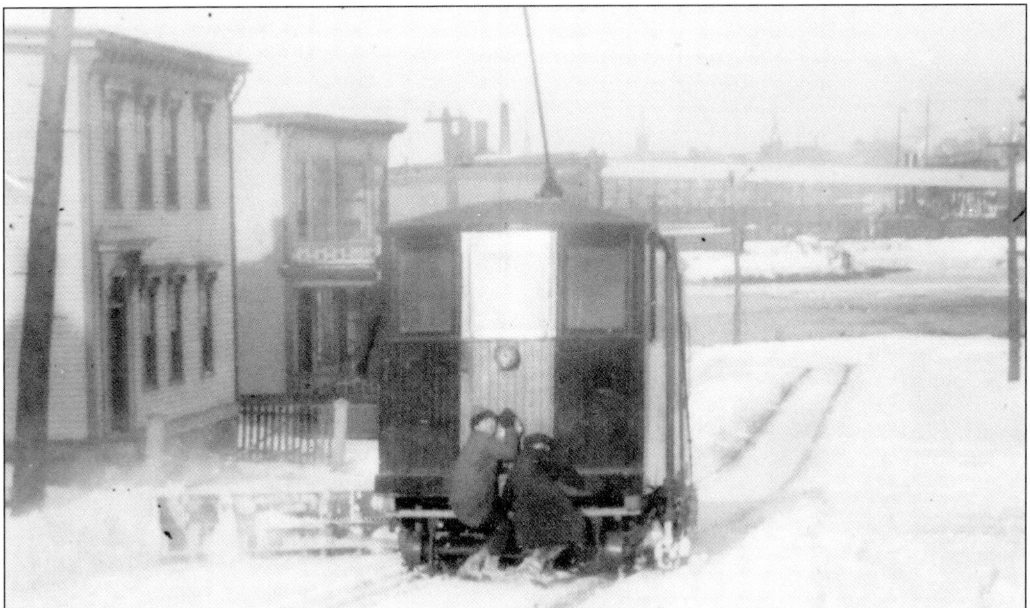

Notice there are no cars in this picture, and the streetplow extended from the left side. This shows that if there were traffic it would still be using this side of the road for travel, which traffic did till December 1, 1922. Note the kids hitching a ride on the back of the streetcar. Later, this was a popular trick when busses pulled away from the "end of the line" on St. John Street.

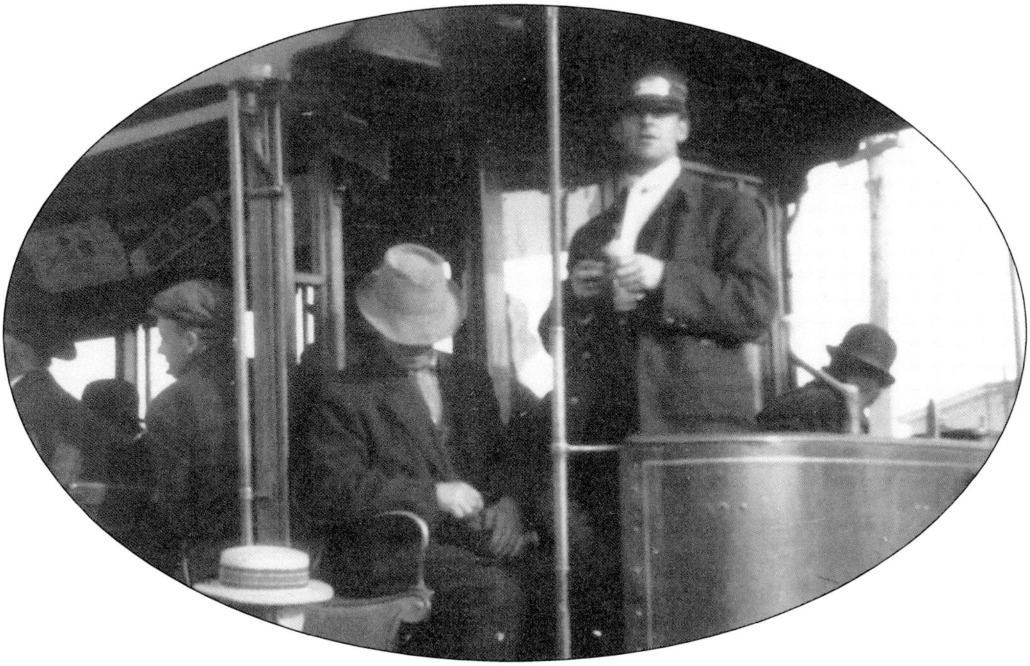

Barney on a streetcar on Tower Street in 1911, is the identification of this A.V.F. Duffy photo, which clearly shows that an open-air streetcar was not limited to the summer runs to Seaside Park. This one is clearly marked "Bridge" and refers to the loop to the Reversing Falls Bridge. West Siders arriving at the bridge had to get out of the car, walk across the plank suspension bridge, and catch the streetcar from Douglas Avenue to the foot of King in what is clearly the downtown of Saint John . . . but, which is referred to as "uptown" Saint John. The streetcar operator is John Vincent Kelly.

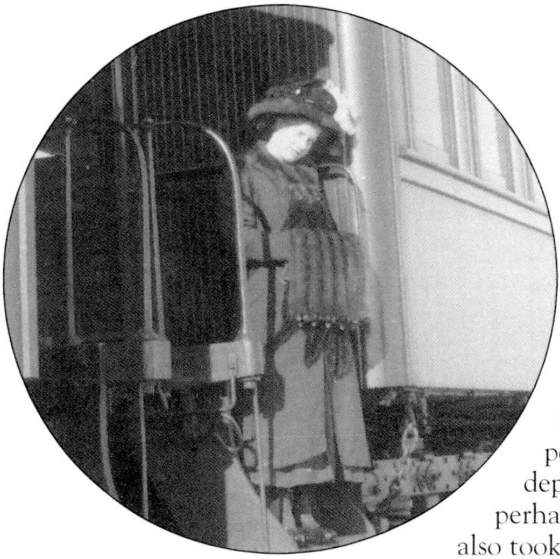

A.V.F. Duffy was courting one of the Wilcox girls, who he consistently identified only as "G.W." in many pictures he took of her. She appears frequently in his photo collection taken in the teen years of the twentieth century. She is pictured at the family business, the Wilcox Shop on Dock Street, seen writing letters to friends (as was shown in "Olde Tyme Christmas in New Brunswick"), portrayed answering telephones, and here, seen departing from the Saint John West train station, perhaps on a trip to Moncton where A.V.F Duffy also took many photographs.

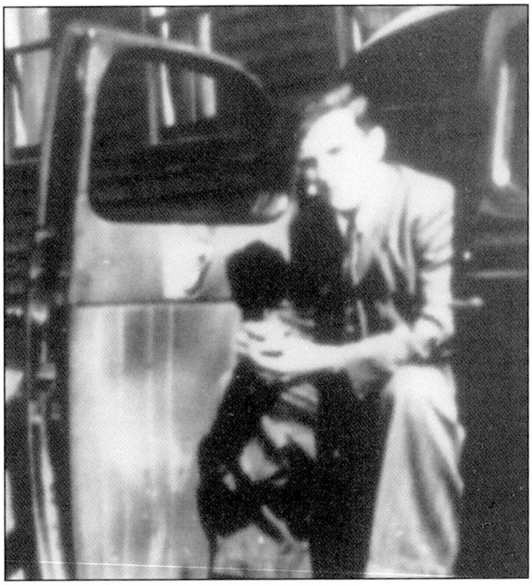

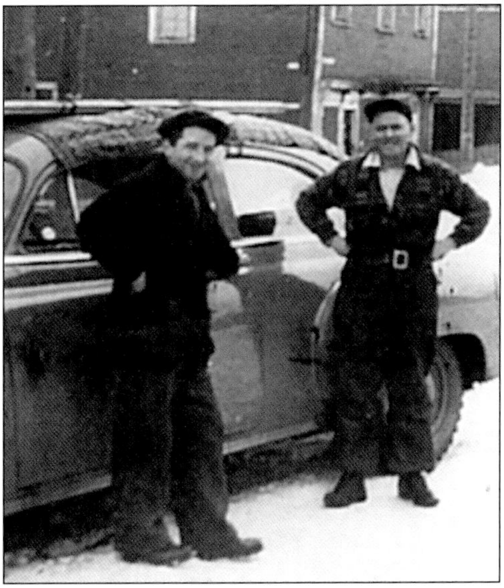

Left: Many West Siders did not have vehicles themselves until the 1950s, so taxi services flourished. This fellow is waiting outside Jim's Restaurant on St. John Street for a fare, perhaps from the nearby Maple Leaf Hotel. *Right:* West Siders were creative with their cars. If they needed to move some lumber they strapped it to their vehicle as these residents of St. James Street did. It appears to be Tuna Silliphant and Bill Guthrie in this mid-1950s photo. Both were innovative with their old cars. If a vehicle needed repairs it was rarely taken to a garage, but the problem was resolved by a bit of ingenuity, and some parts pirated from an older vehicle that had been put to rest.

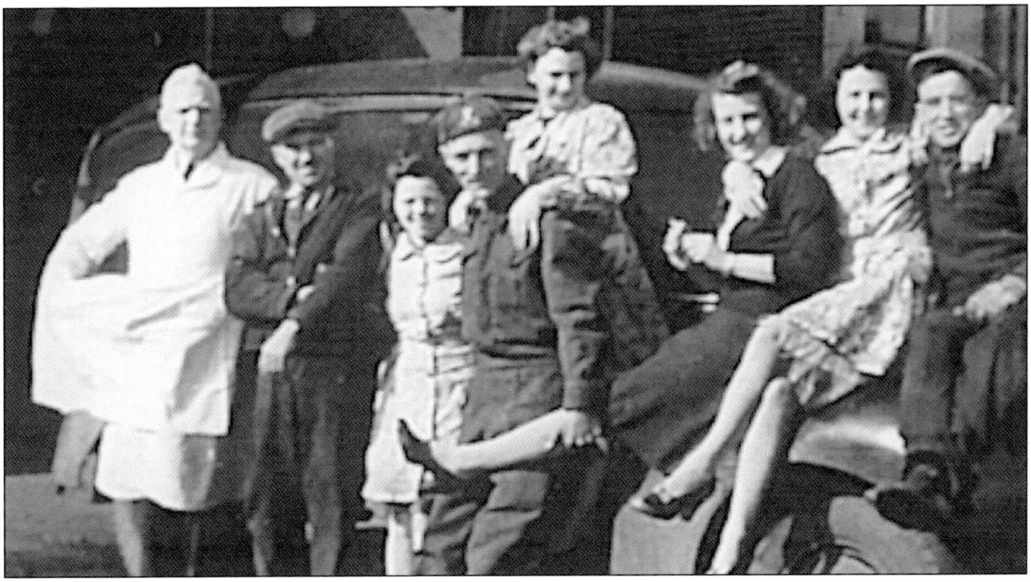

The staff of Donovan's Store at 203 Queen Street are gathered in the early 1950s around the delivery wagon. This is typical of many such portraits that were received. This one was chosen because the names of all the participants are known. From left to right are the following: Leo McGuiggan, Bill Galbraith, Marie Driscoll, Gerry Russell, Helen McGuiness, Pat Ring, Ali May Murphy, and Fred Graham. (Courtesy Alice O'Brien.)

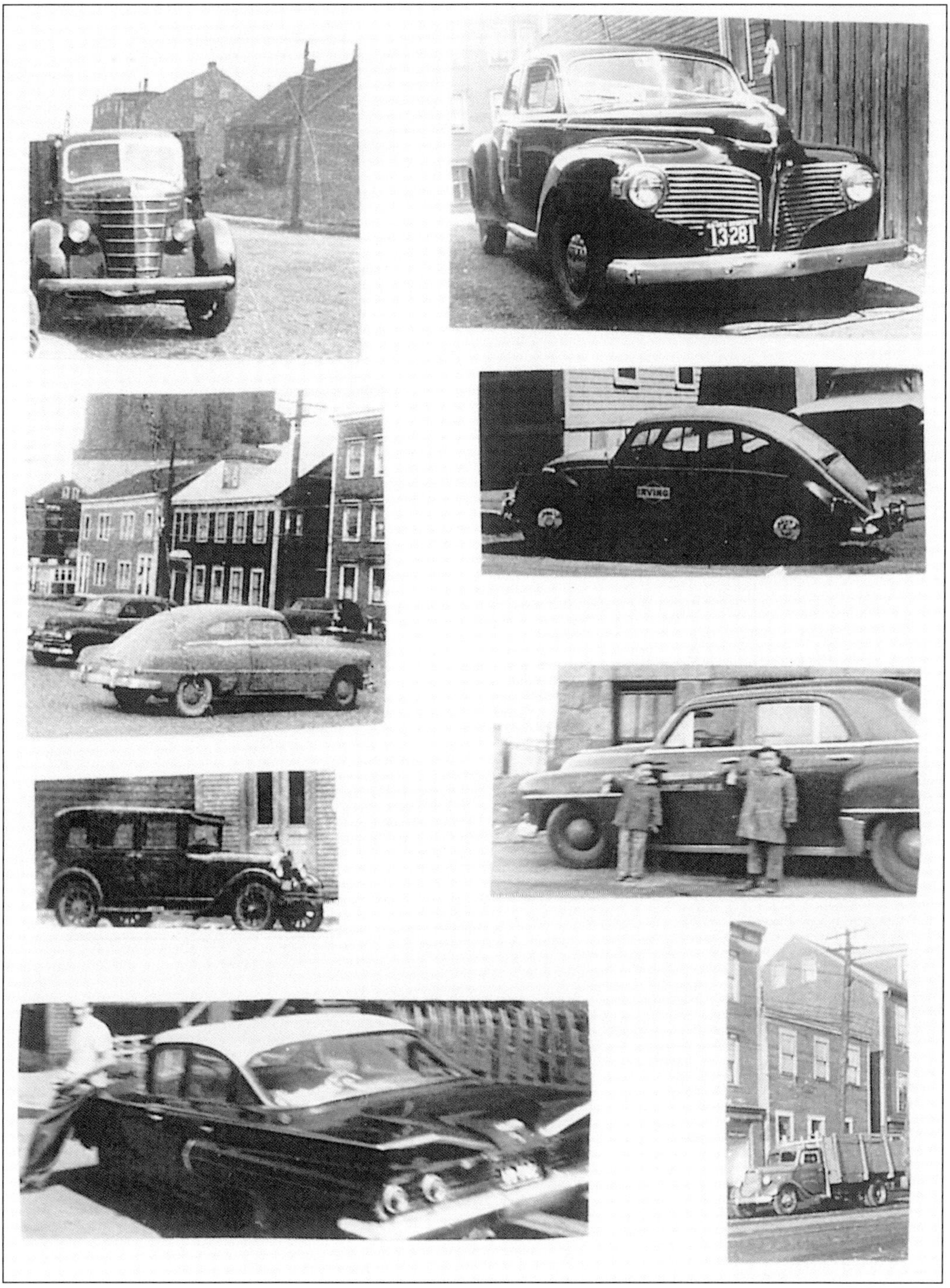

This concludes our look at cars on the West Side with this collection, which has been cropped from a variety of shots presented to us for use. Down the left side are a 1939–1940 International truck, a 48 Oldsmobile, a Model A, and a 57 Chevrolet. Down the right side are a 41 Plymouth, a 59 Volkswagen, a 48 or 49 Chevrolet, and a 1929 Ford truck. Thanks to Evelyn and Raymond Speight for identification of the vehicles.

Seven

The Port and Railway

The port of Saint John has had to constantly reinvent itself in order to take advantage of the economic opportunities of the wider world. At first, it was furs that were shipped from the shoreline; no wharves were needed for that. Lumber and limestone required some structures, and this conflicted with the productive fish weirs strung out from the shore of the inner harbour below the Reversing Falls. Space was needed, too, to build the wooden boats that carried forest product overseas. Individuals built what was needed, and not much more, to get the job done . . . mostly small cribwork wharves, and they maintained them, too. With the coming of the age of steam and the railway, bigger wharves were needed, and in the closing years of the nineteenth century, this began to happen. But it was a struggle . . . the railways wanted the city to pay the bills, and the city felt the railway should foot the cost of development. Saint John was pitted against rival developments in such places as Portland, Maine, and Halifax; railway lined up against railway in attempts to wrangle money from the various governments, and they generally got it. The taxpayer funded most of the development, but in return the rail lines and port facilities provided work as they were developed and seasonal employment for some 4,000 men moving goods. Fires, landslides, and labour unrest were also factors in the story.

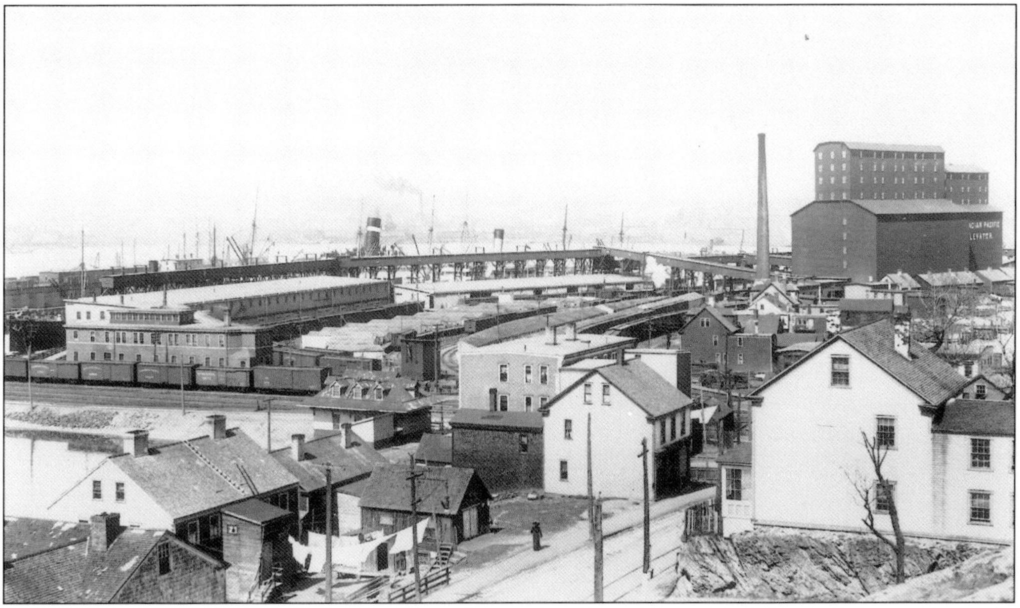

This view of the Millpond and the Sand Point slip was taken from Blue Rock Hill in 1912 by Isaac Erb, the same year the 800 strong Longshoreman's Association was granted a charter and became ILA #273. (Courtesy Vintage Photo and Frame.)

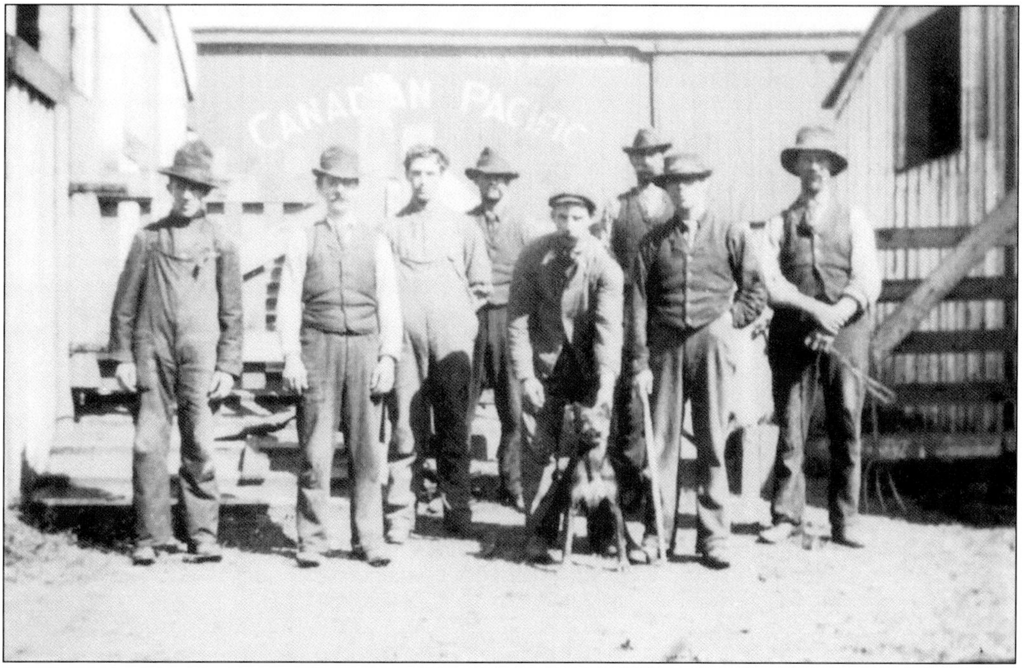

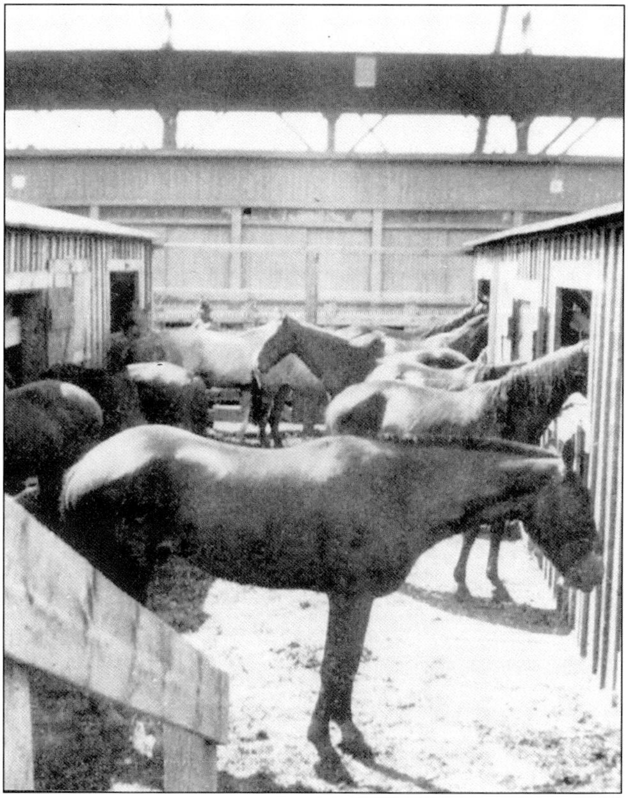

Look back on page 19, bottom, and see the sheds that are shown on page 79. Cecil E.R. Strange took the page 19 photo from atop the grain elevator, then moved closer for the second shot of the workmen at the sheds and the horses that were being shipped through the port in 1910.

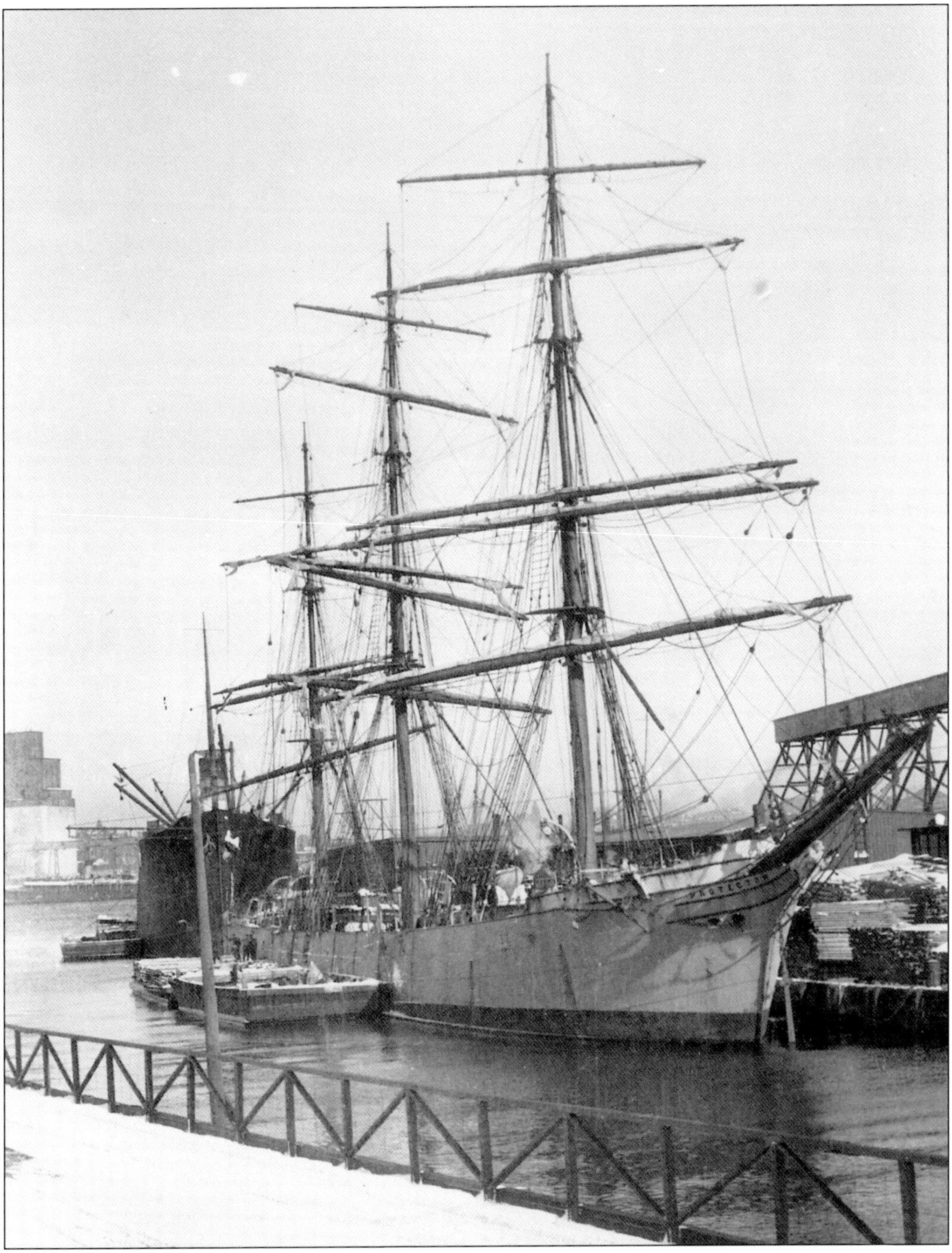

This is the ship *Protector* in 1921. It is loading lumber from the dock at the Sand Point pier. From the time of Simonds, Hazen and White, wooden ships like the *Protector* were built in the area, and lumber products like those on the Sand Point wharf were an important export from the port. As we approach the year 2000, forestry products such as lumber and paper are still the chief commodity shipped from the West Side terminals, but wooden ships are no longer built, and only infrequently berth in the area.

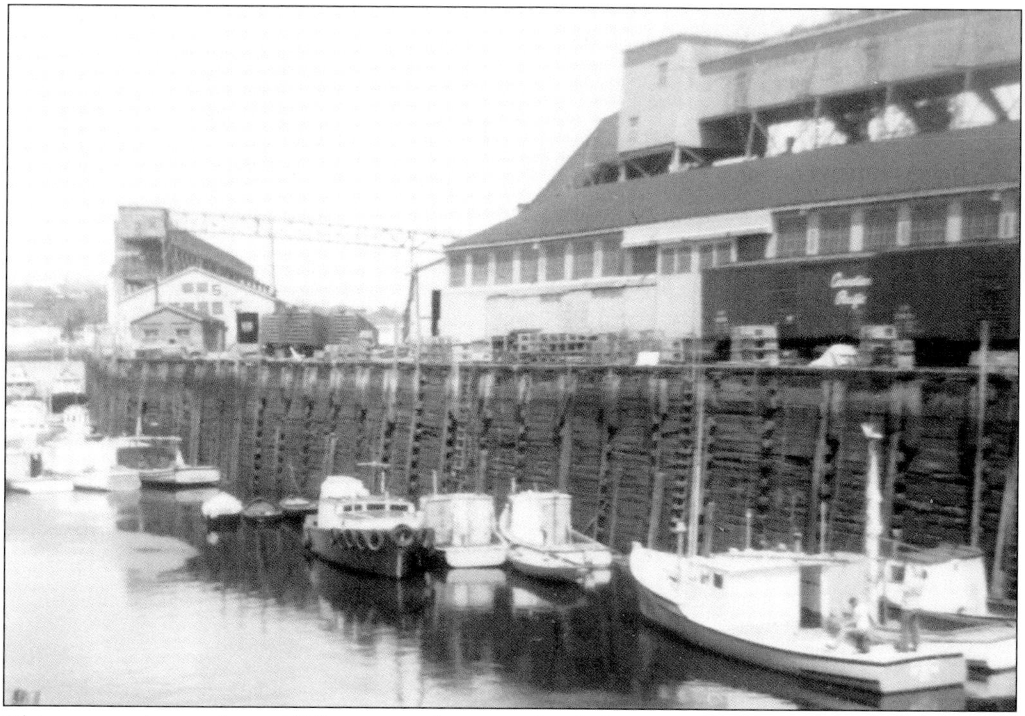

Thirty years later, about 1950, we see the same berth between Rodney Slip and Sand Point where the *Protector* was docked in 1921. It was in use then by much smaller lobster boats doing seasonal off-shore fishing in the Bay of Fundy. Now, 50 years later, the fish are much depleted, and the boats do not berth in Saint John. This area is now landlocked and in the middle of a container terminal developed in the 1980s.

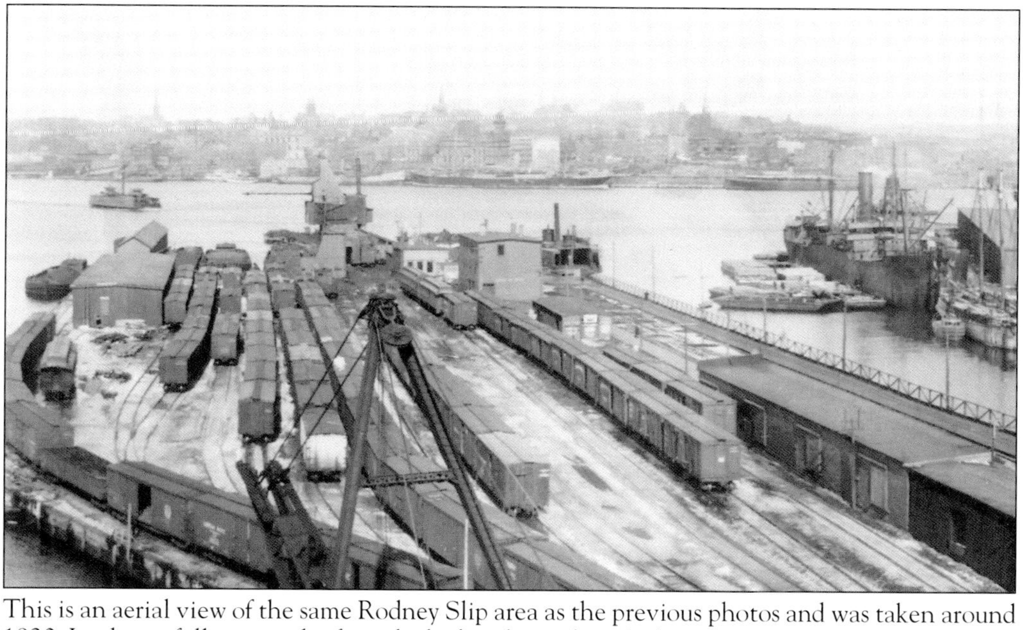

This is an aerial view of the same Rodney Slip area as the previous photos and was taken around 1920. Look carefully to see the ferry docked at the end, and when you turn the page you will see the same ferry enlarged and crossing to Saint John.

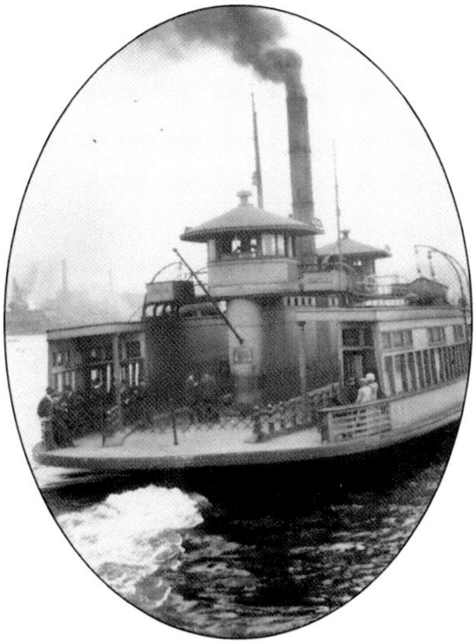

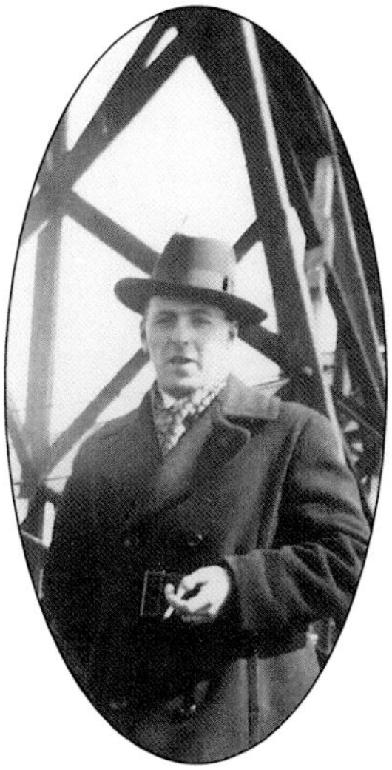

Left: Here is the ferry *Ludlow*, as seen on the previous page, leaving Rodney Slip in 1913. The *Ludlow* was launched on July 6, 1905, from Hilyard's shipyard at the foot of Sheriff Street in the North End of Saint John. It was the first propeller-driven ferry and first steel vessel on the crossing. It had 82 seats in each of the male and female cabins and room for 500 standing. It served till 1933. *Right:* A.V.F. Duffy is shown on the ferry landing at Rodney and Union Streets. He took quite a few of the older photos in this book, but as the photographer, it is rare to find a shot with him in it among his extensive collection. When we found this one, we thought it was worth showing the man behind many of our good photos.

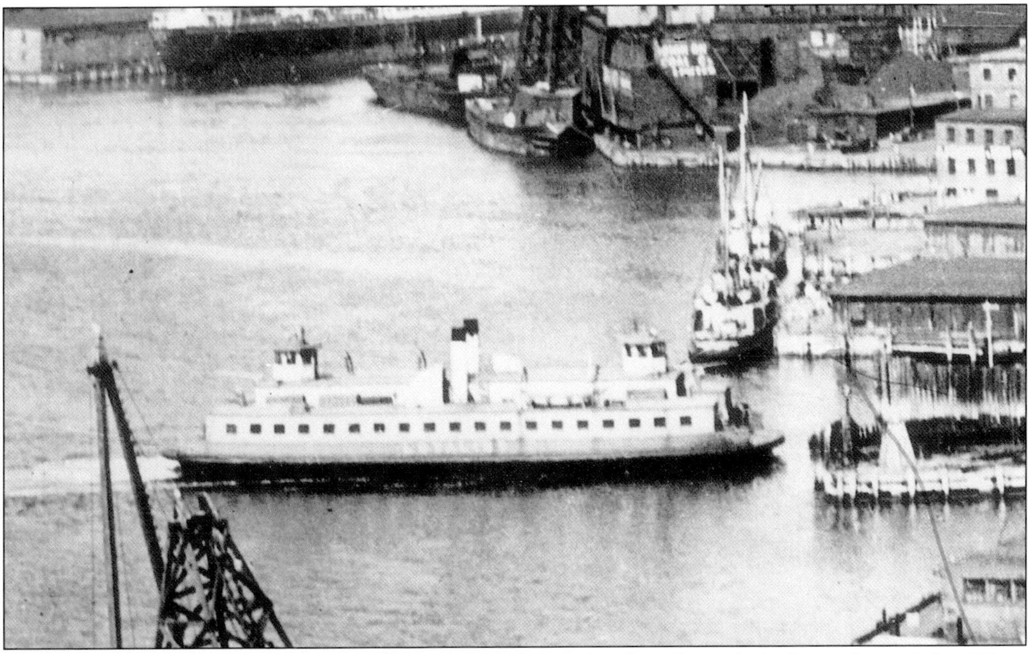

The *Loyalist*, built in 1933 in Shelburne, N.S., was the last ferry link from Saint John West to the centre of Saint John. Officially it ended its schedule on December 31, 1953, but many residents claim it ran till the spring of 1954. It was towed out of the harbour in July of that year, and later served on the Miramichi between Newcastle and Chatham.

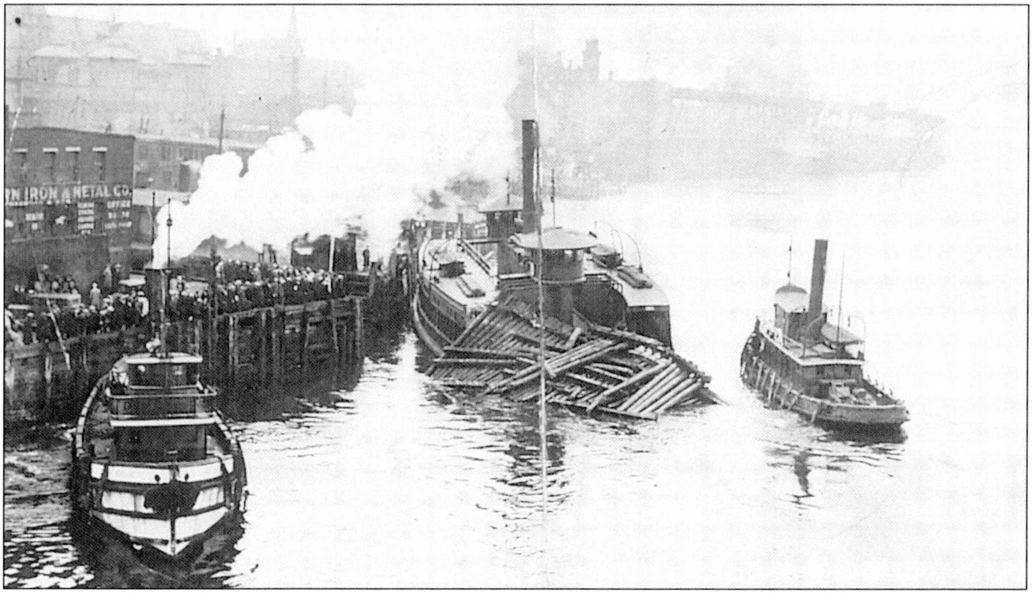

There were numerous collisions and sinkings in the harbour over the years. Even though the area has a reputation for being a difficult tidal zone in which to navigate, the number of problems has been negligible in comparison to the vast number of ships that have travelled into the harbour. However, accidents did happen as we see in these pictures. April 23, 1928, the *Ludlow* collided with a wharf, and damage was estimated at $20,000. In the second picture the *Beaverhill* is shown aground on Hilyard's Reef on November 24, 1944. It proved impossible to refloat it, so it was disassembled in the harbour at low tides. It was done quietly as it was carrying powerful munitions for the war effort overseas. Few pictures were taken and those that were, were censored. This one is marked, "Nov 30, 1944, District Intelligence MB No.7". It was 1947 before the final pieces were removed from the reef.

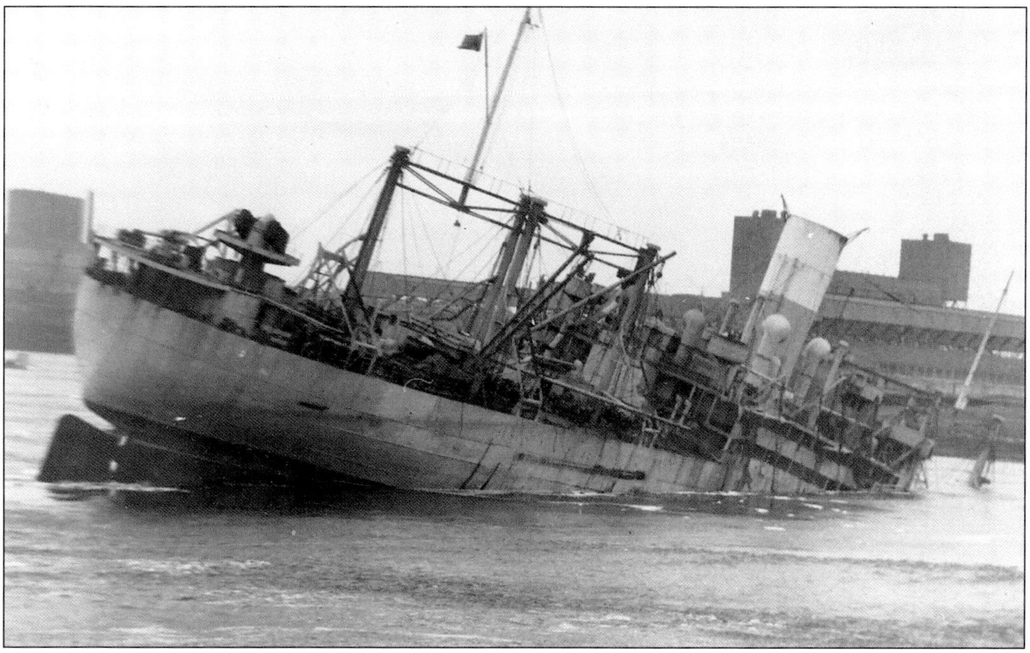

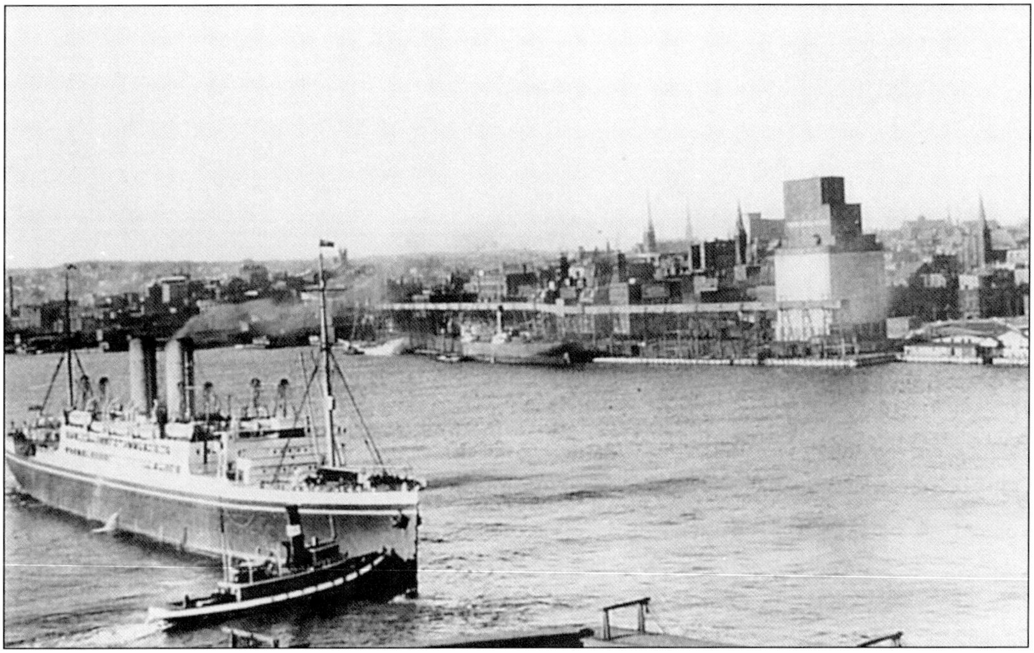

Here the Canadian Pacific mailboat is assisted by the tug *Ocean Hawk*, leaving the city in the late 1940s. The CP mailboats and vessels of the Beaver, Head, Furness, and Donaldson Lines provided lots of work, and the city's men hoped that several would arrive at the same time so the high-numbered gangs who didn't always get work would then be called. Mail arriving in the city would be loaded in railcars the same day as arrival and sped across the country. (Courtesy Dyson Thomas.)

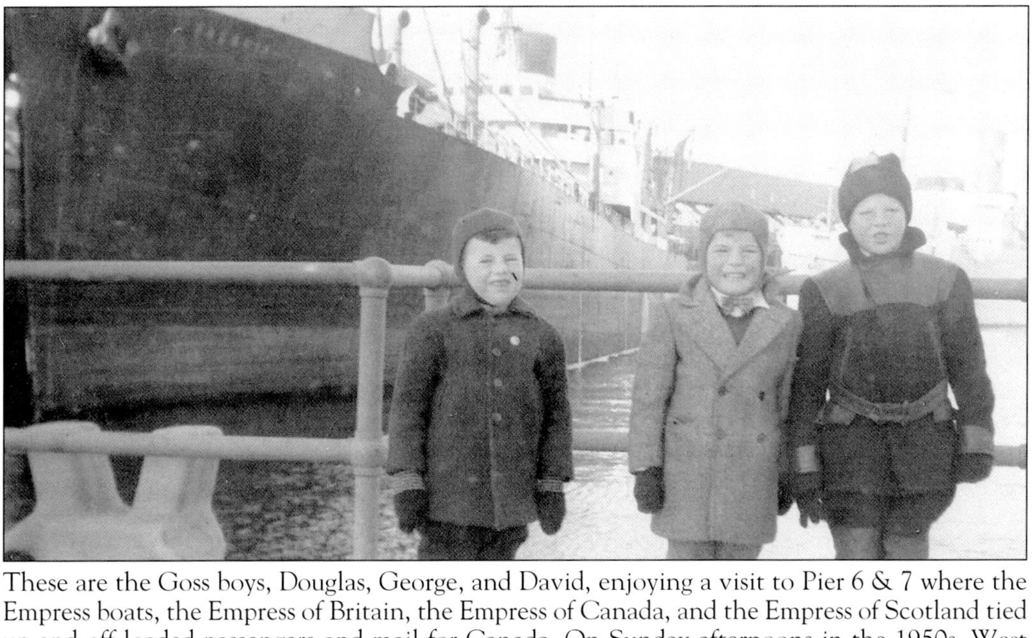

These are the Goss boys, Douglas, George, and David, enjoying a visit to Pier 6 & 7 where the Empress boats, the Empress of Britain, the Empress of Canada, and the Empress of Scotland tied up and off loaded passengers and mail for Canada. On Sunday afternoons in the 1950s, West Side children would be allowed aboard, as was the case when this photo was taken. (Courtesy Abe Goss.)

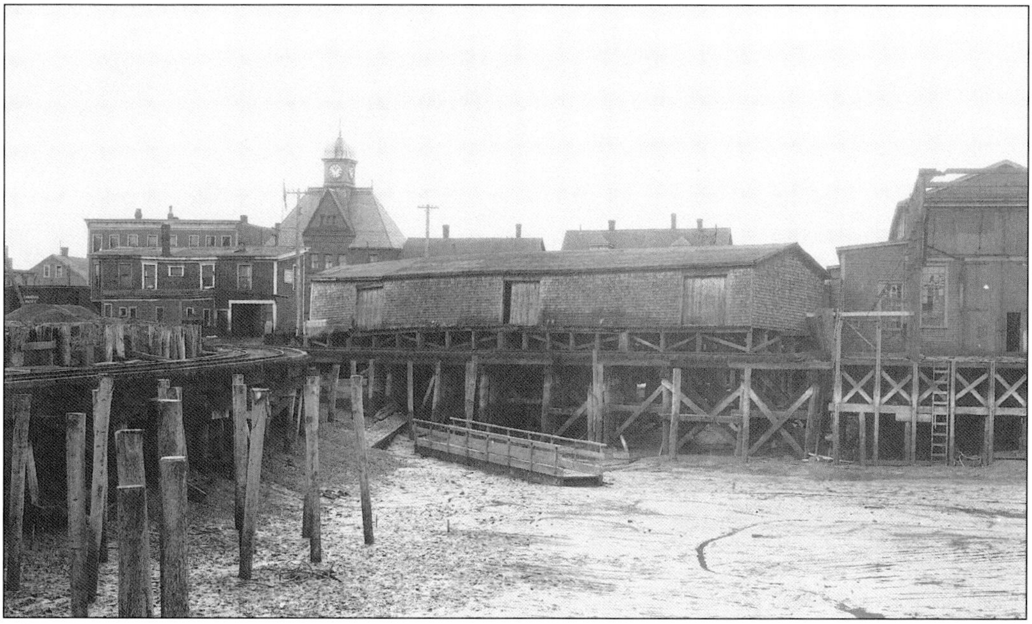

This top photo shows the typical West Side wharf—a combination of pilings and cribwork laid in the mud flats. It had been developed as a practical solution to the tidal variations in the days of wooden ships, and when there were still lots of trees in the woods to use for the cribwork. By the 20th century, such wharves were inadequate; many had rotted, others were slipping into the channels, and there was a need for much improvement. There was constant wrangling between railway, shipping lines, local, provincial, and government as to who would do the job, but it was usually the taxpayers who ended up footing bills. In the second photo we see improvements underway to the area below King Street and Middle Street, which eventually became the Navy Island terminals in the early 1930s.

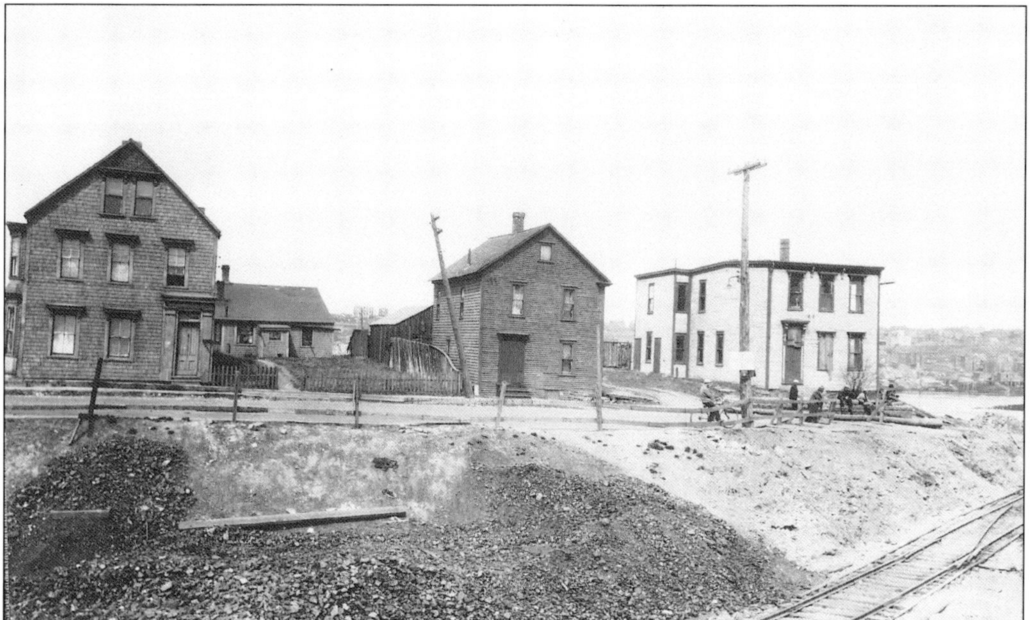

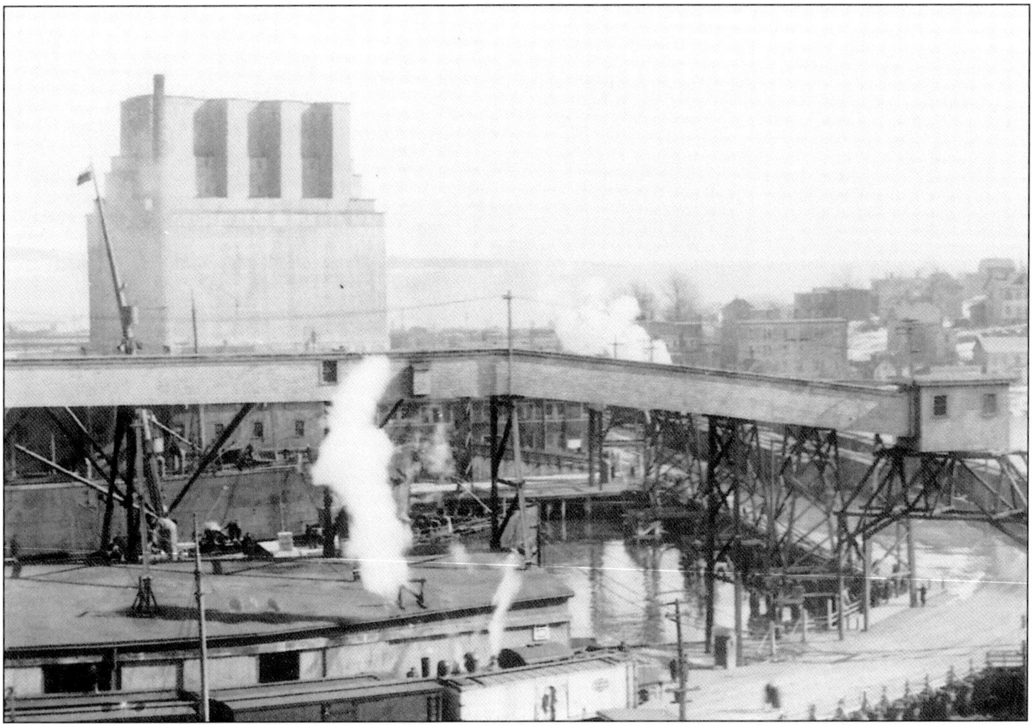

These two views were taken 30 years apart from the top (200 feet 6 inches, Jim Donner told me!) of the 1929, 1,500,000-bushel grain elevator on Union Street. It shows the Pier 8 area and the Millpond, considered for a dry dock project in the 1890s. In the top photo the tidal Millpond is still flooding, and trestles are supporting the trains. In 1958 the trestles are gone, the Millpond is filled in, and there is a railcar yard where the sea once surged. (Courtesy Dyson Thomas.)

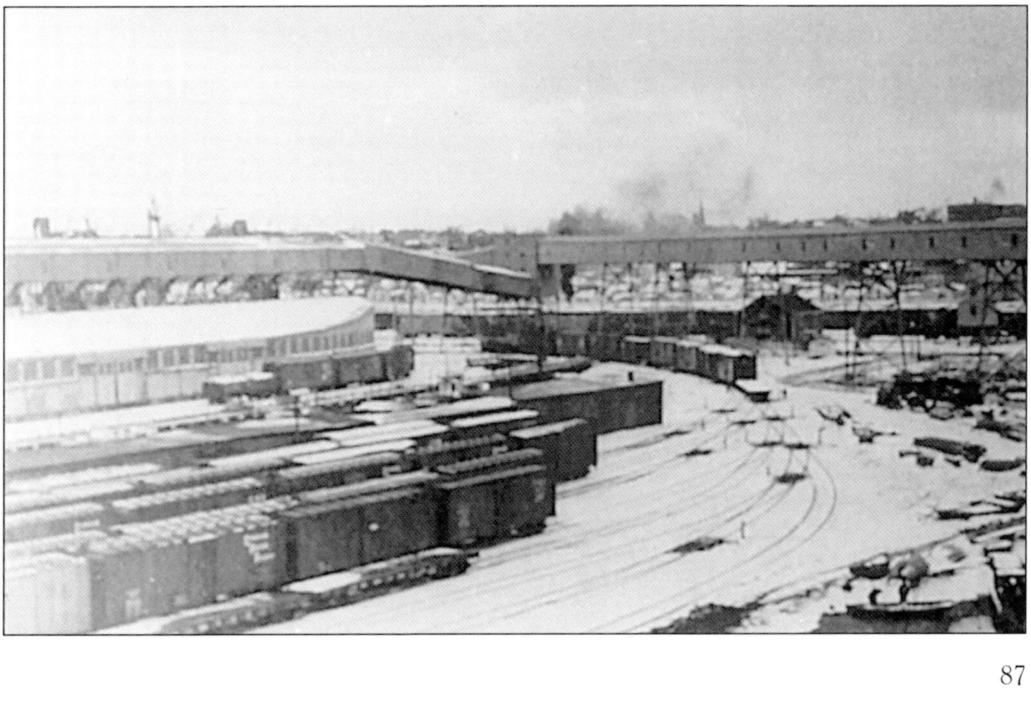

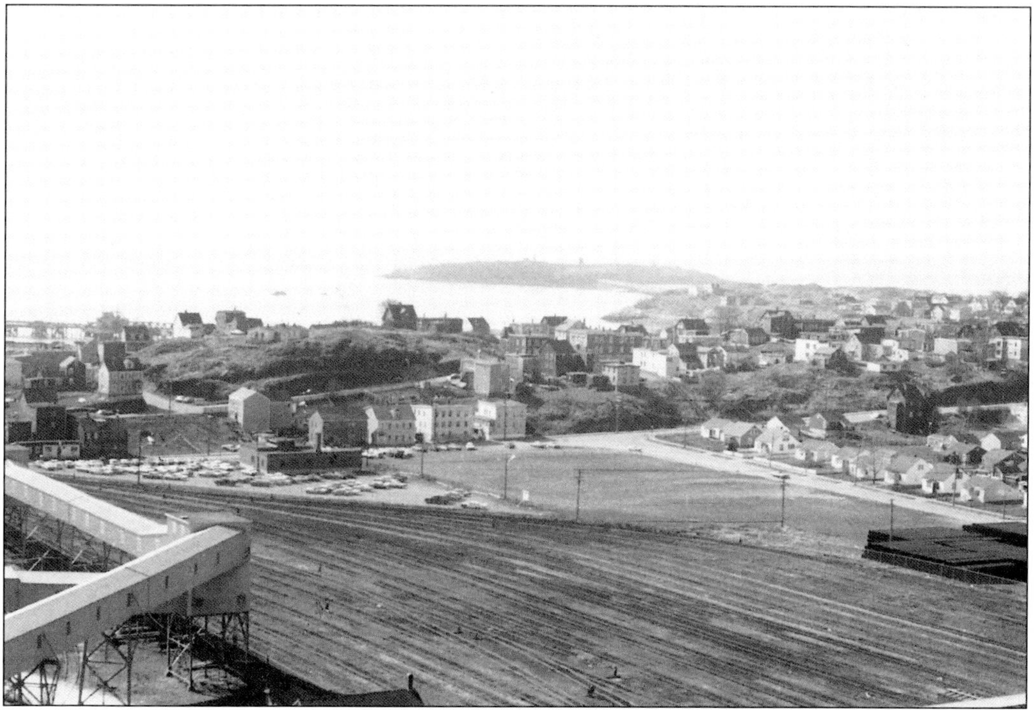

A dozen years later, in 1971, Malcolm Somerville was atop the grain elevator and took these pictures of a largely empty railyard. There was a considerable difference between winter and summer activity at the port—and of course this affected rail traffic. By the early 1960s ship traffic was moving up the St. Lawrence year-round, making winter and summer traffic in the port comparable and with containerization—many less workers—and many fewer box cars were needed.

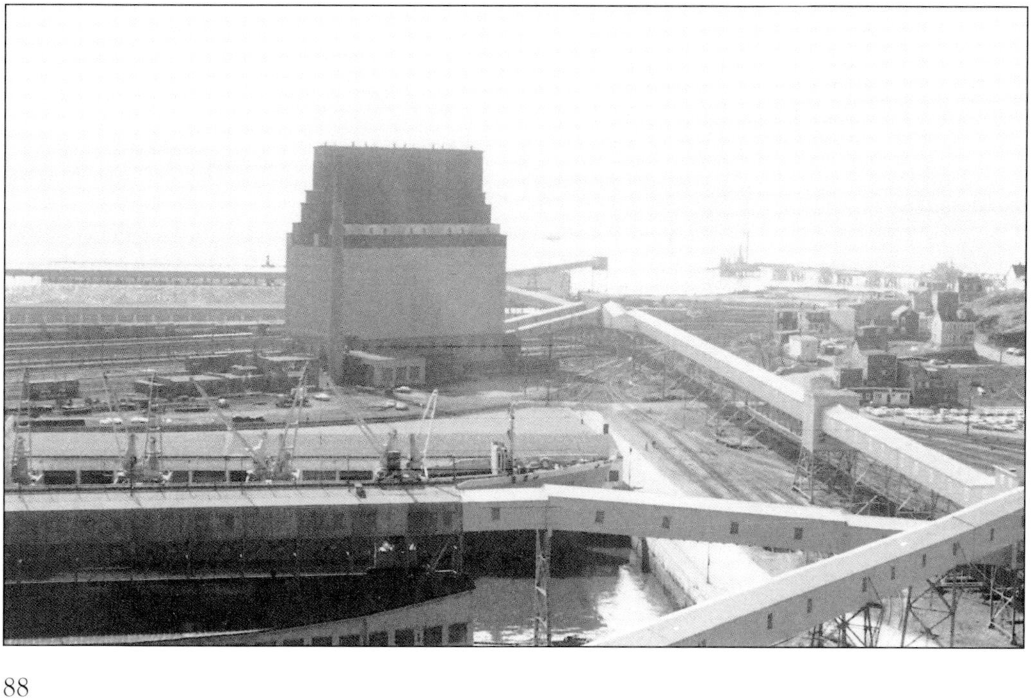

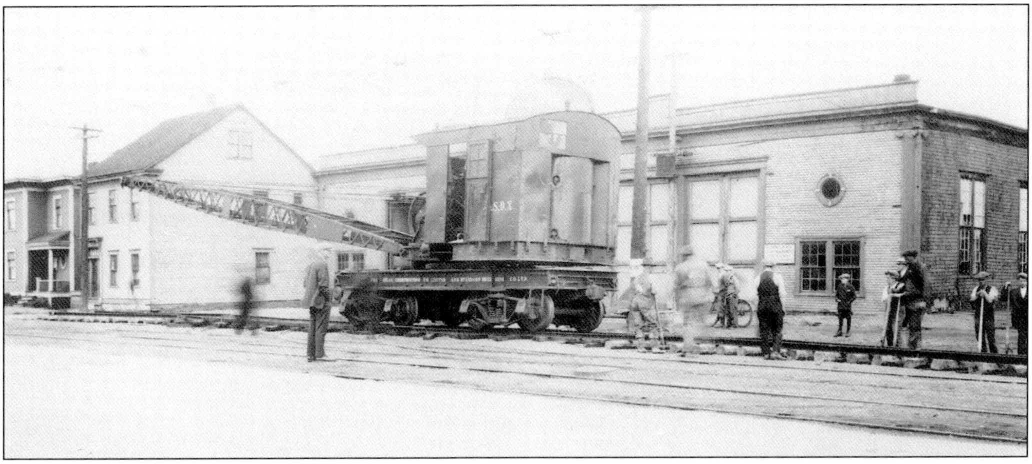

A crew of workers is pictured around a railcar on the Atlas Company crane. It is September 20, 1928, and they are on Union Street in front of the car barn working at ballasting the tracks. It was in this area that the Carleton Electric light company produced through steam dynamos, the power to light 29 street lamps, and claimed they could light 1,800, even as far away as Fairville in 1884. These were the first electrically lit streets in Saint John as the uptown area was still lit with gas, and would be until 1891.

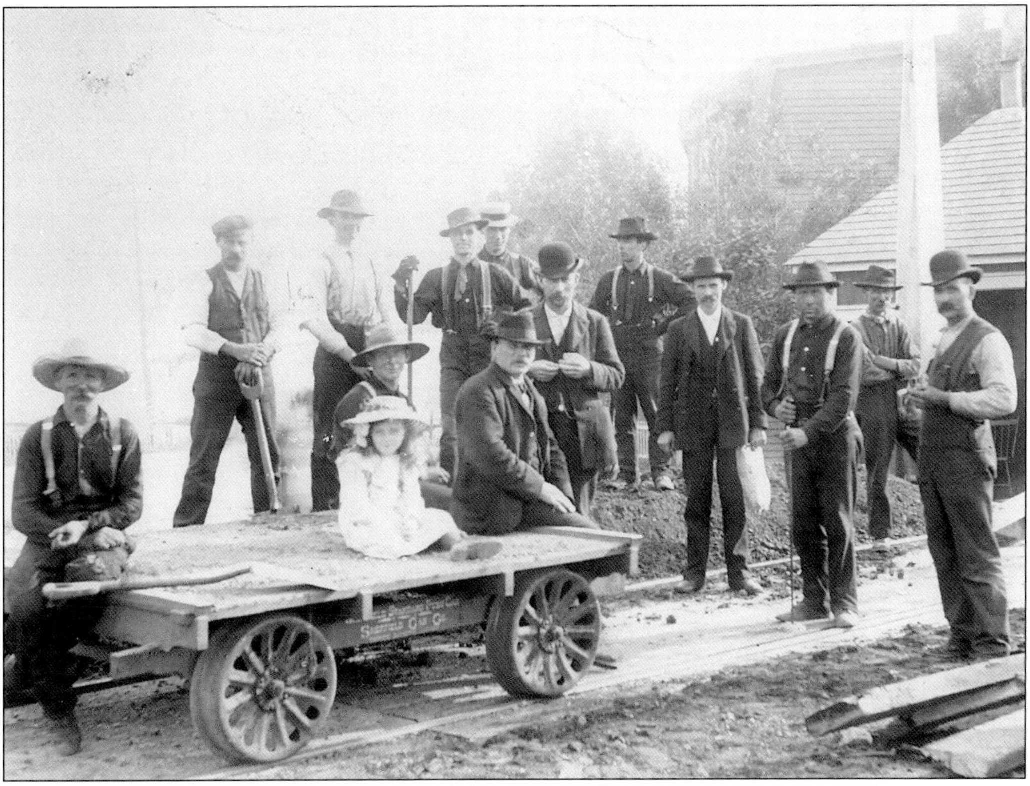

This is a work crew typical of the turn of the century; however, we cannot say for sure it is in the West Saint John area, as this photo was given by Alice Huige, who couldn't identify where it was taken. Still, it does illustrate track work that was typical of all areas of the city in the days of the iron rail.

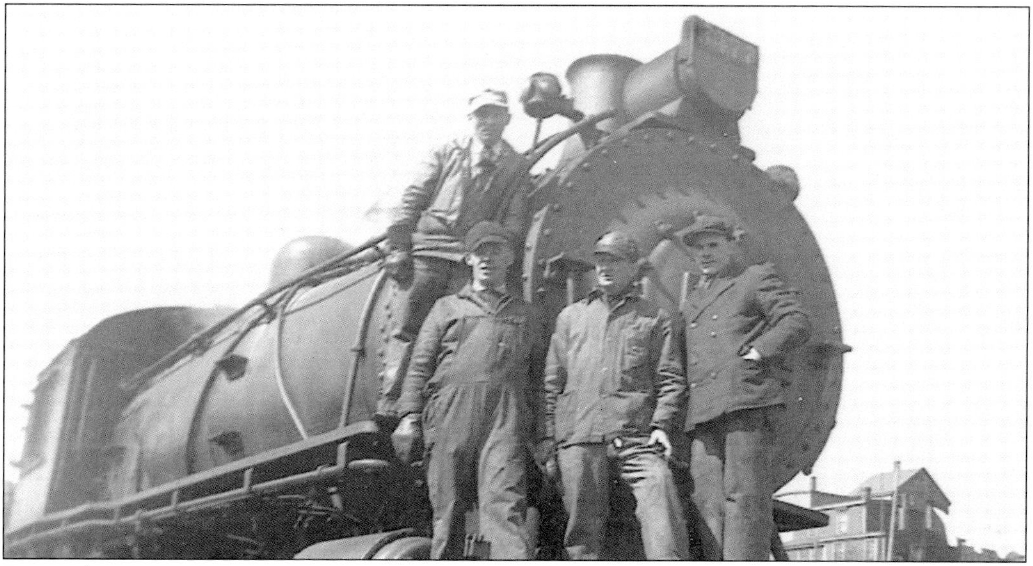

Pictured are James Moyer and crew on the "King" line leading to Saint John West in 1940. There seems to be few pictures of the men who operated the huge engines, but in this instance they paused parallel to Germain Street for the photo. In the background, on St. James Street is the Oliver home. James Moyer is nearest to the smoke stack and from the left below him are, Herman Pitre, Diggs Jennings, and Gerry Fowler. (Courtesy Dawson Moyer.)

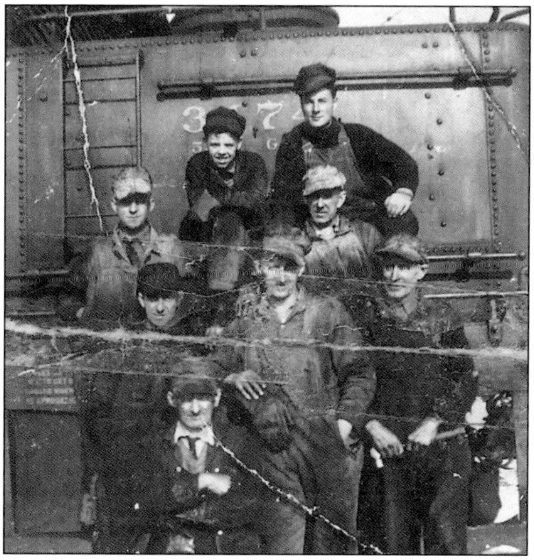

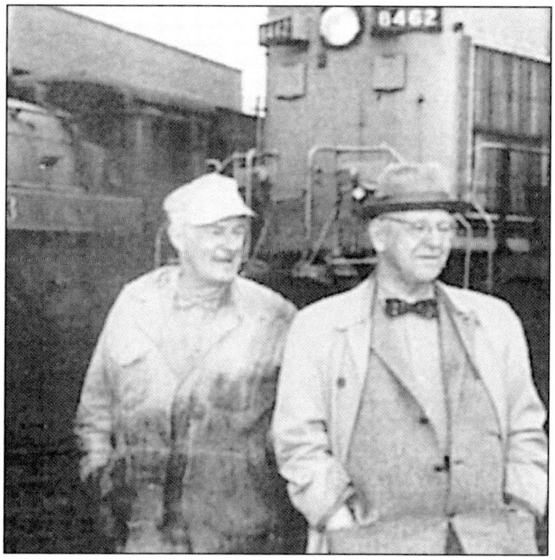

Left: Many of the photos collected were cracked and taped. Some have been enhanced for reproduction, but no effort has been made to correct this one from the 1940s, as it shows how people treasured the few pictures they had of their fathers and uncles at work. In this case, Lorraine Jeffers has provided this picture, which shows from top left, J.R. Butler and George London. In the second row are P. Watters and B. Barlow. In the third row are W. Campbell, Bill Quilty, and R. Lawson. Seated is C. Raynes. *Right:* Dyson Thomas labeled this shot: "Two Browns, CP's Bayshore yard with one of the last P2 locomotives and one of the first diesel locomotives." This is likely the late 1950s or early 1960s. Before the turn of the century it was believed the port would grow to the Bayshore roundhouse area, about 2 miles from the original St. John Street station.

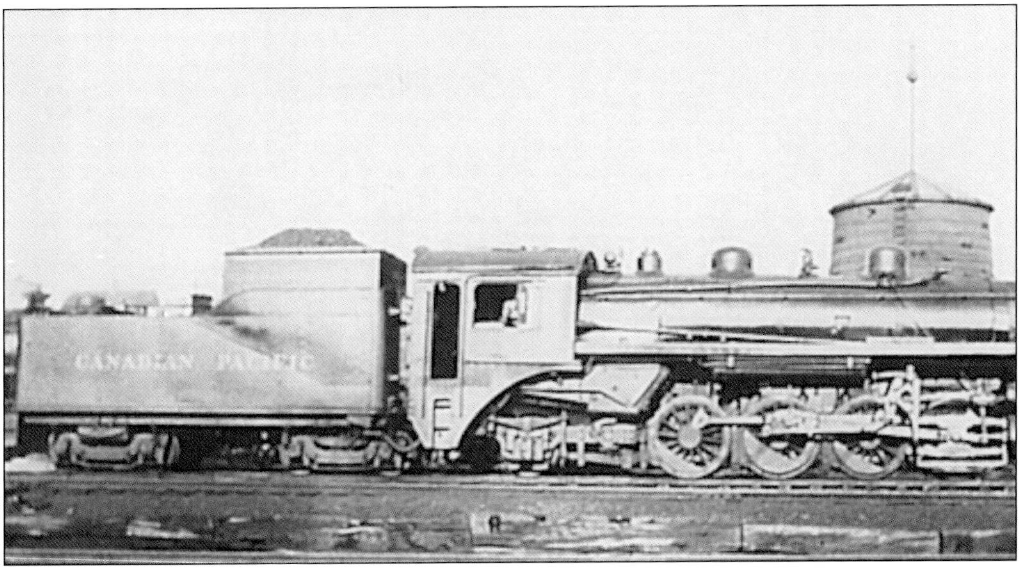

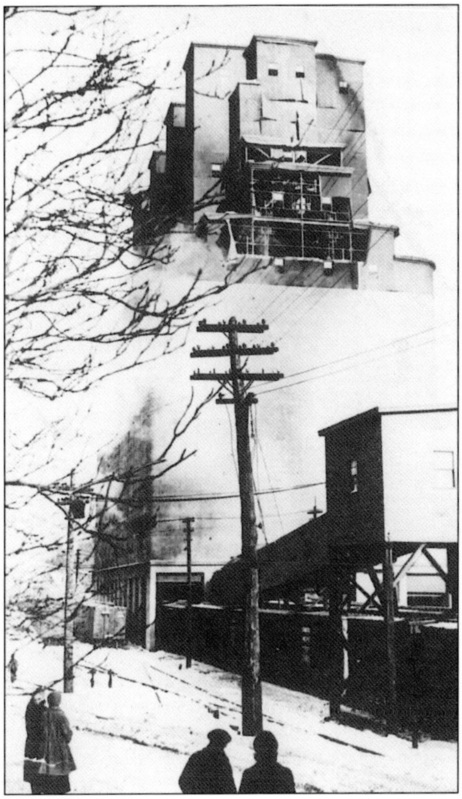

This train in the Bayshore yard is shown prior to World War Two. How do we know? It is Martello Tower in the background on which there has been no fortification added, which was done for World War Two, as it served as a radar and observation point overlooking the city. This type of engine is known as a P2 and would have pushed hundreds of thousands of railcars into the 1912-era grain elevator on the right. The elevator has had sheet metal ripped off in a windstorm and has attracted curious West Siders, who are looking over the damage while out for a Sunday walk. (Courtesy Dyson Thomas.)

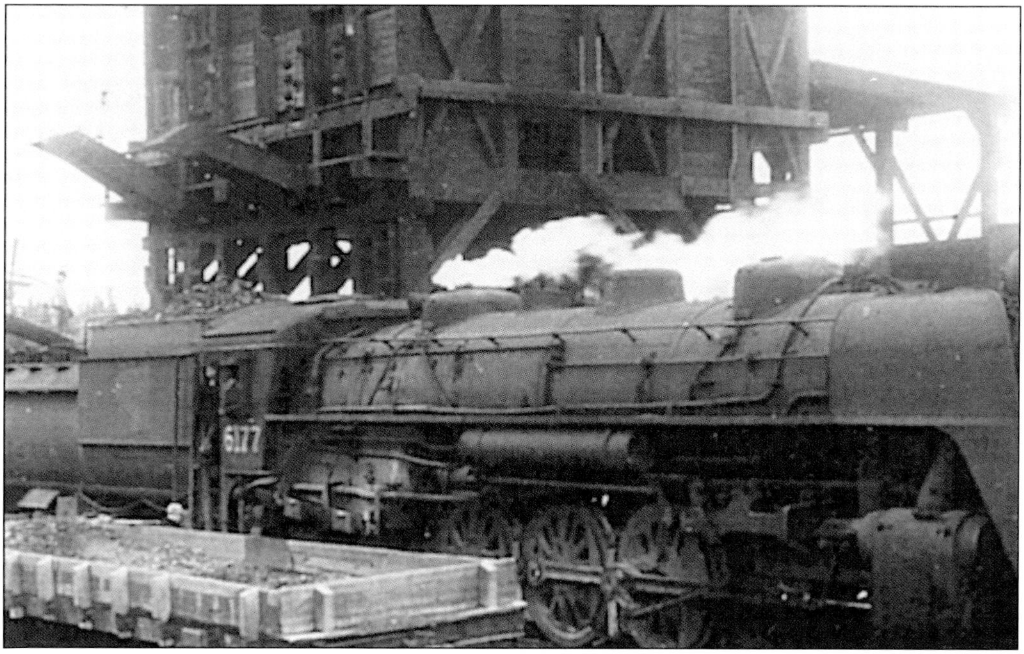

These are the coalshoots at Bayshore for loading the engines up with their fuel. There were always a few lumps that escaped, and the yardmen made no attempt to pick these up knowing that West Siders, hard pressed to keep their houses warm in the Depression years, would be by to scavenge the pieces of coal. (Courtesy Dyson Thomas.)

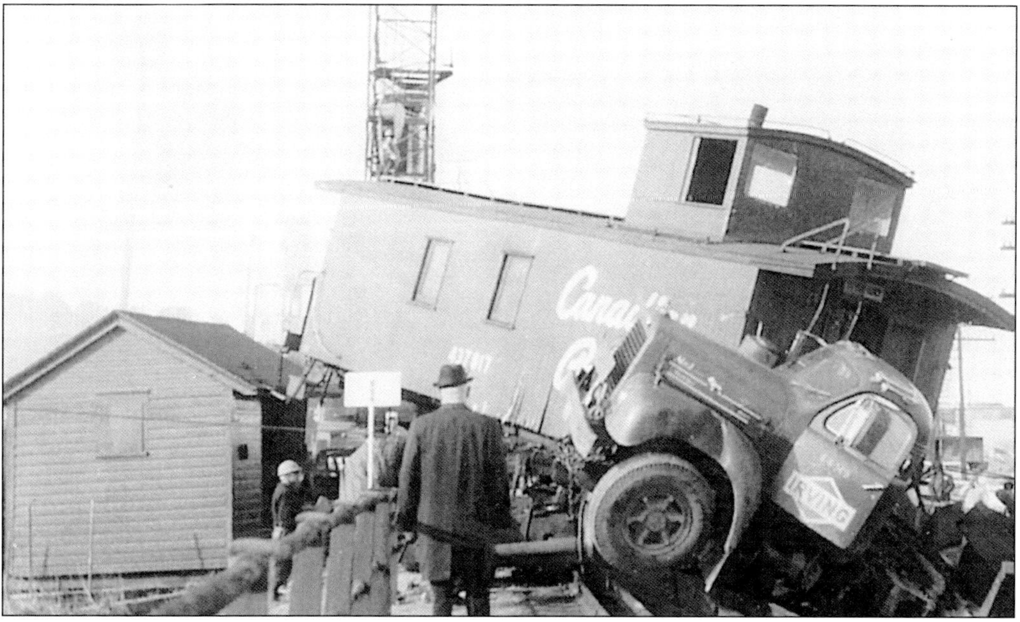

This wreck at the Reversing Falls, which Dyson Thomas took a photo of in November 1966, is typical of what happened when cars met trains at level crossings, which happened more often as cars became popular. Residents would rarely pass such collisions as many family members or friends worked on the railways, and one never knew if someone near and dear might be involved and need help.

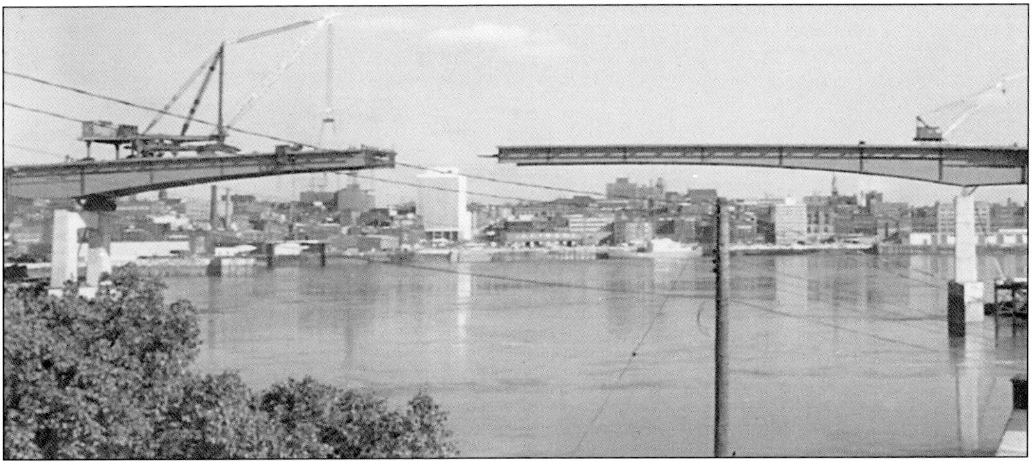

To build a bridge across the harbour was a considerable challenge. The first attempt to connect Watson Street to Merritt Street fell in 1837 when the engineering technology was not yet up to the distance that had to be crossed–1,400 feet. Kilby Reynolds built a suspension bridge in 1853 at the Reversing Falls, a shorter 623 feet. By 1915, with heavier traffic such as streetcars on the roads, it was necessary to replace the first bridge, and the current 565-foot steel arc spandrel bridge was built, again at the Reversing Falls, and has served to the present. It cost $350,000 to build initially and $400,000 to paint it in the 1980s. Until 1968 it was the only way to travel from East to West and carried 30,000 cars daily. With the opening of the Harbour Bridge in 1968 (shown under construction; the piers in the bottom picture and the extension pushing out from East and West Side in the larger picture) there was an end to lengthy traffic jams. The Harbour Bridge fulfilled a promise to the residents of Carleton made regularly and that almost came to fruition in 1857, 1889, 1909, 1929, and 1952. It cost $20 million, is the only toll bridge in the province, and it has been said it will never be paid for! (Courtesy Jane Hemmings for top photo.)

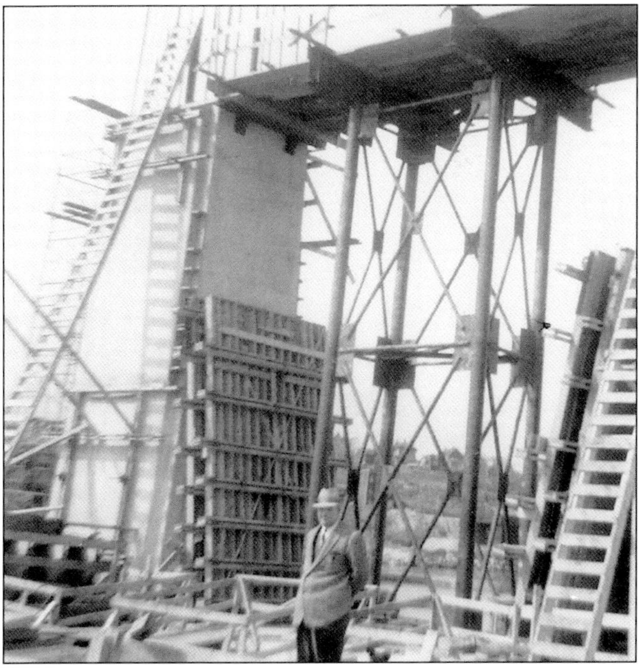

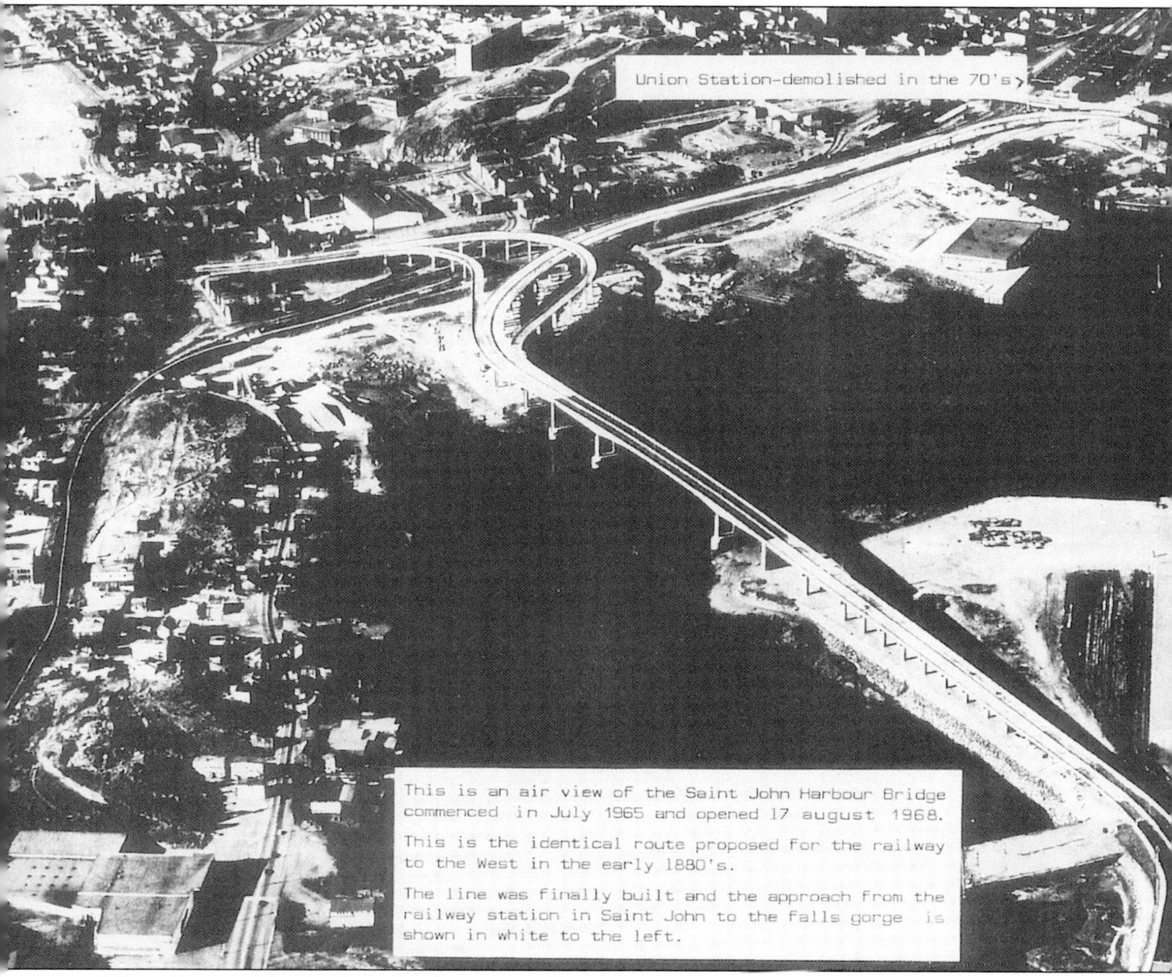

This photo of the harbour bridge was collected by Dyson Thomas, who added his interesting self-explanatory comments.

Eight

Schools, Churches, and Fraternities

The official education of a West Sider took place in the home, at church, then at school. The youngster began his education, perhaps on a walk with his parents through the streets of the West Side, down by the piers of the harbour, or up to the heights of Martello Tower, or to visit parks or play areas, or short cut along the rail tracks to the pebble shore for a picnic.

In this chapter we continue with pictures that have come to light since the last book, which pertain to the churches, schools, and other organizations that provided the "glue" that held the community of Saint John West together.

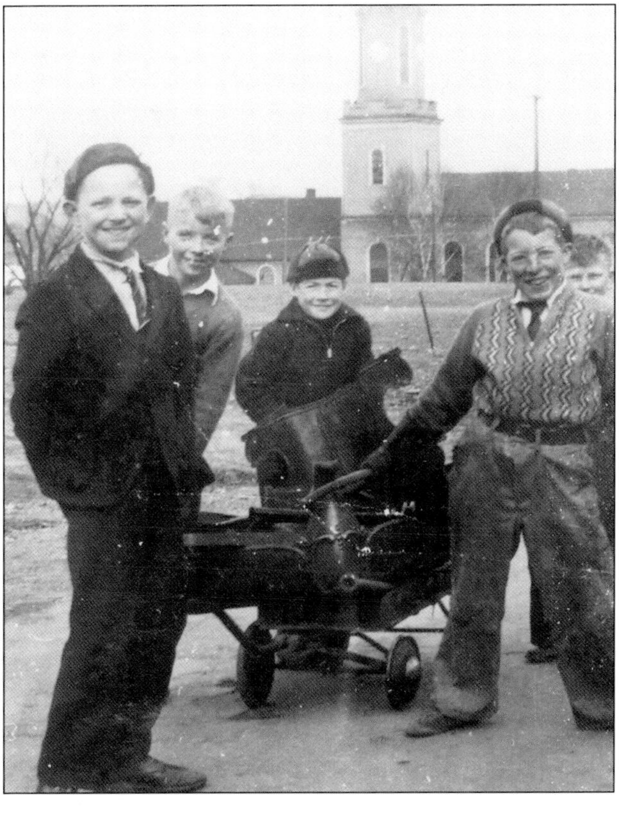

We begin with these five boys. Dressed in outlandish costumes, the boys are gathering junk during the Second World War outside New Albert School on Courtenay Hill, not far from St. George's Church. In Saint John West it was hard to find a place where one of the schools or churches wasn't visible and exerting its influence upon the citizens. (Courtesy New Albert School archives.)

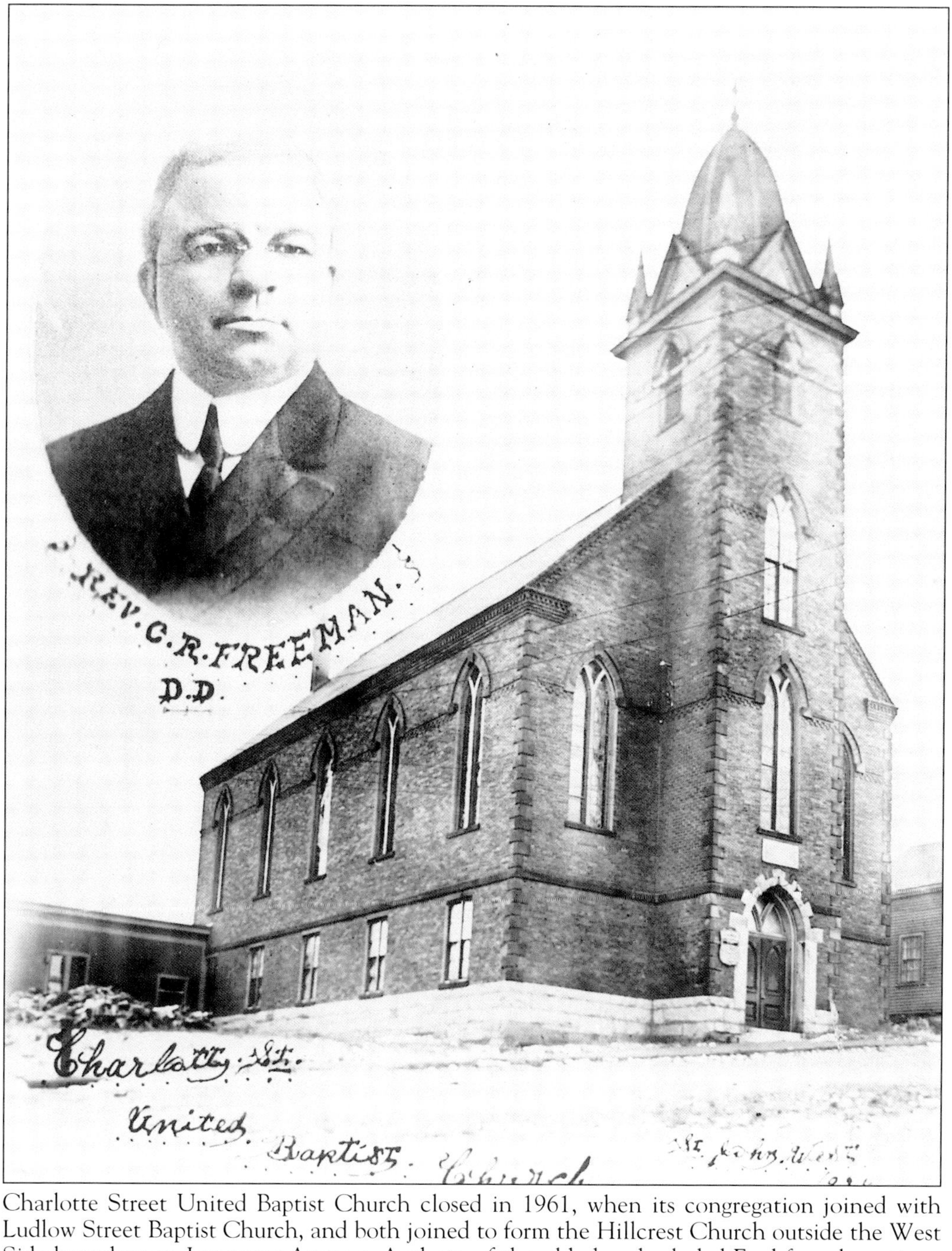

Charlotte Street United Baptist Church closed in 1961, when its congregation joined with Ludlow Street Baptist Church, and both joined to form the Hillcrest Church outside the West Side boundary on Lancaster Avenue. A photo of the old church eluded Fred for a long time, but he was successful after the first book was published, and so we include this photograph to complete our look on churches in West Saint John. The building lives on, without the tower, as an apartment building.

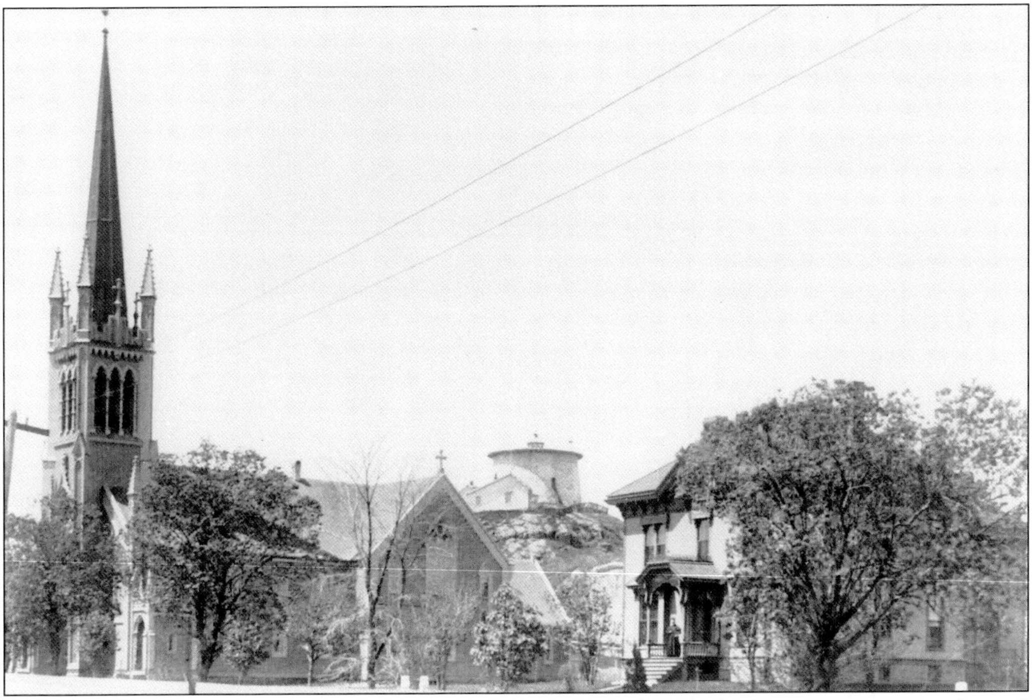

In the previous book we showed the original Assumption Church, built in 1849, and we showed the current church dedicated on March 6, 1907, but not this church. It was built about 1885 perhaps incorporating the superstructure of the first church. It was struck by lightning and burned on October 26, 1904. The resemblance to the present-day St. Rose of Lima Church in Milford is striking, but not unexpected, as both were built around the same time and St. Rose was the mission church of the Assumption parish.

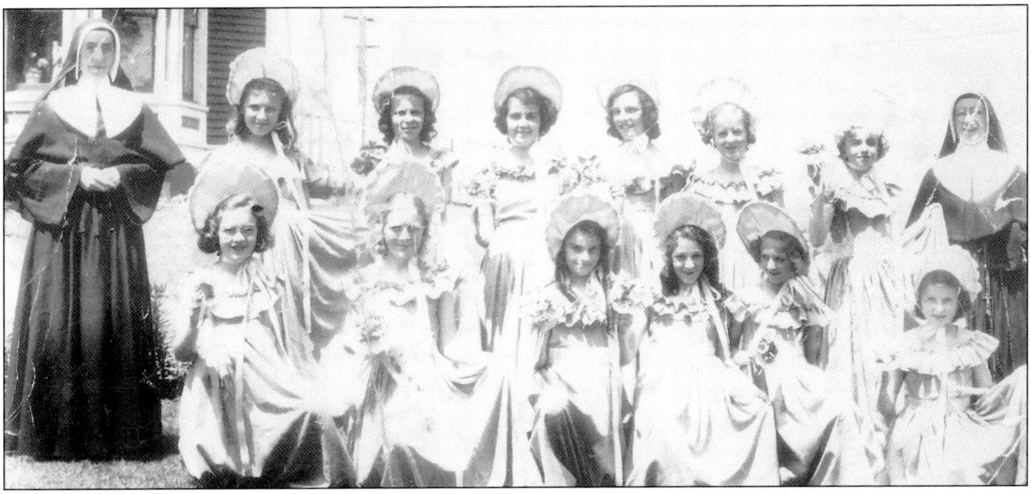

Continuing with the Assumption's story, beginning in the 1920s, under the direction of Father John J. Ryan, St. Patrick's School was built on City Line. Property opposite the church was acquired for the Sisters of Charity with St. Joseph's Convent opened at 40 Dufferin Row. We see two of the Sisters of Charity, at the property at 175 City Line opposite the school, which later became the Children's Aid Society and is now apartments. These girls seem prepared for their first Communion. (Courtesy Mary Ellen Kindred.)

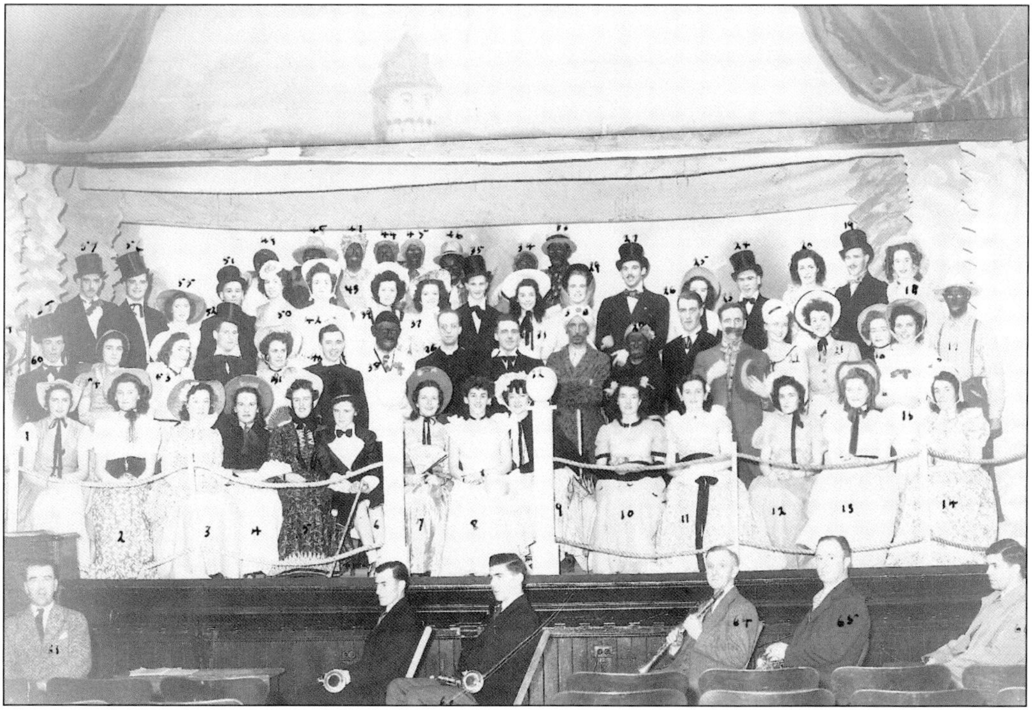

This is a presentation of the show, *An Old Kentucky Garden* on April 28–30, 1946. Tickets were 50¢ for the presentation, which was given at St. Patrick's Hall by the Assumption chapter of the C.Y.O., 60 strong. Patricia Owens had the lead as "Jeannie", with the light brown hair, and Larry Murphy played the northern boy who loved her but was forbidden to court her. Stephen Foster's music was directed by Rev. T.C. Beck, and F. Joyce directed the stage action. Percy N. Woodley was the photographer.

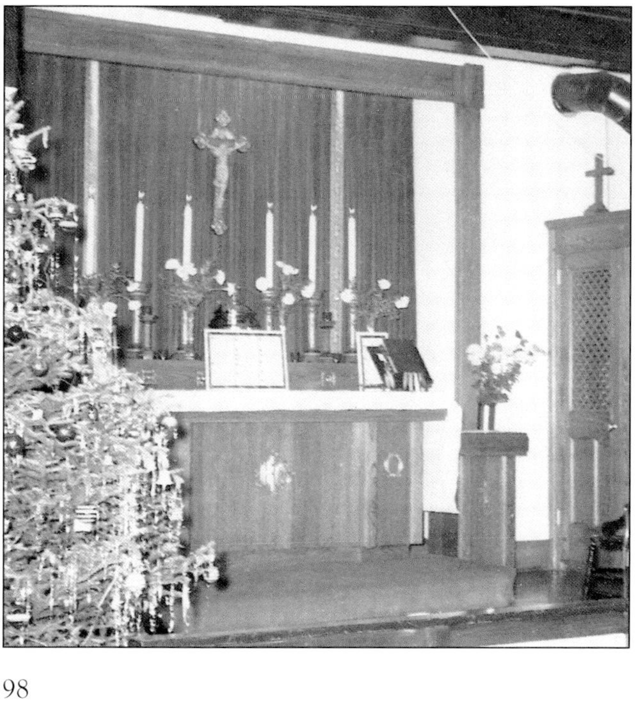

The Catholic Sailor's Club on Rodney Street provided a recreational area, as well as the opportunity to participate in the Mass for those arriving from sea. It is shown at Christmas in 1960. The first Seaman's Mission was started by Lady Alice Tilley in 1897. It was one of many social programs she got underway, such as the Fredericton Hospital and the Saint John Council of Women. The Seafarer's work continues to this day in a building east of the Carleton Community Centre on Fred Miller Way.

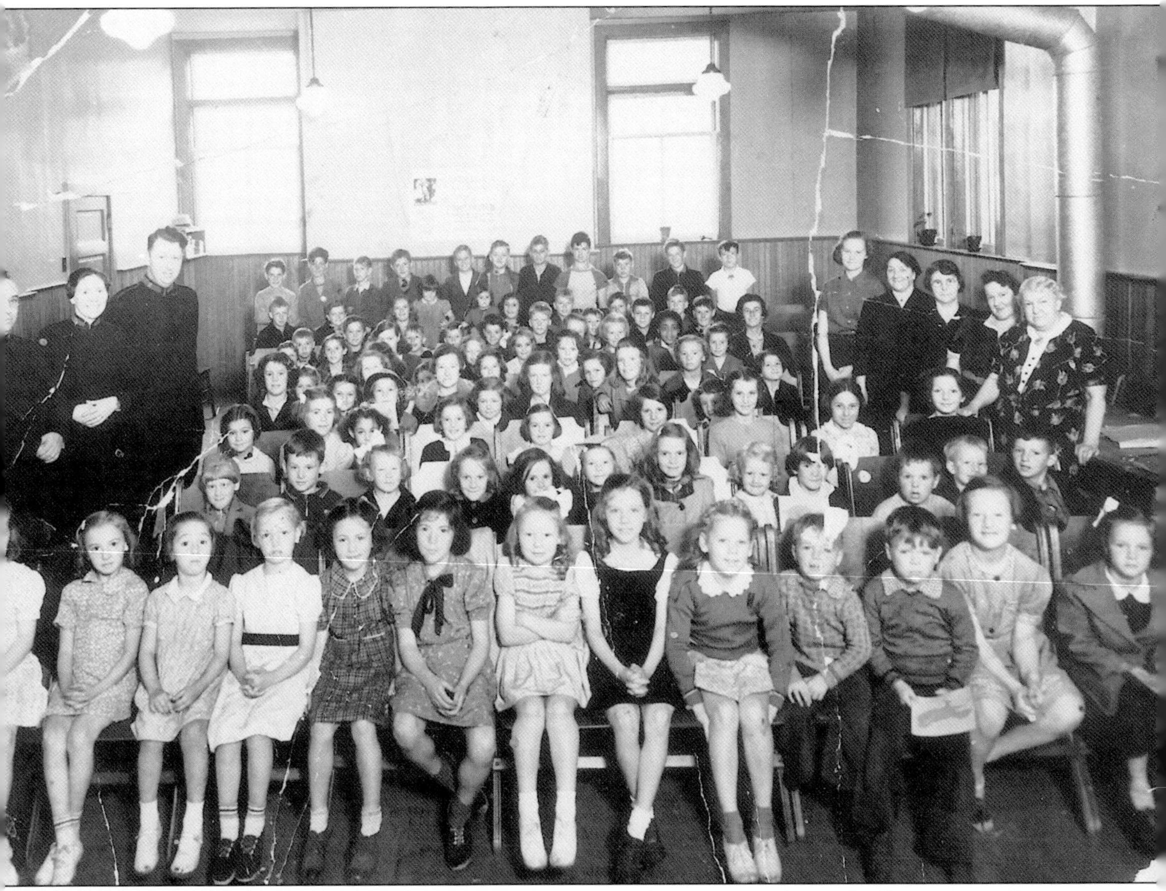

This group of children, over 100, are at the Salvation Army Citadel on Guilford Street for a presentation, perhaps a magic show or puppet show, which the Corps used effectively to attract children and lead them into a relationship with God. Perhaps they are being told about the program advertised on the poster at the back of the room for July 1, 1941, involving the Army cadet band. The Army bands played regularly on King Street as a way of attracting new members to their work in the Saint John West area.

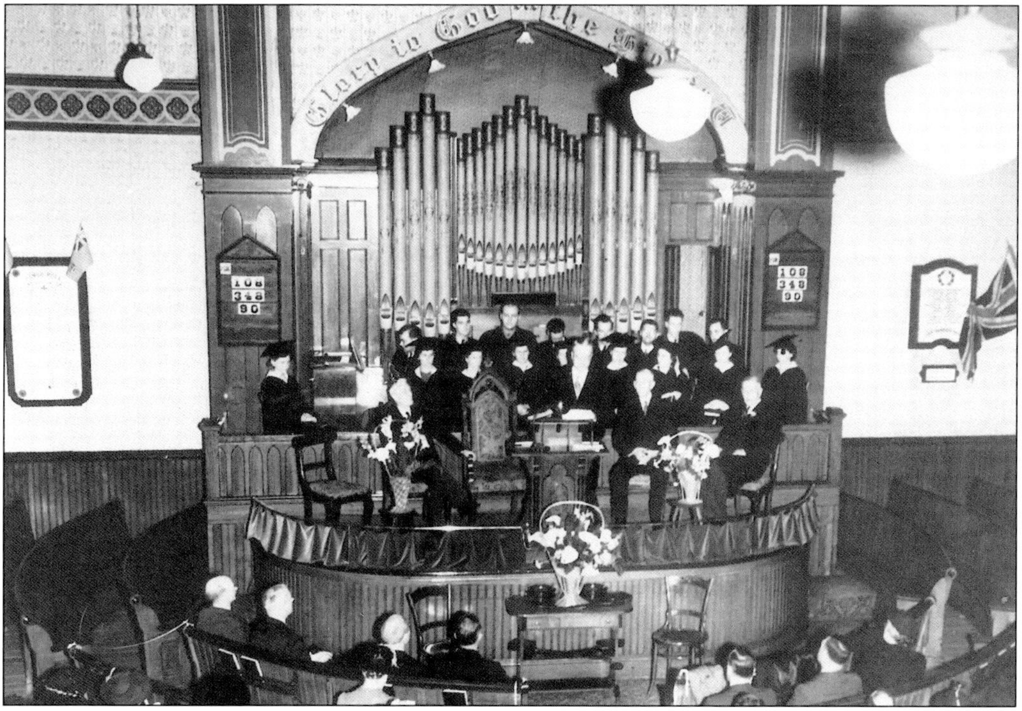

Here is the interior of two churches that no longer stand. Above is the Ludlow Street Baptist Church (1841–1961), and the bottom photo is of the Carleton Methodist Church, which stood from 1841 to 1979.

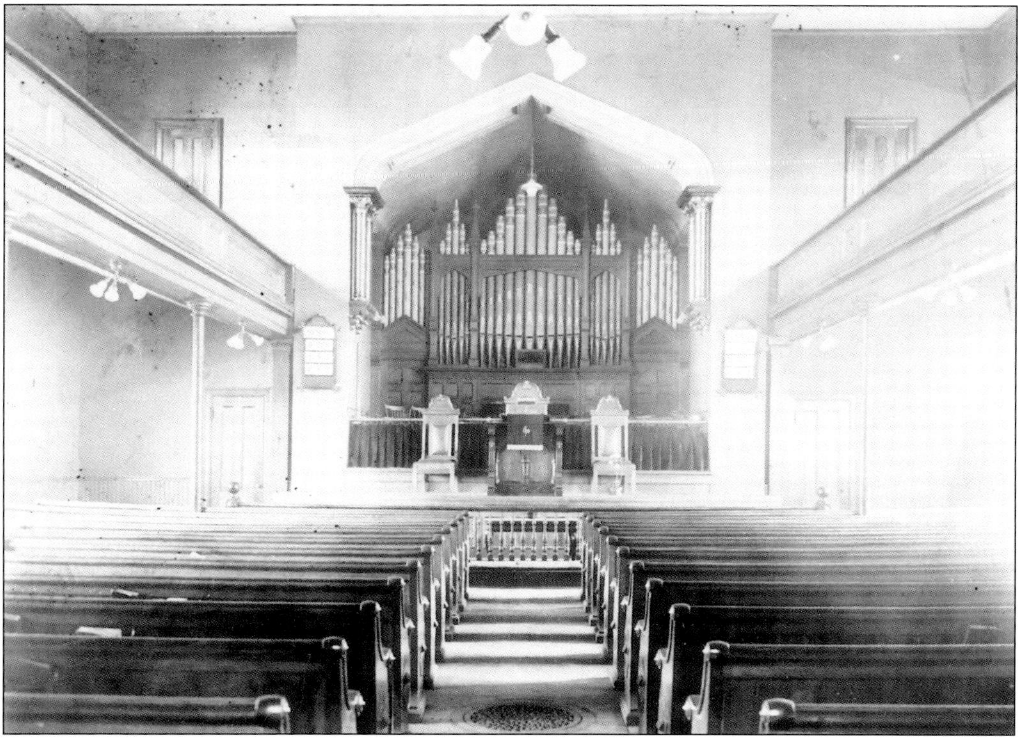

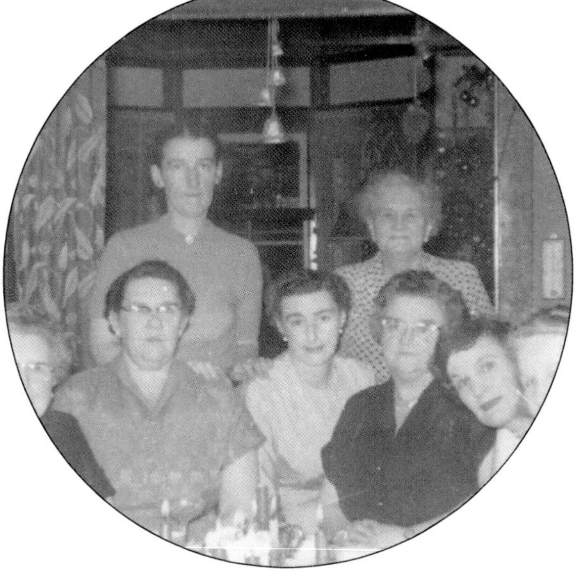

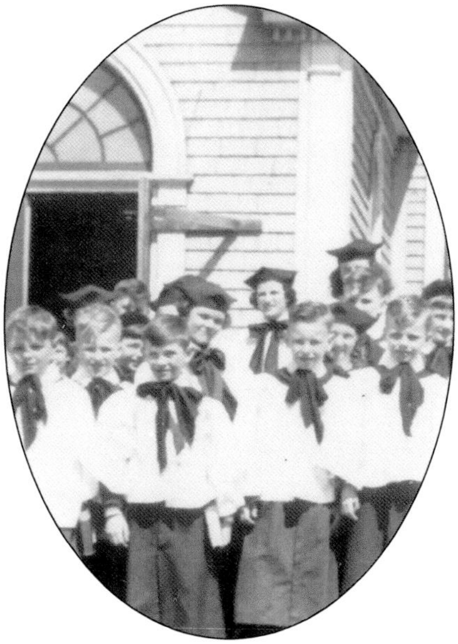

If you were a church member, your life might include club night, such as shown in our top left photo being held by the Ludlow Street Baptist Ladies' Group in 1959, or you might sing in the St. George's Church choir, posed on the lawn in 1952 (top right photo). You might meet at the Carleton Church for a boys meeting (bottom photo). The members in this photo, from left to right, are, Jimmy Fox, Walter Scribner, Jimmy Estee, Arthur Wilson, Malcolm Harned, Ronald Galbraith, Hunter Parsons, Harold Ring, Clint Regan, Mr. Woods, Donald Regan, Whitney Moore, Mr. Crosby, and Jack Galbraith.

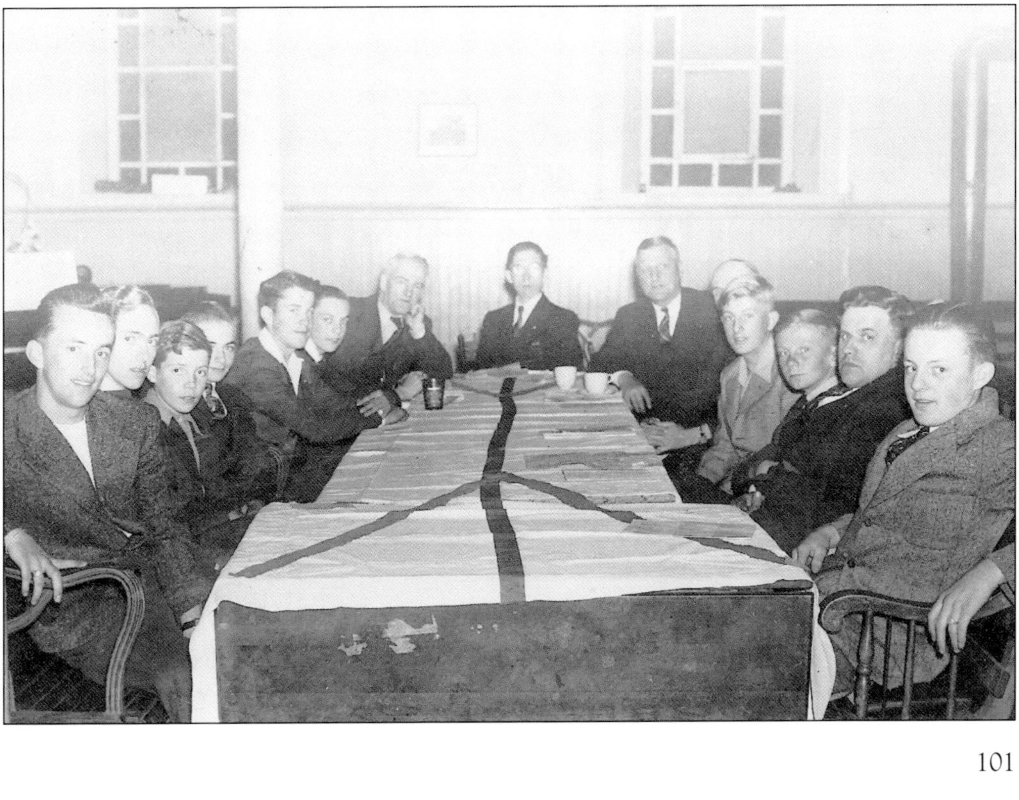

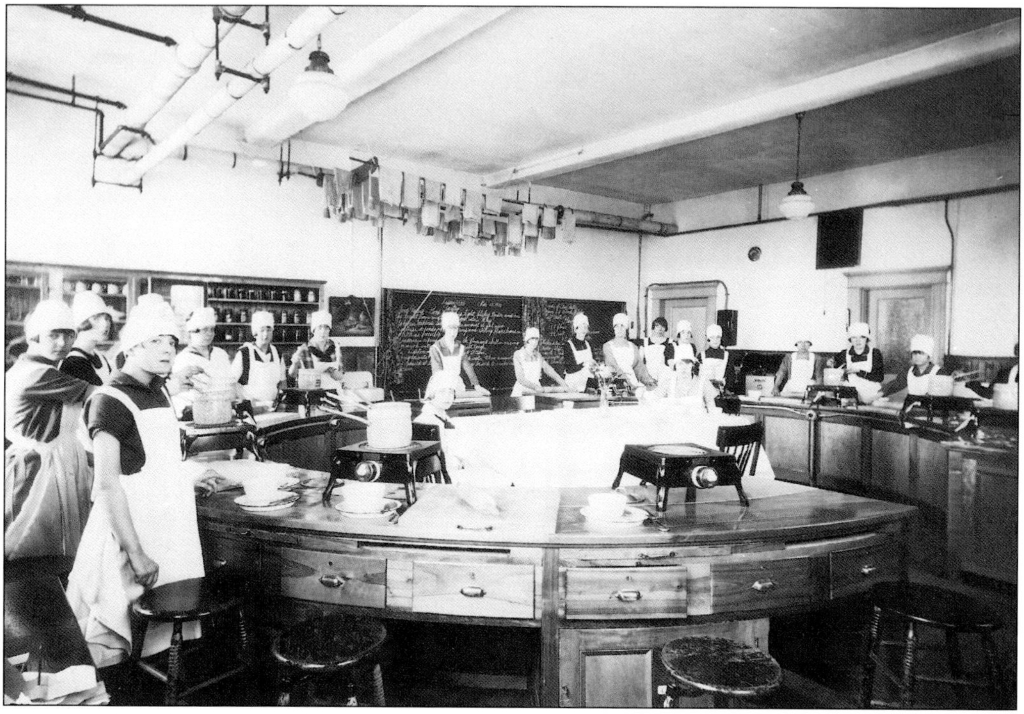

Top: At New Albert School, Lesson 27 is given in Pastry-making on March 12, 1926, in the very well-furnished Domestic Science Department. *Bottom:* Red Cross Clubs were a big hit in schools, and New Albert had one of the best for the years following World War II. David Goss, left, and Ian Wilson, right, pack items for arriving immigrants at the pier just down the street.

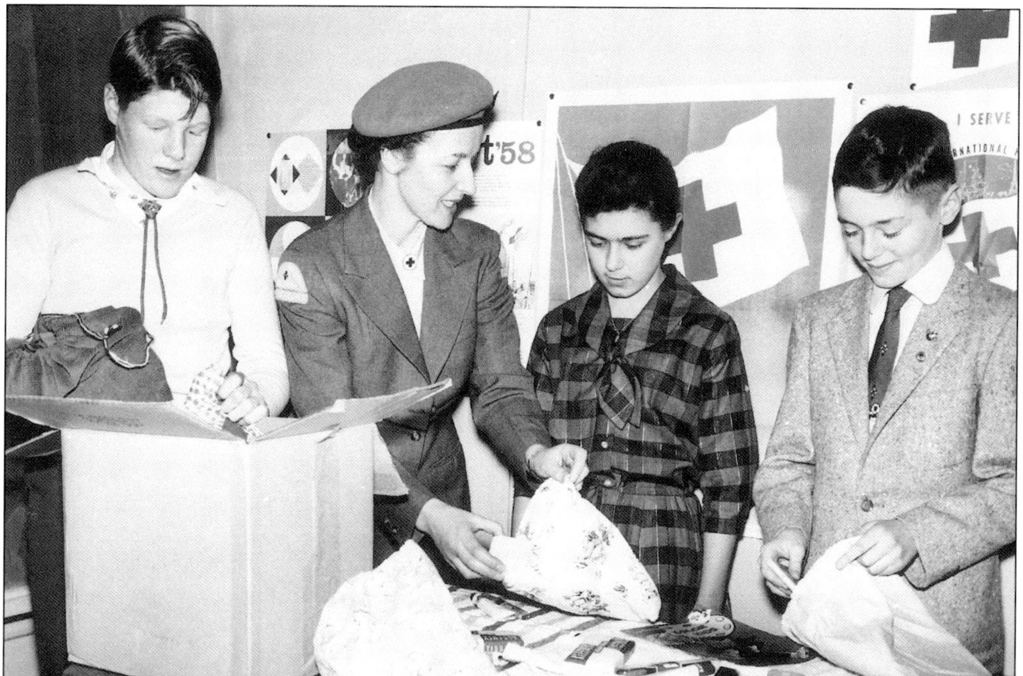

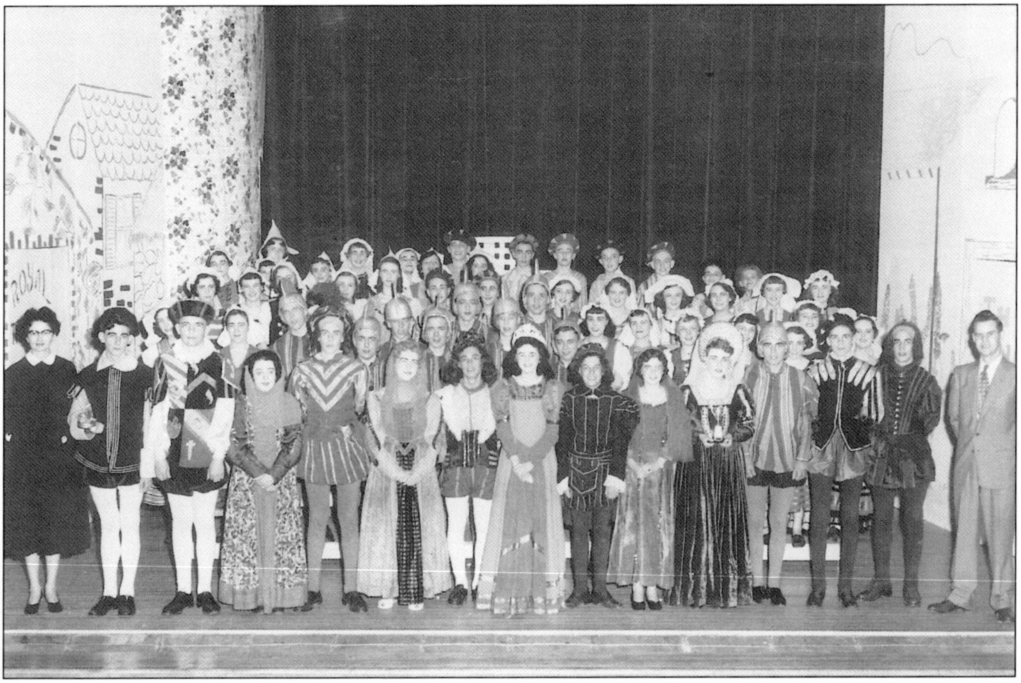

The New Albert School Dramatic Club presented Williams and Steckel's *Captain of the Guard* with 50 members in 1955. As a tryout, it was first taken to Grand Manan Island, as Miss Mary Ingalls, the music director, was a native of that Fundy Isle. Then on May 4 and 5, 1955, they performed at Barnhill School in the new city of Lancaster, then, a few nights later they gave their final performance at New Albert School. Many of the members who played in the production went on to become stalwarts in the musical life of Saint John in the years to follow.

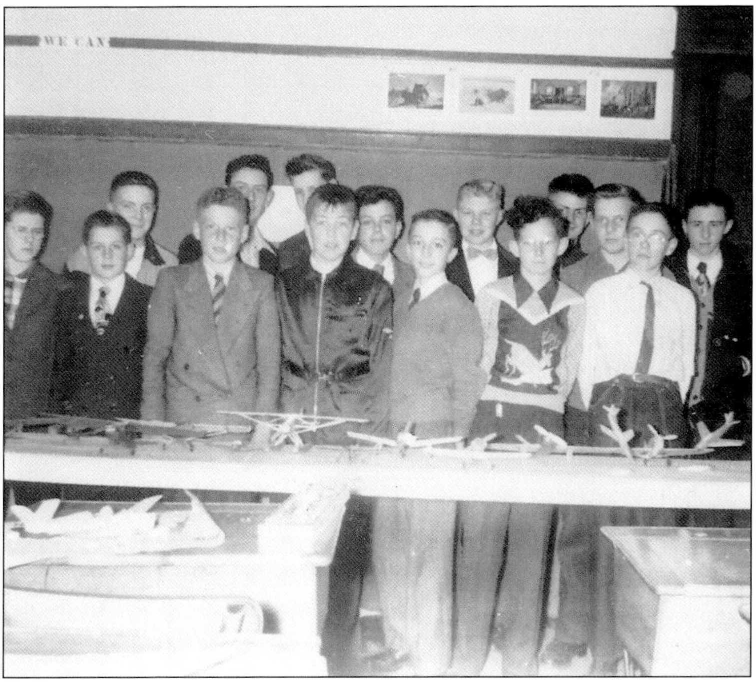

Hobby shows were a 1950s rage, and New Albert School didn't miss this. Participants, from left, are, Robert Mills, Calvin Lee, Keith MacCollum, Billy Weaver, David Thorne, Carl Tippett, Malcolm Campbell, Donnie Walker, Fred Hersey, Charles Buchanan, Billy Miller, Burton Alderman, James Ryan, Lawrence Kincade, and Donald Corkum.

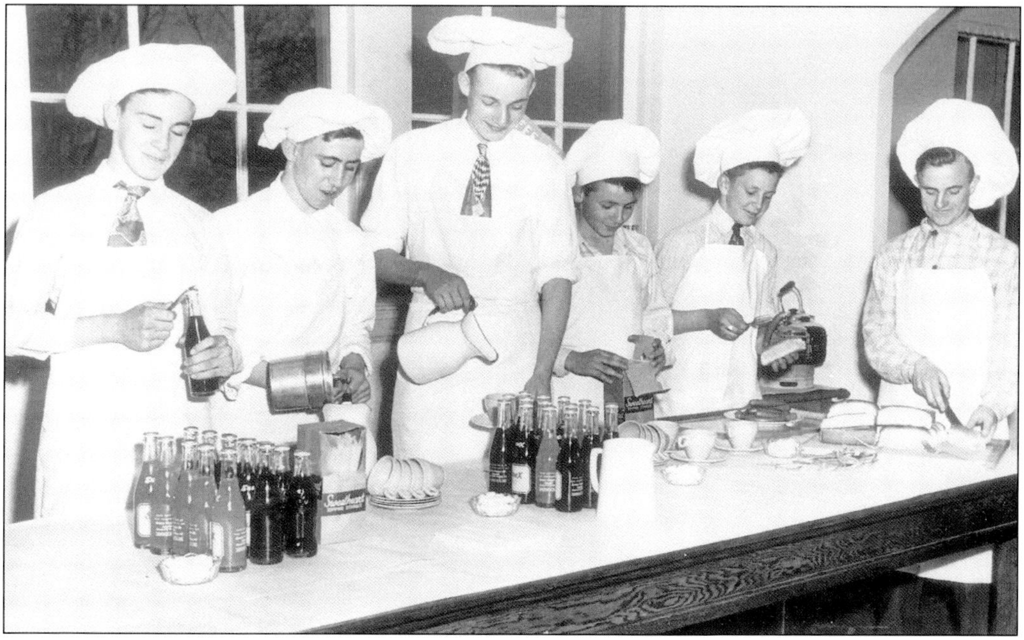

This scene is of Hobby Night on June 5, 1952. Ross Whalen, Donald Allaby, Harry MacFawn, Wayne Murphy, Paul Ellis, and Arthur Robson prepare pop and hot dogs at this popular school event.

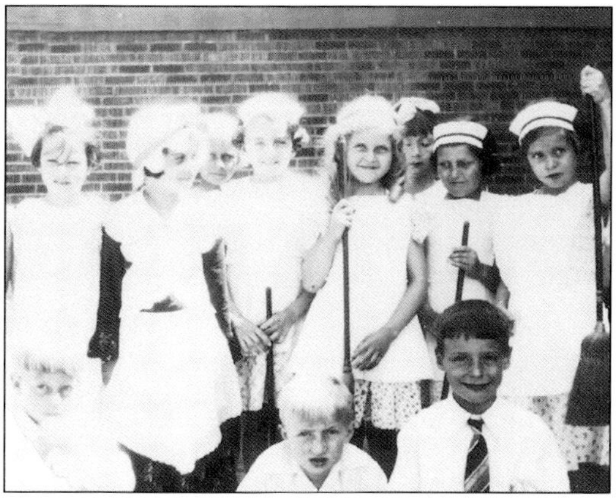

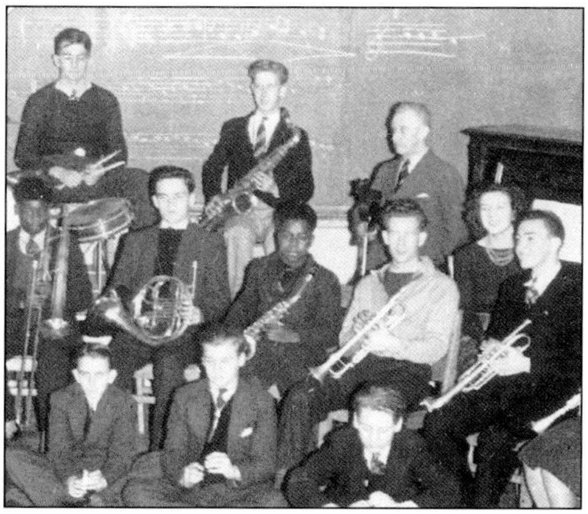

Left: Norma Beville's photo of the cast of *Old woman who lived in a shoe* is proof that dramatics was part of New Albert's program from the earliest days, as it was taken in 1933. *Right:* Music was an integral part of New Albert School life. Professor William C. Bowden (well remembered as he taught music for 57 years in city schools) addressed this card to David. However, that is all we know of this particular musical moment. Music was one of the last programs to disappear from the school as orchestra practices continued in the closed school almost until it was torn down in 1999.

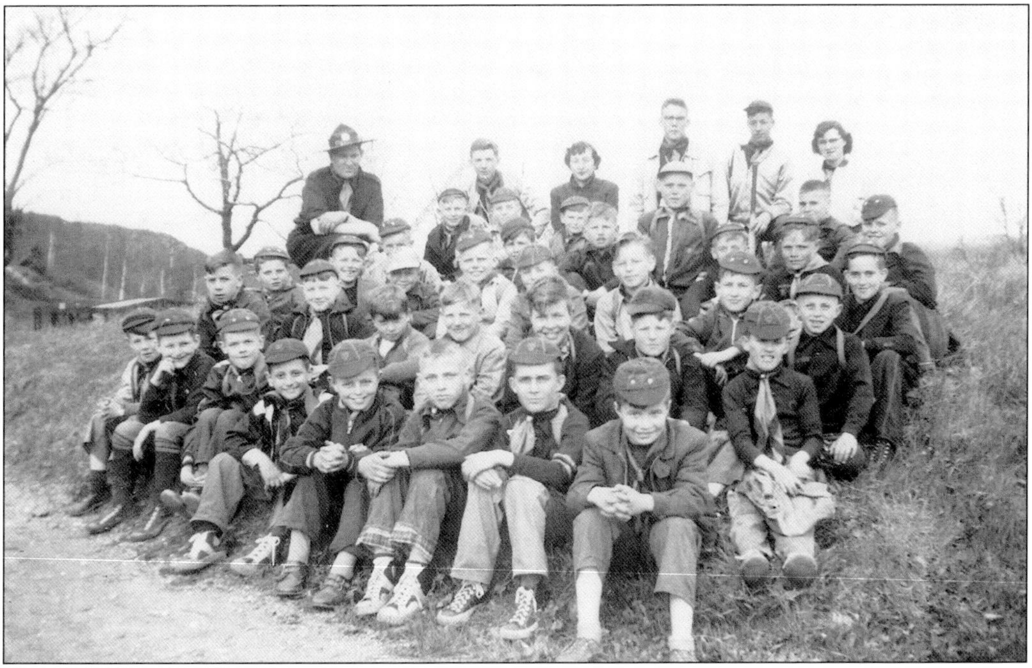

Scouting played a huge role in the Saint John West area. The 5th Troop of Saint John was founded in the city about 1912 by Stanley Olive, and later he moved across Carleton to St. George's Church, where he founded a Boy Scout Troop there in 1922. Olive began a tradition of hiking, which continued as shown with the St. George's Cubs in 1954 in Rockwood Park with Akela Abe Goss. In the photo below Scout Grant Kelly (now owner of Vintage Photo and Frame, who helped with this book), Andy Stark, and Ron Roy look on as Roy Melvin is presented the Canon Haigh "Scout of the year award" by G.A. (Barney) Goss, representing the Royal Canadian Legion #2, in 1979.

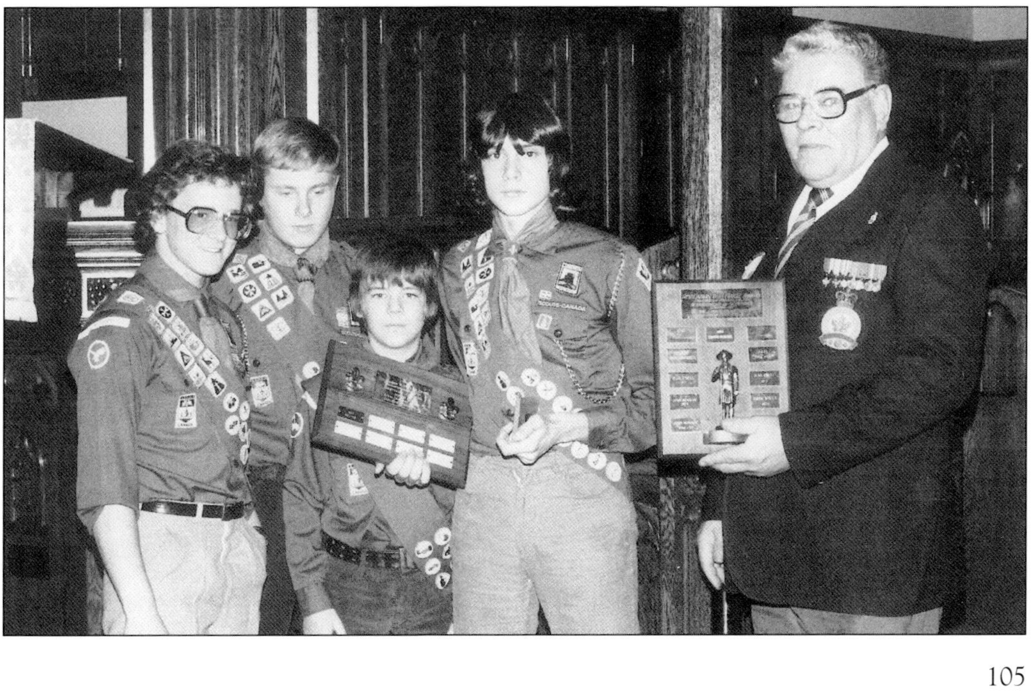

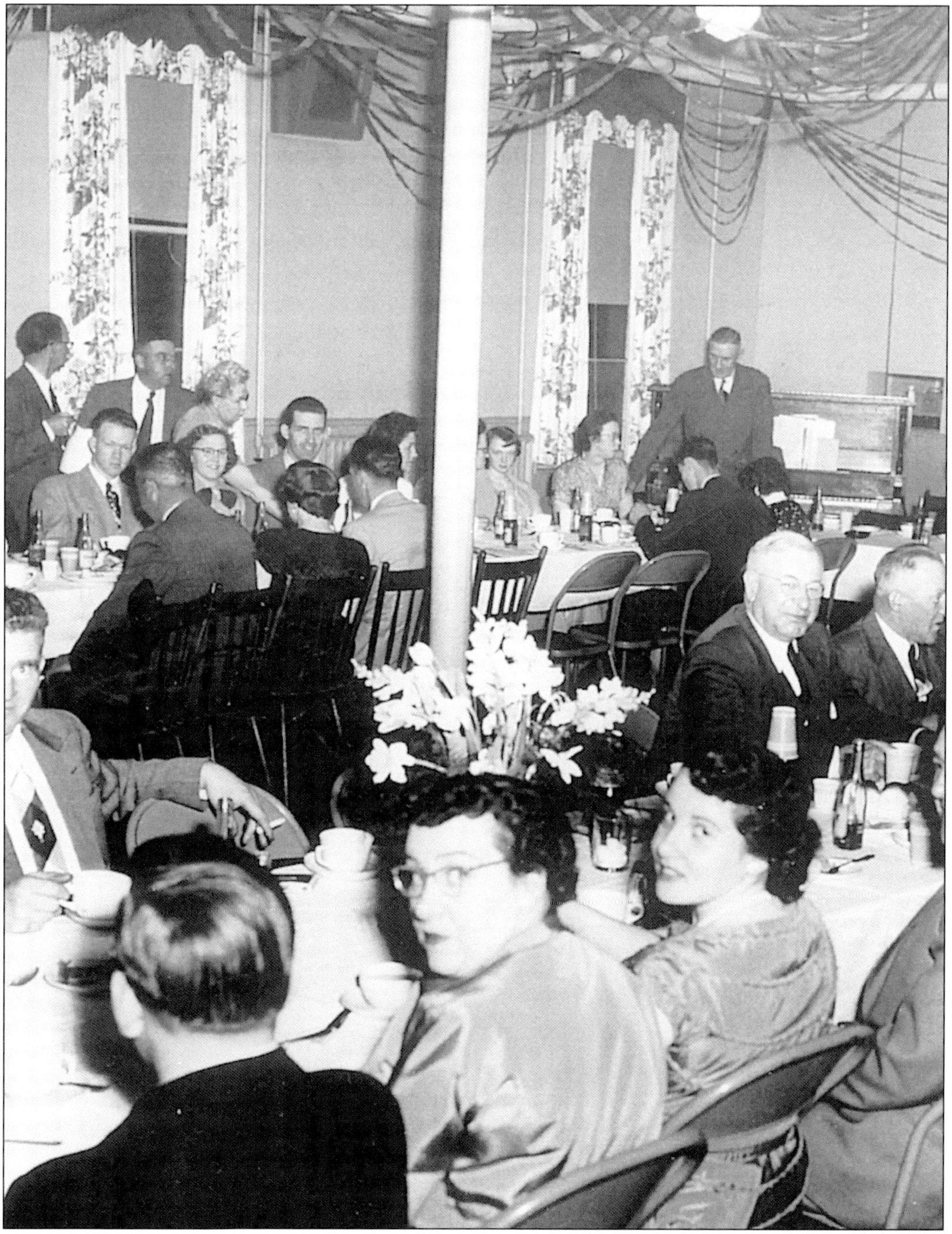

West Siders loved to eat, especially if someone else was preparing the meal. Thus, church societies, fraternal groups, and clubs were kept busy serving one another with sit down dinners. Here the hosts are the members of the Masonic Order, and it is being held inside the 1869 Masonic Lodge for the International Brotherhood of Railworkers sometime in the mid-1950s. Dawson Moyer provided the picture and would love to have all the people identified. He does know his father, James Moyer, is in the background standing in the frame between the flowery drapes.

Nine

The Streets of Saint John West

Paul Beddell was the man who originally planned the streets of the city of Saint John in 1783. He chose their names from among the pioneer settlers, as well as from well-known men and women of the empire. Later, natural features, such as the Martello Tower and the breakwater, and the water itself superseded some of the early choices.

In this chapter we have tried to select a photo representative of every street in Saint John West. There are, unfortunately, a few exceptions for one reason or another. We've started with Water Street on the north, the street nearest the St. John River, and worked across the peninsula to the south until we've come to Germain Street, being closest to the Bay of Fundy. Then, we've started at the harbour, with Union Street, and worked our way criss-crossing the north-south streets till we've come to the boundary of Saint John West, appropriately named, City Line. We've tried to use pictures with views different from those shown in any other chapters of this or our previous book.

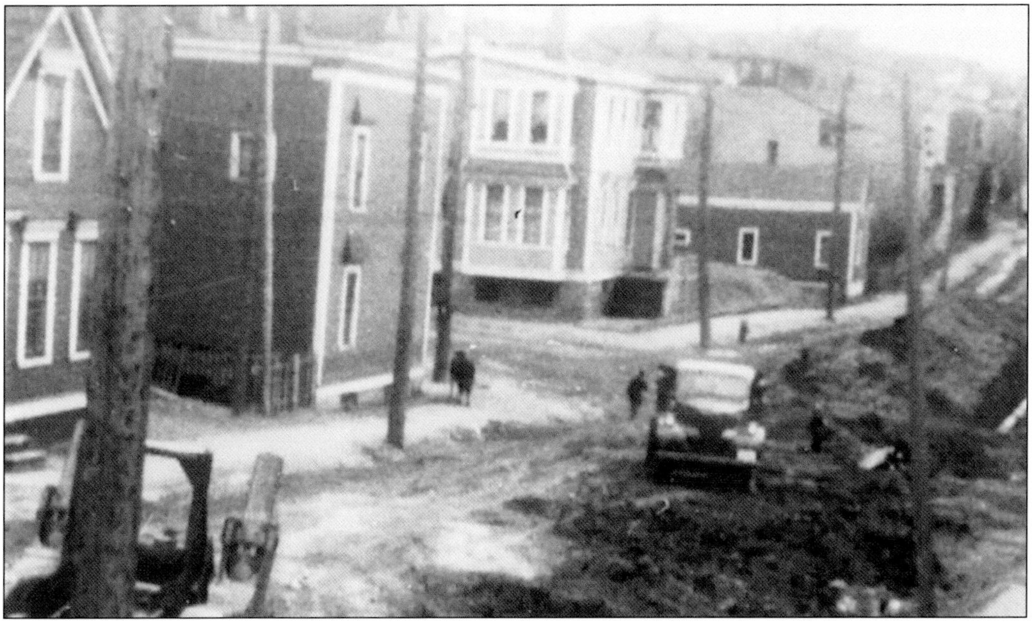

Riverview Drive, formerly known as Water Street, is shown when the waterline to the pulpmill was laid in the 1950s and the street was extensively dug up.

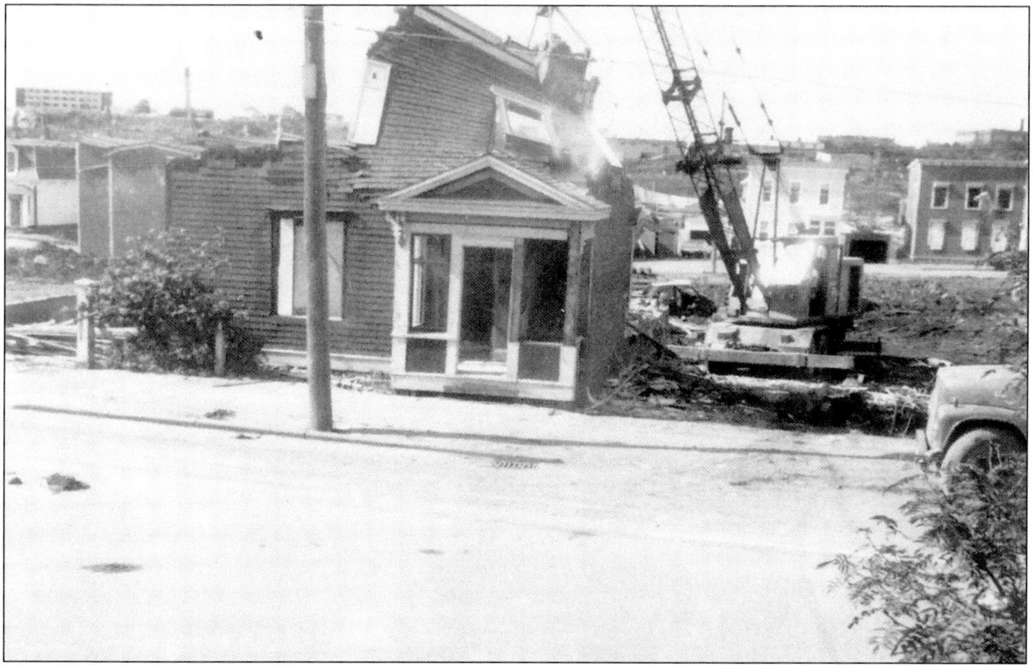

About 80 houses were torn down on Water, Prince, and Ludlow Streets for the construction of Harbour Bridge and the building of the throughway from 1964 to 1968 in the lower West Side area. Many were also lost in the North End. This was William Maxwell's house at 65 Prince Street. In the background on the left is the home of Malcolm Harned, and on the right is the home of Eric and Frances Taylor on Riverview Drive.

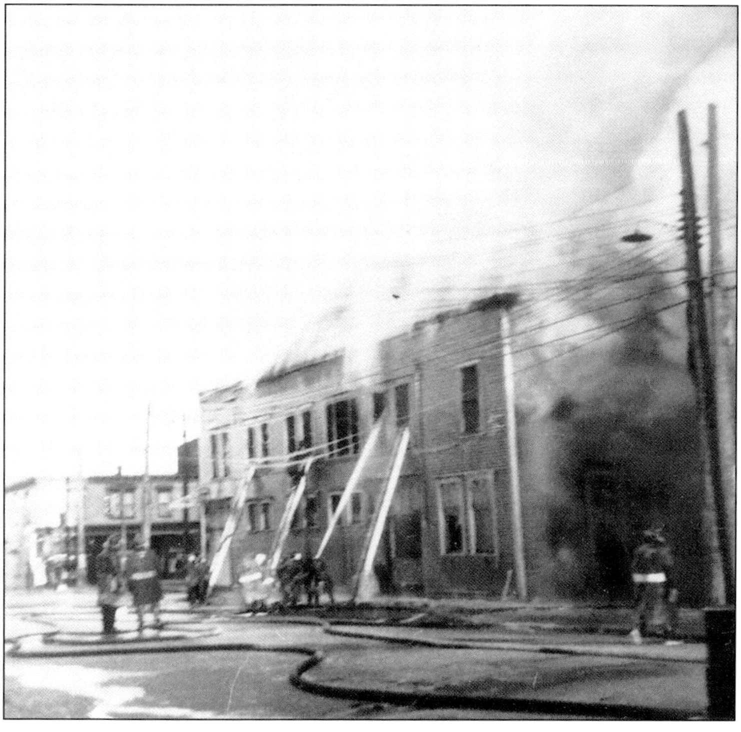

This view is of King Street. W.E. Emerson, built in 1930, was destroyed by fire in November 1957. It was rebuilt as the New Brunswick Liquor Commission Store and now serves as Snack's Convenience store. They were the top sellers of the first book on this area, *Saint John West and its Neighbours*, in November 1995.

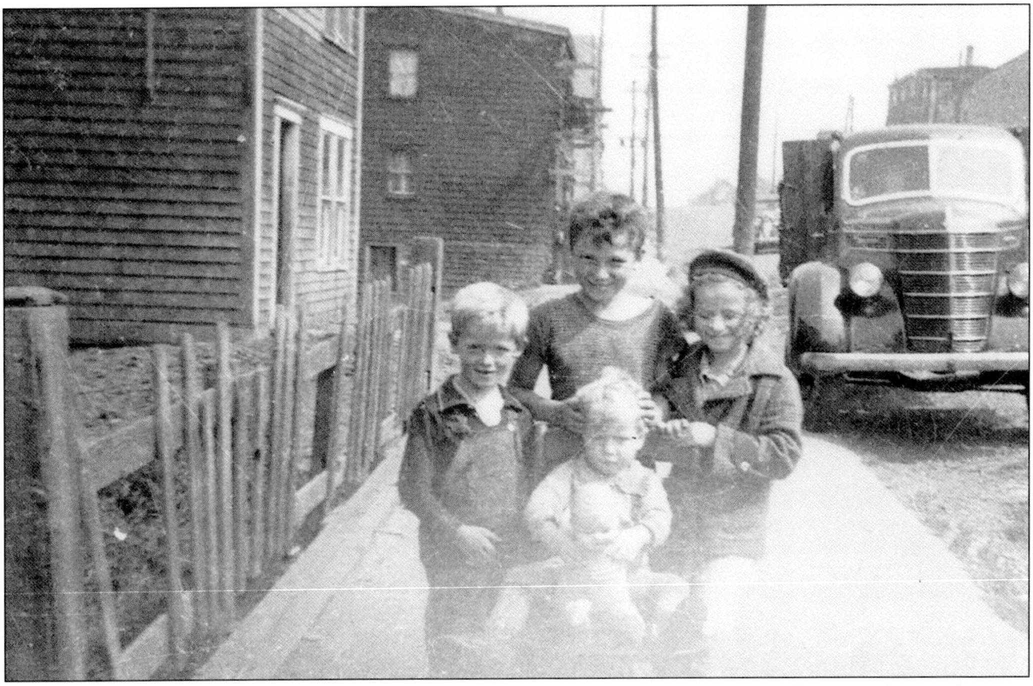

Four children have gathered at the bottom end of Duke Street to play, perhaps in the apple trees that were a popular attraction on this corner in the 1950s. The trees may have been remnants of a farm in the area in earlier times.

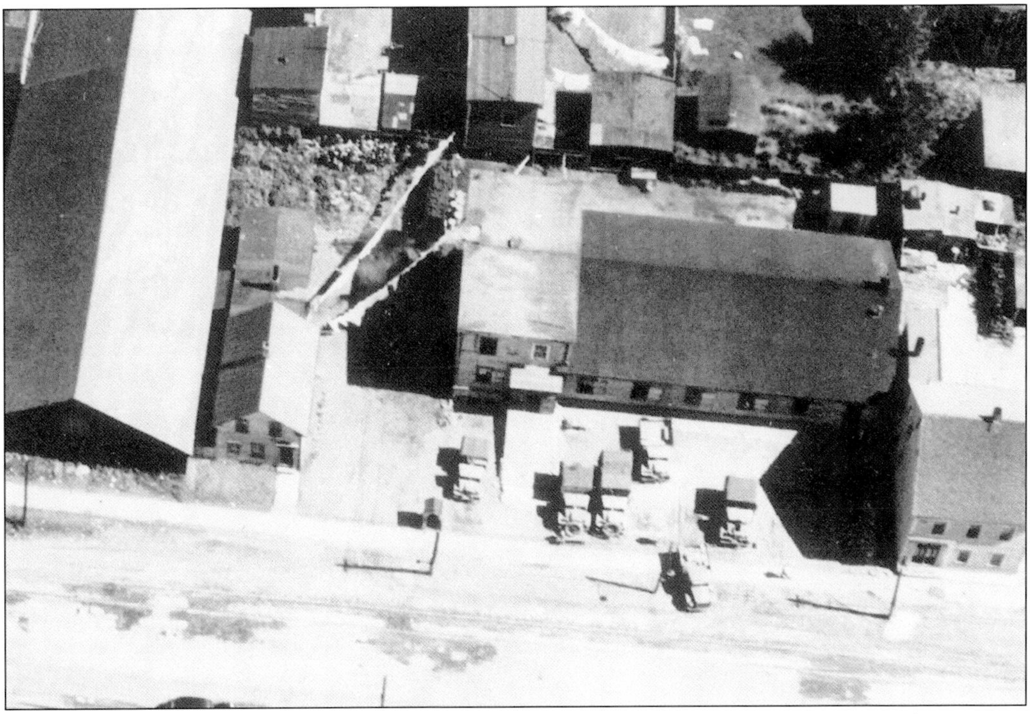

In back of the various jeeps are the Army Barracks shown in this aerial view on Winslow Street. Today the barracks have been converted to apartments.

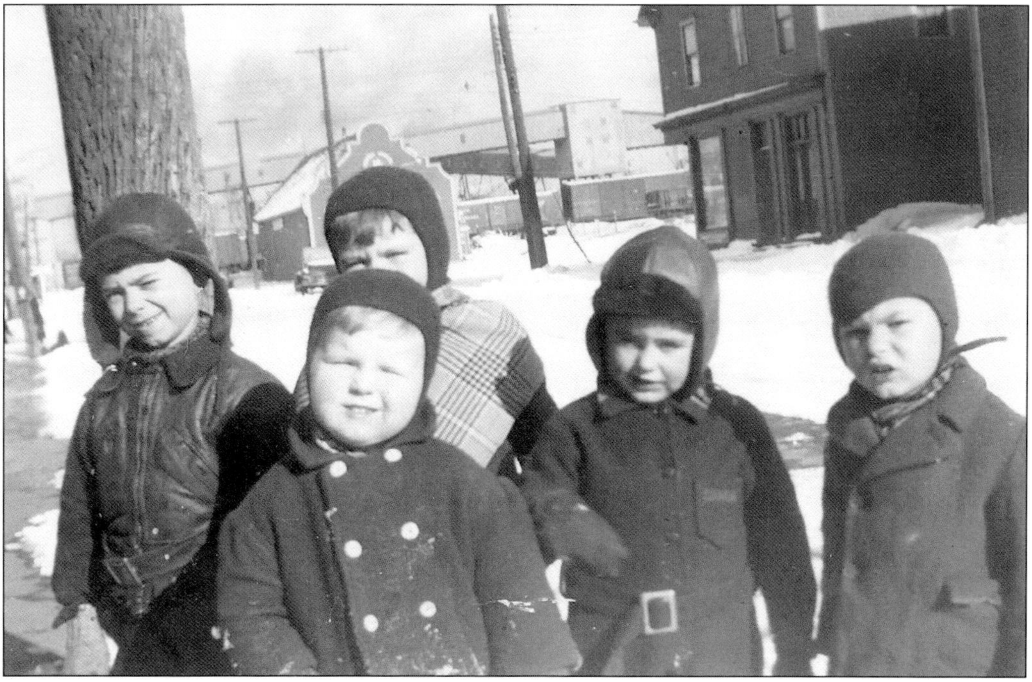

These five children dressed for a winter outing are believed to be Bobby and Jimmy Orr and friends. They are at play on Rodney Street with the Seaman's Mission in the background in 1944.

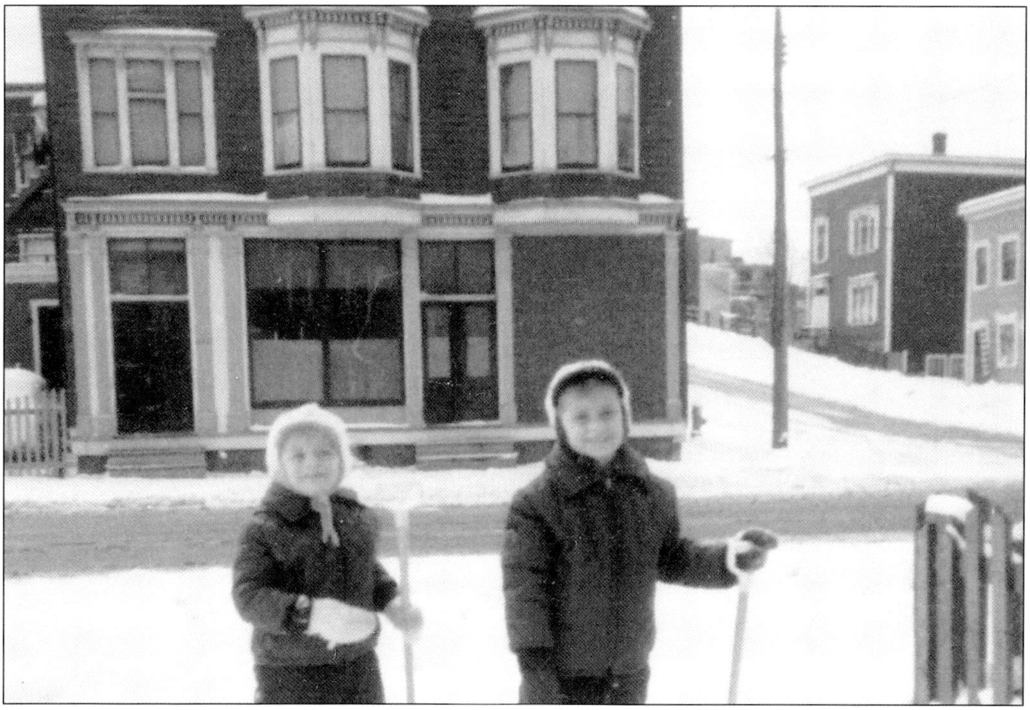

Mrs. George Stackhouse's Grocery, one of about 20 family shops left in the '50s, is shown at the corner of Charlotte and Ludlow Streets.

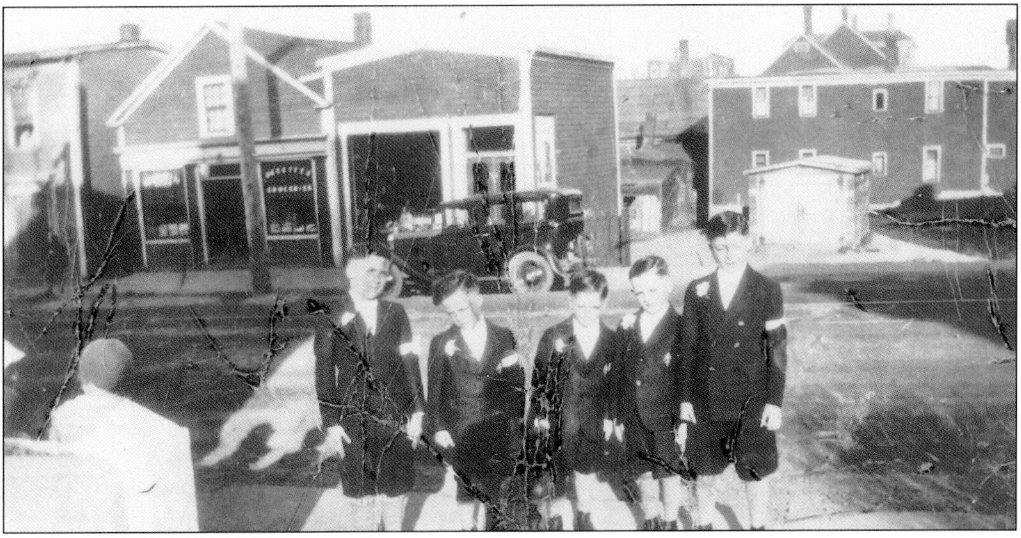

The five boys in their very smart suits are standing in front of the Lynch House on Tower Street, probably about 1935. They are decked with a boutonniere and white armbands and soon will be off to either Confirmation or first Communion at Assumption Church. Besides being a general store, O'Keefe's, seen in the background, also served paperboys as a depot for the *Telegraph Journal* and *Evening Times Globe* paper pickup for many years.

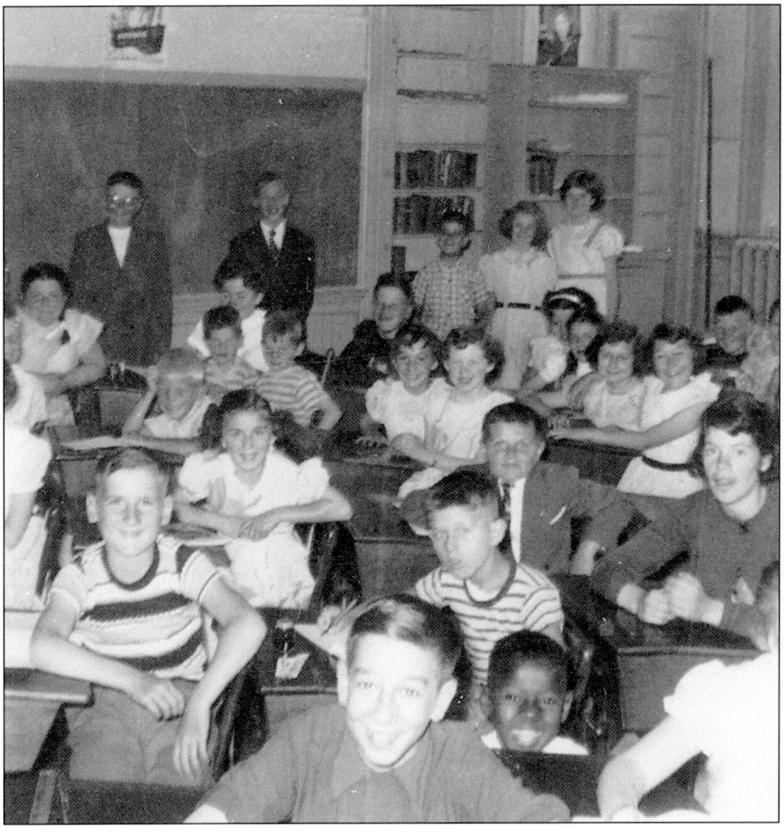

La Tour School was built on St. John Street in 1901 and served students who lived from Rodney to Germain Street—222 in all, till 1958. Doug Spinney taught there in 1954 and 1955, and this is his photo of the fifth-grade class of the latter year. He presented it to me as I was in that class, but I don't recall the occasion, and unfortunately, can't identify half my classmates, or find myself! Still the photo is important, as very few exist of La Tour.

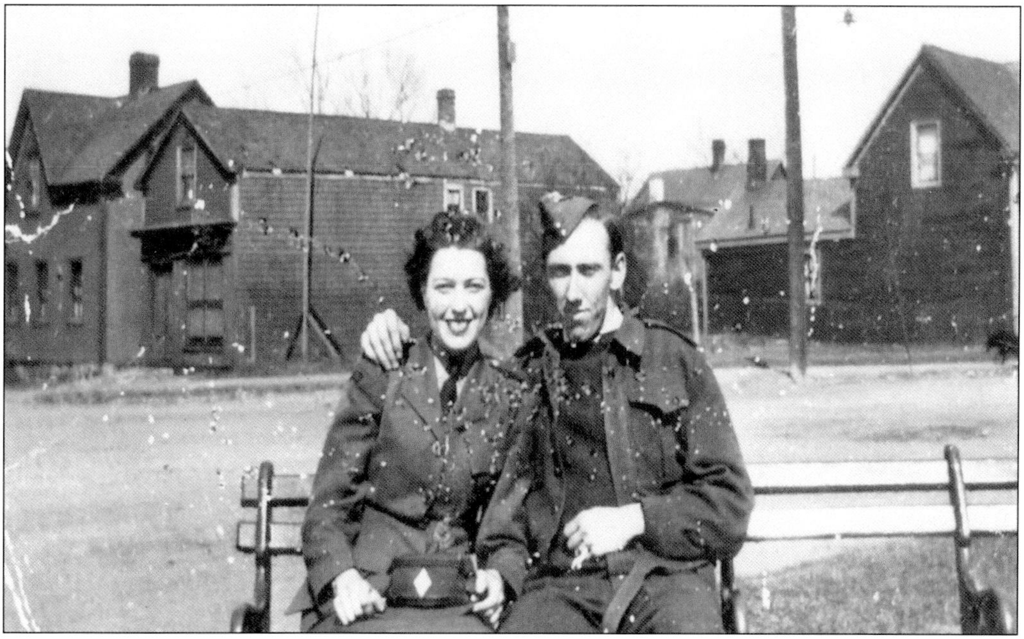

Queen Square on Queen Street was a popular courting spot. If a sailor or soldier had a date he could go to admire Johnny Duncan's well-kept gardens and his date in Queen Square. Note the store in the background behind the girl. It was McManus Ship Chandlers (1880–1940) and also served as a grocery, bakery, and library since the early 1880s.

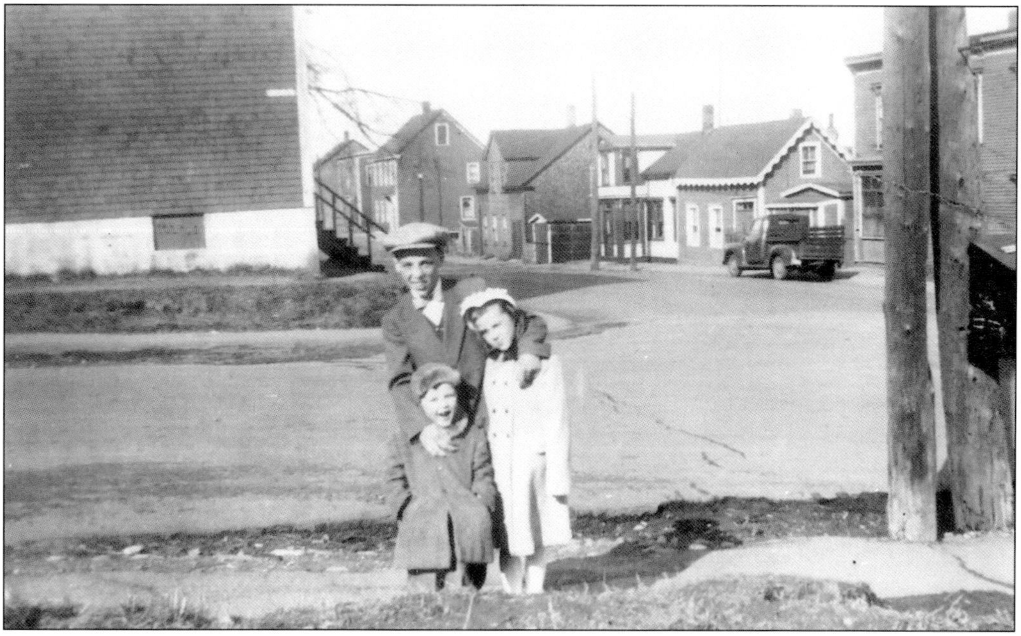

Big brother Doug Carter, with left arm around sister Betty Ann, and younger brother Fred pose at the corner of St. James and Ludlow Streets. Across the street, Ludlow Street drops precipitously to the rail tracks. It was a favorite, though dangerous, sliding spot for the Carters, as well as for members of the Lee, Goss, Cogswell, Journeay, Finley, Till, Byers, and Price families, whose homes are seen in the background. (Courtesy Douglas Carter.)

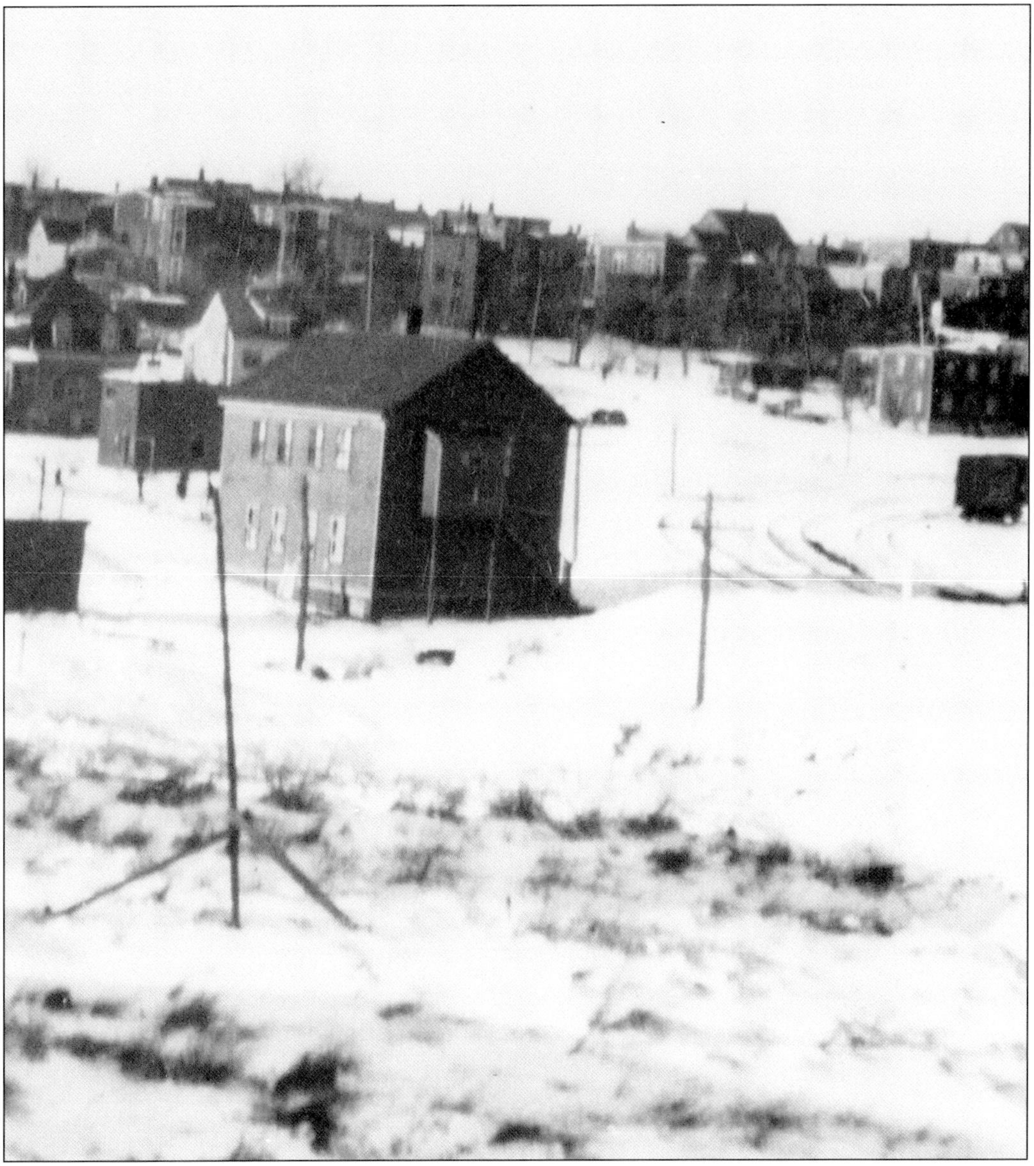

Pictured here is Germain Street in the early 1950s. In the foreground is Buckley's Pond, a popular rafting and skating location for area children. To the right is the pulpyard of Harry A. Corey and Son. To the left is what the locals called Sewer Hill, an unpaved portion of Germain Street used as a popular sliding spot. In the background, to the left is Queen Square. To the right is the ridge of Blue Rock Hill. The railroad tracks cut into the hill, but it was not until the grain elevator was built in 1912 that a large portion of the hill had to be excavated. Beatteay's Beach, which would be to the lower right of the photo, was destroyed in this process. Today, a terminal for the ferryboat to Digby is located where Beatteay's Beach and the weirs on page 33 were located.

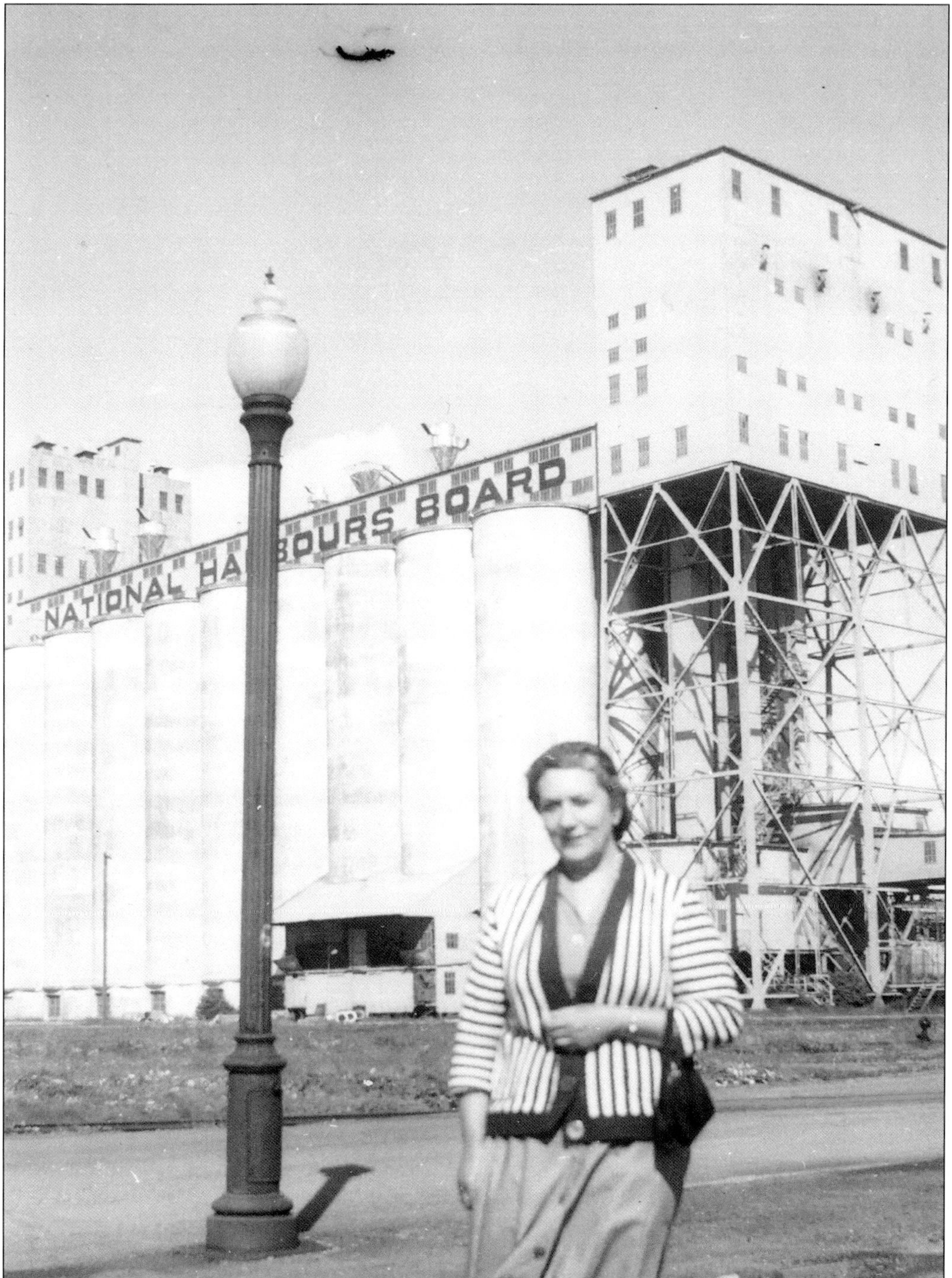

Now we come to the streets that cross the ones already mentioned. Union Street, or what remains of it, is shown in July 1960 with Betty Cormier by the 1929 elevator, which was used by Malcolm Somerville for his photos on pages 21 and 88. In the summer there was not much traffic in the port, which made this a great place to take your girl for a walk.

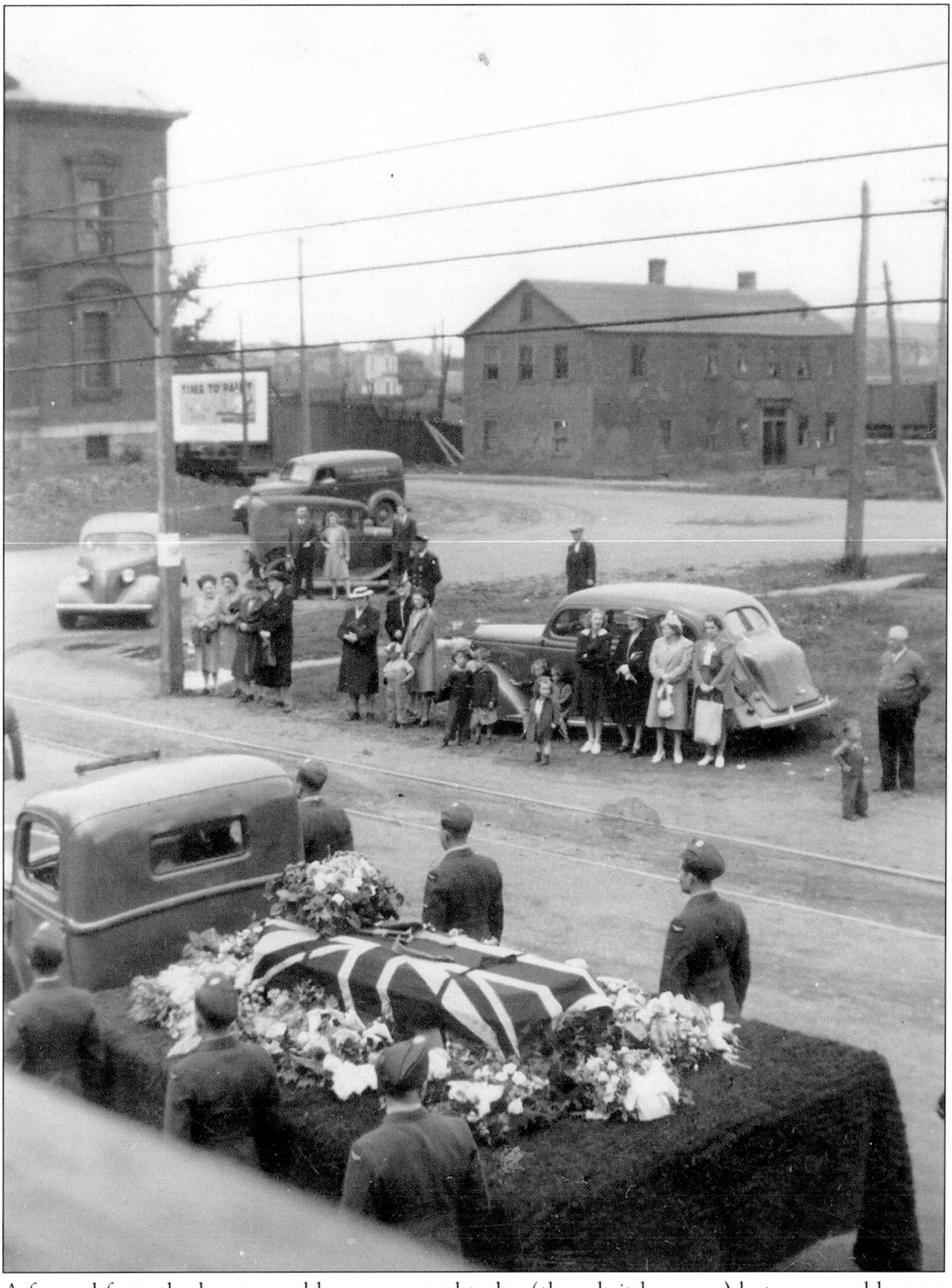

A funeral from the home would seem unusual today (though it happens) but one would never see a truck converted to a hearse, as this family has done. It stands outside a Market Place home, near Cameron's Barber Shop. Perhaps it was borrowed from Driscoll's or another lumber yard where the deceased believed to be Lawrence Babkirk may have worked. It has been carefully covered with black material to make a suitable and low cost conveyance and was no doubt a great help to the family in paying their last respects.

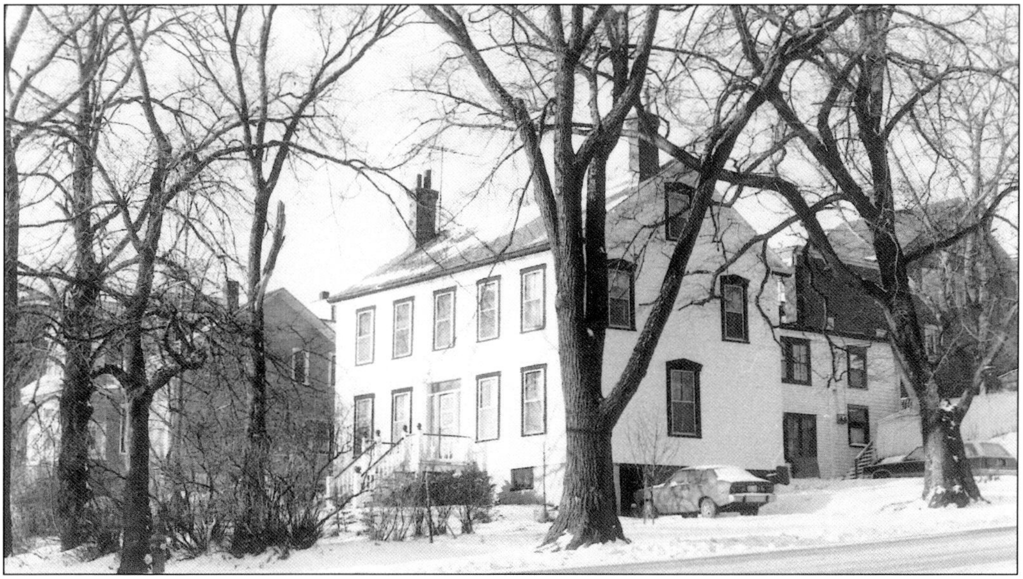

One of the older houses in Saint John West is pictured here at the foot of the Ludlow Street hill at Winslow Street. The style is Greek Revival, popular in the 1820s through the 1860s. Also in the photo are what are thought to be remnants of the 10,000 Elm trees, scions of those on Tremont Street in Boston, which were planted to commemorate the 100th anniversary of the city. Only a few remain, and appropriately, these are on Winslow Street, named for Edward Winslow, who held lot 202 in Carleton and was prominent in the negotiations separating New Brunswick from Nova Scotia.

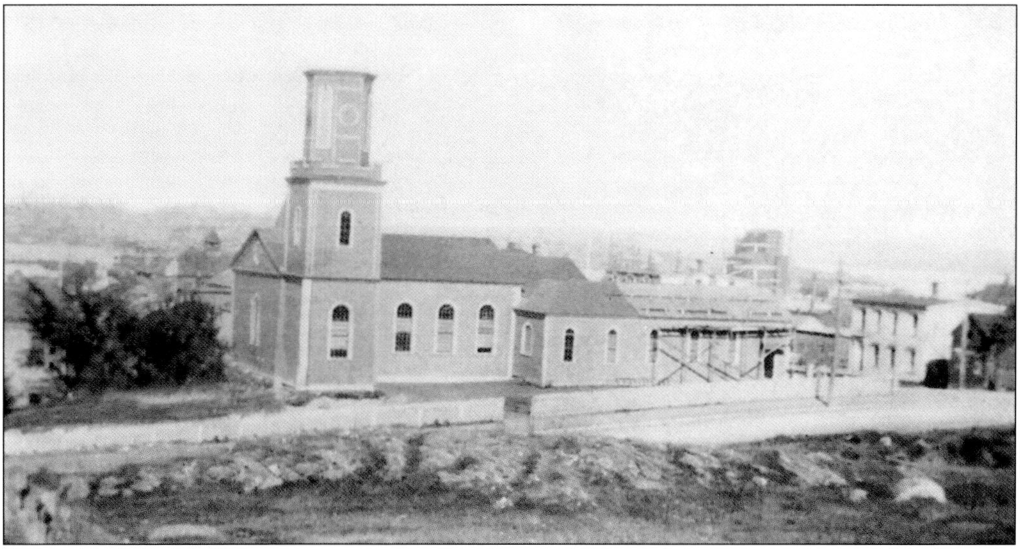

St. George's Church, on Watson Street, has been changed dramatically over the years. The central nave was built in 1821 and hasn't changed much on the exterior. This photo, taken by Cecil Strange, shows the original portion, with the Georgian windows prior to their beautification with stained glass. The original Sunday school hall is being built on the right, or the south end of the church. The year is between 1890, when the tower was constructed, and 1921, when the Sunday school hall was torn off the south end and the present hall built on the north end. (Courtesy Robert Taylor.)

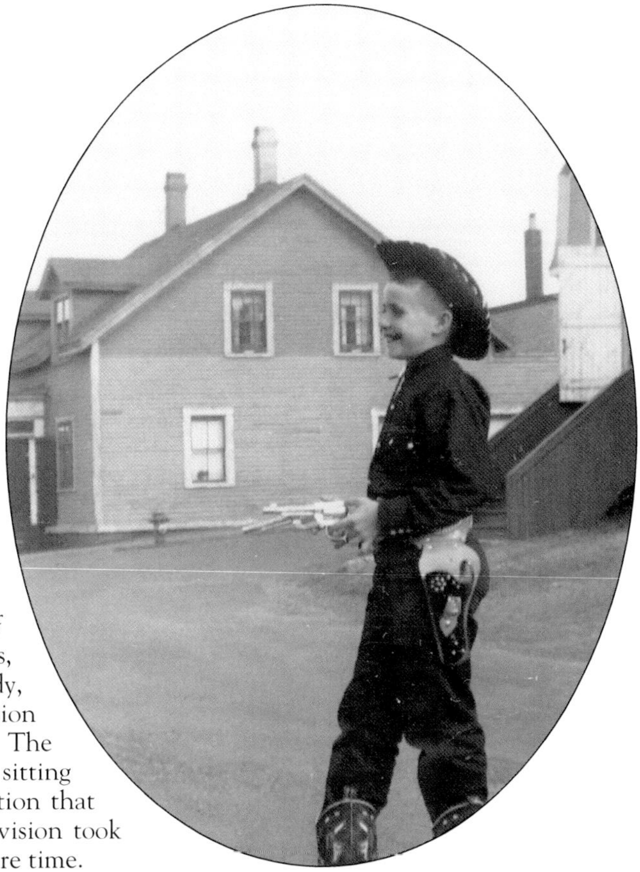

David Yelle is pictured here on Albert Street playing the part of the cowboy, perhaps Roy Rogers, Gene Autry, or Hopalong Cassidy, who were popular stars when television arrived on the West Side in 1954. The second picture is of Thelma Robson sitting in Queen Square, a longtime tradition that began to lose its popularity as television took more and more of West Siders' leisure time.

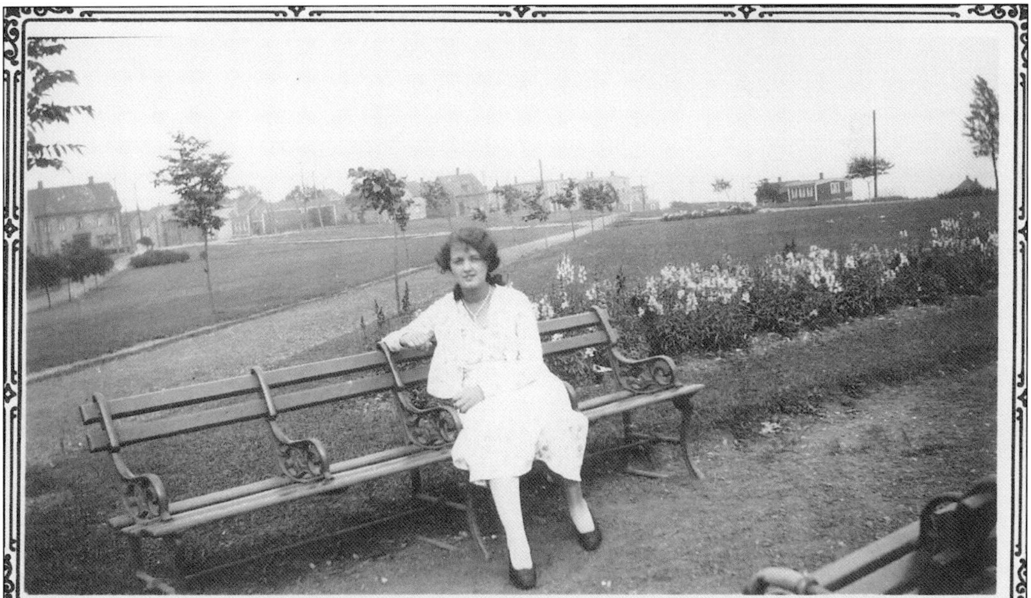

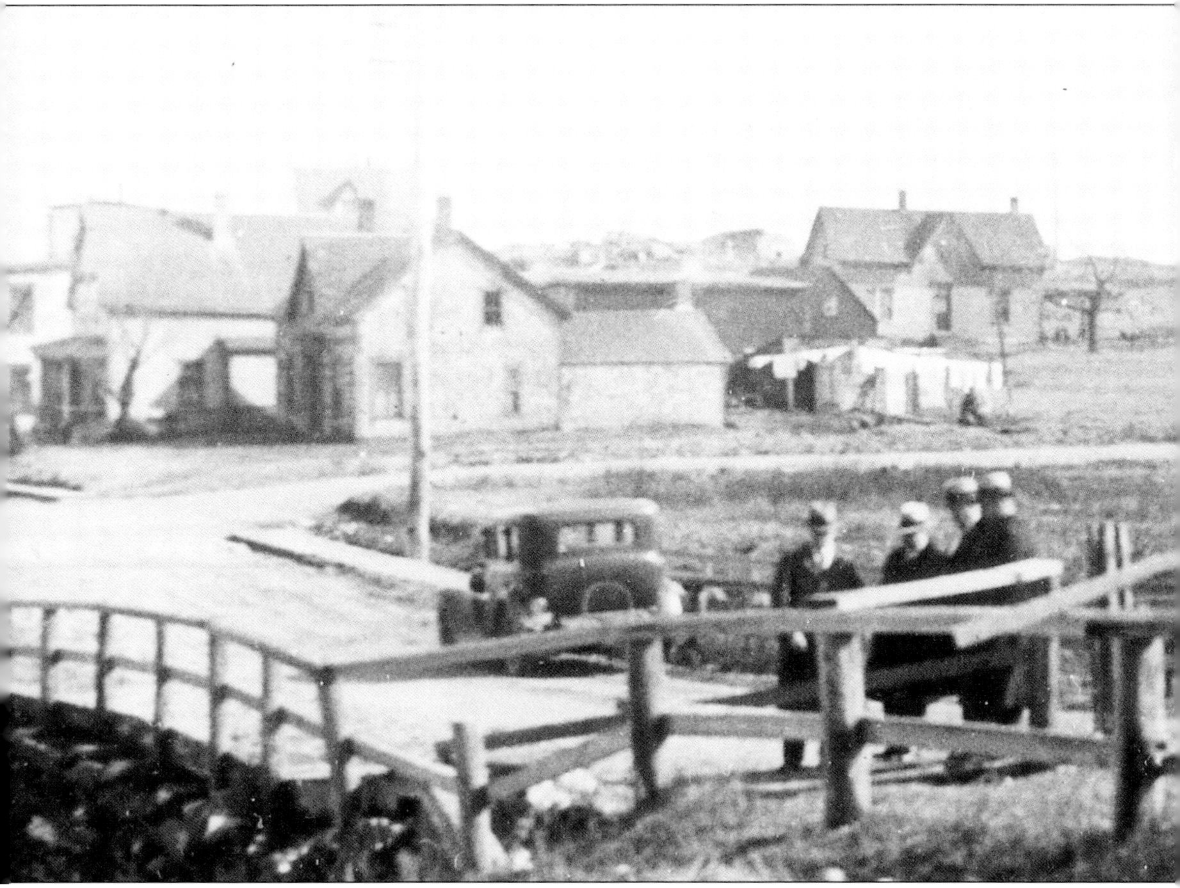

City Line is pictured here with Fort Dufferin in the background. This was a training ground for the Artillery each summer, and they chose it for their campground, as they could fire their cannons over the Bay of Fundy at the Shag Rocks about a mile off the shore. At the time it was an acceptable practice, and was not thought to have been doing any damage to the environment. The workmen are standing on a bridge that once covered a gulley separating Fort Dufferin and the McNulty Gravel Pits from Saint John West proper. Many Saint John West residents used the area as an easily accessed, yet quite private parking spot, when they were able to get dad's car for a Saturday night date.

Ten

FINAL LOOK AND NEIGHBOURS

In our final chapter we will take a wider look at Saint John and at some of the places where the residents went to work, to shop, or enjoy their leisure time. The ferry service provided easy access to the downtown core, and there was reliable streetcar service, too, and after 1948, good bus service. These were used not only to get to work at plants such as Simms in Fairville, but they also made it possible to travel to recreational sites farther afield. Sometimes this would include parades uptown, a visit to the Rural Cemetery, or a sit down to people watch in King's Square. Dominion Park on the St. John River and 2,000-acre Rockwood Park in the city centre were popular spots, too. We get a glimpse of these, as well as other recreational and work sites in outside neighbourhoods in this closing segment of the book.

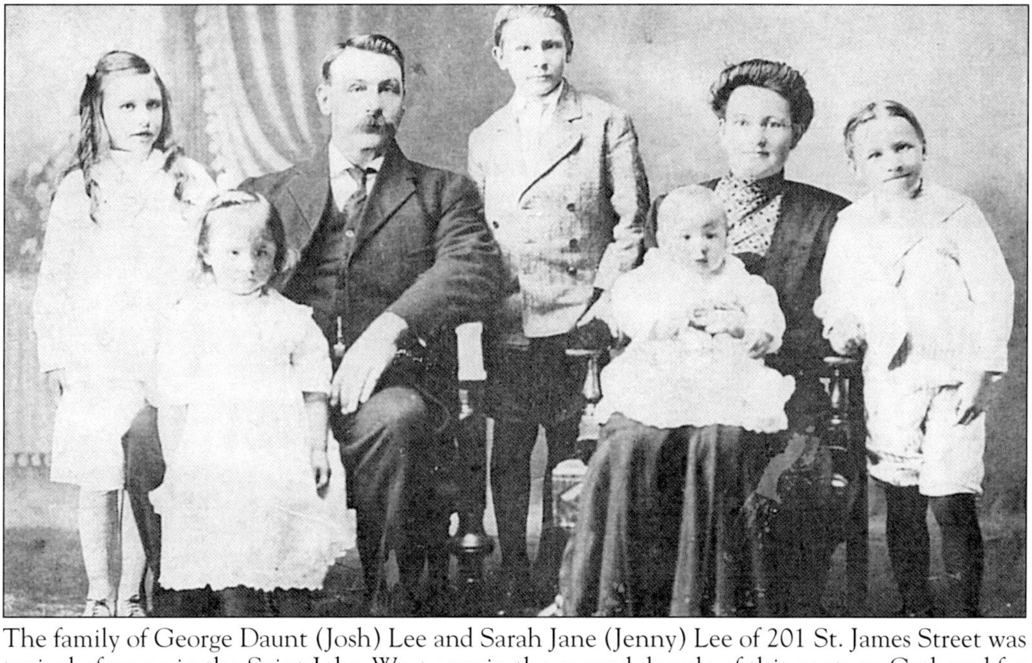

The family of George Daunt (Josh) Lee and Sarah Jane (Jenny) Lee of 201 St. James Street was typical of many in the Saint John West area in the second decade of this century. Gathered for a family photo, from left to right are the following: Sophia Lee, Alice (Drillon) Lee (the only one living in 1999 and who provided the photo), Alice's father George, her brother Allan, her mother Sarah (holding brother Dick), and finally brother Harry.

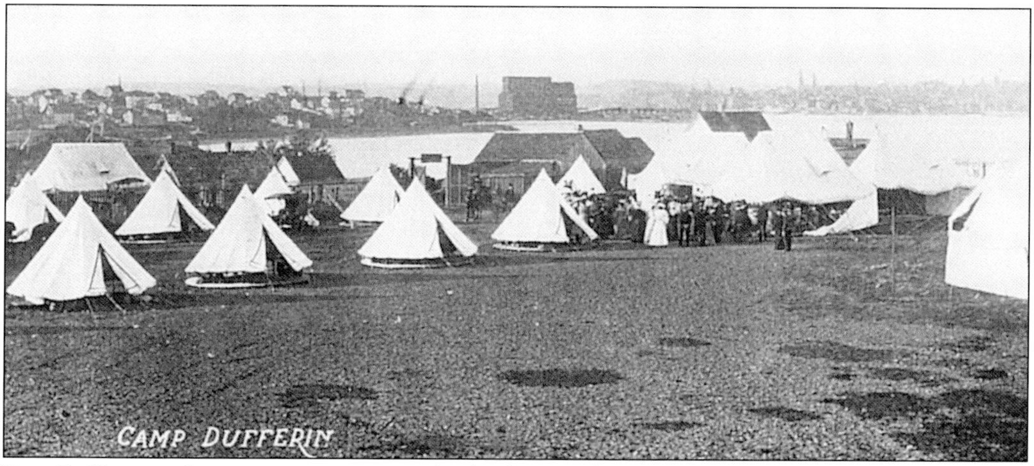

Fort Dufferin is shown on page 118 in the background of the photo. This closeup view shows the artillery camp. It was a 30-minute walk from "Carleton proper" Saint John West to watch them shelling the shag rocks, and it must have been quite an attraction. The booming guns would have alerted West Siders to the possibility of seeing the shells shattering the rocks.

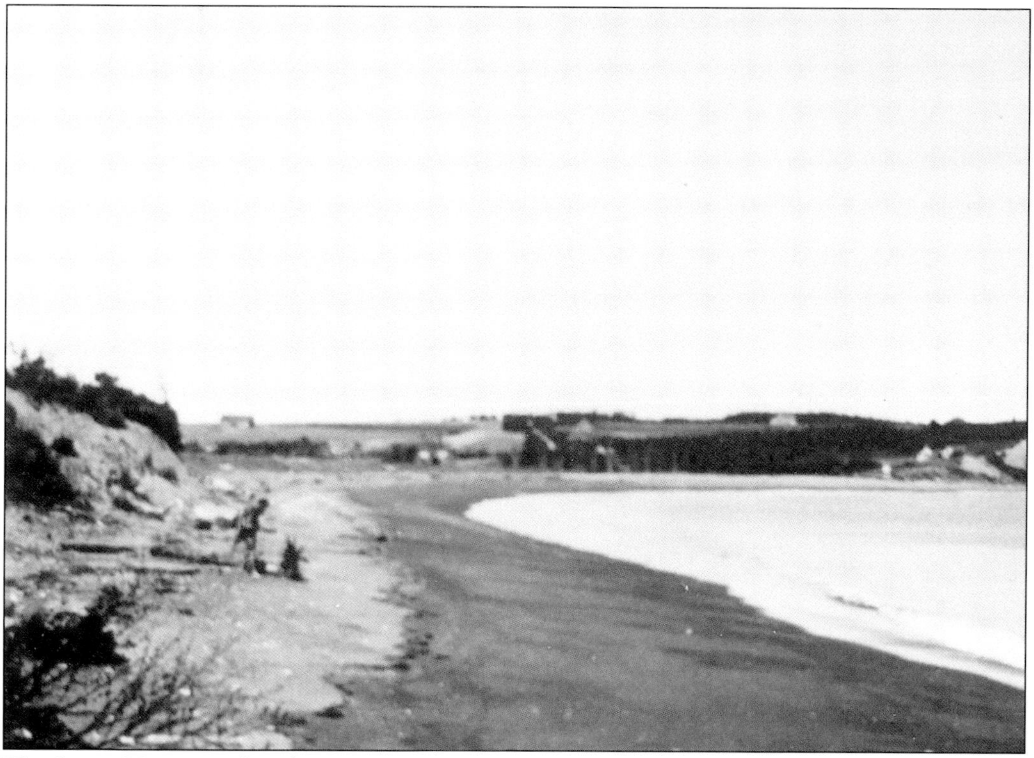

The Irving Nature Park today is a great attraction for the public. This photo was taken in 1936 by a worker named John Lockhead from the ship *Saint John*. Each week when the ship arrived from Boston, Lockhead made visits to various Saint John locations like Drury Cove, Long Lake, and one week he visited Taylor's Island. To go there he had to walk across a farmer's pasture and the marsh from Manawagonish Road, not Sand Cove Road as is the case now. He noted the area was the popular escape from the city for West Siders, as it is to this day. (Courtesy of Harold Wright.)

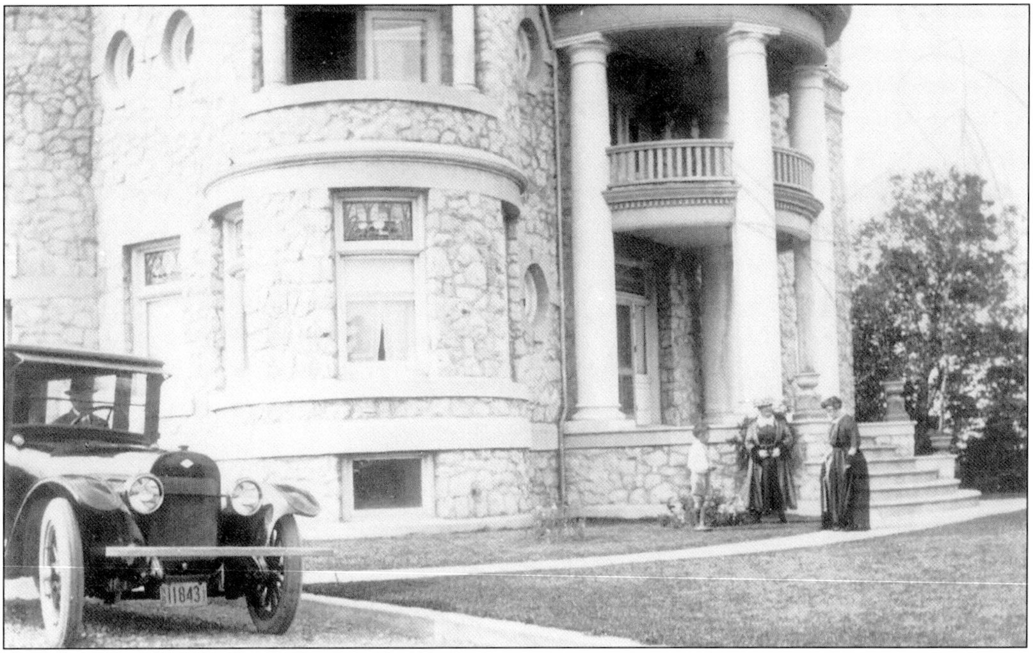

This is Emerson's castle, formerly the Baker castle, which was built for Mrs. E. Baker from a design by F. Neil Brodie in 1915. Considered unusual for the time (and still quite an attraction today), it is of stone-cased limestone from Randolph's and Baker's quarry across the river from South Bay at Greenhead. The rocks were floated over the river by barge. It cost $25,000 to build, with MacDonald of Sussex as the stone mason and J. Medley Belyea of Saint John West as the carpenter. Near it was the Ridgewood Golf Course (below), which was developed just off the road to Westfield just below the main rail line, and what was called Bogg's crossing. Today it is the site of Centracare. (Courtesy Ann Baker.)

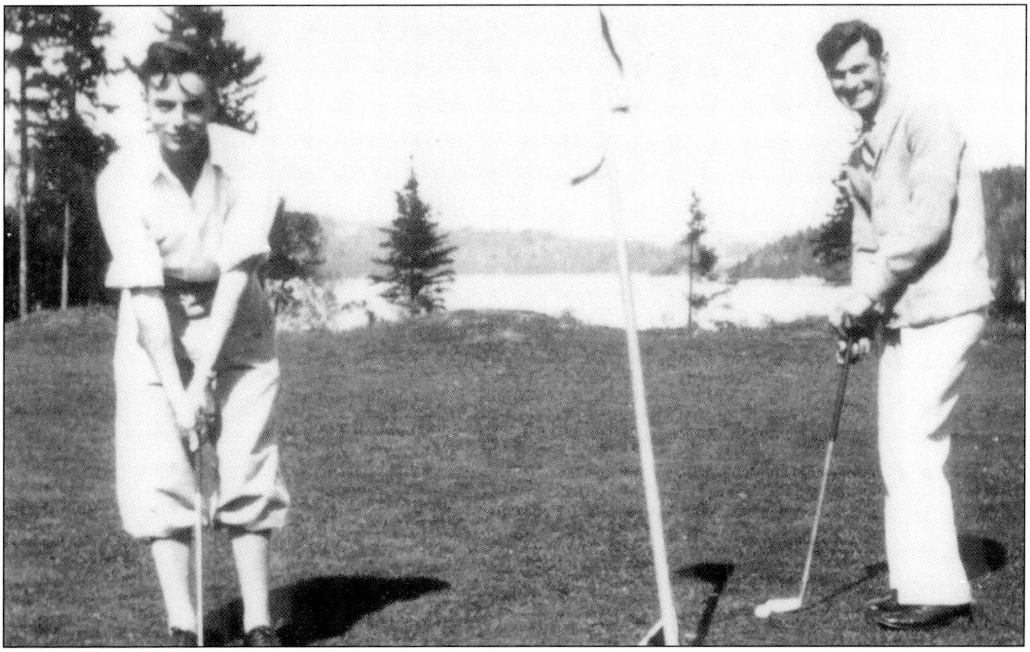

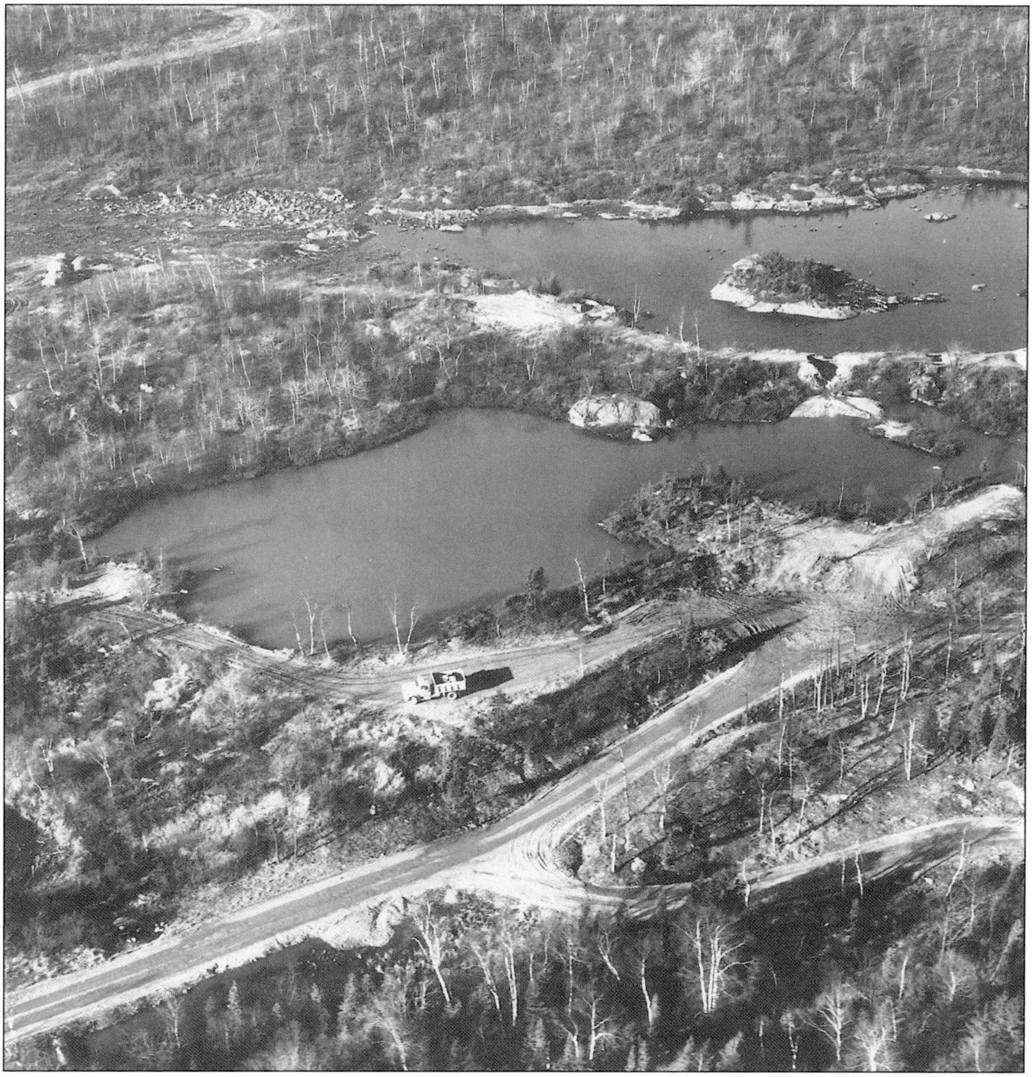

Rockwood Park was developed in 1894 as a playground for the Saint John residents, though it had been used informally for that purpose since the 1840s when Oliver's Cave was discovered. It was also the city's first water supply. This aerial portrait shows the park under redevelopment in 1966 when the artificial lakes, which had been dug out in 1906 by chain-gangs, were drained. The old dam was reinforced and the water allowed to gradually refill the depression to form the present lake system. The award-winning design also included picnic sites, an animal farm, a children's playground, and horse and walking trails were developed, along with several new swimming areas. West Siders flocked there following the redevelopment, and like most, could not believe the change that had occurred. Sadly, it has since been allowed to deteriorate, and many of the attractions developed in 1966 are gone. (Courtesy Vintage Photo and Frame.)

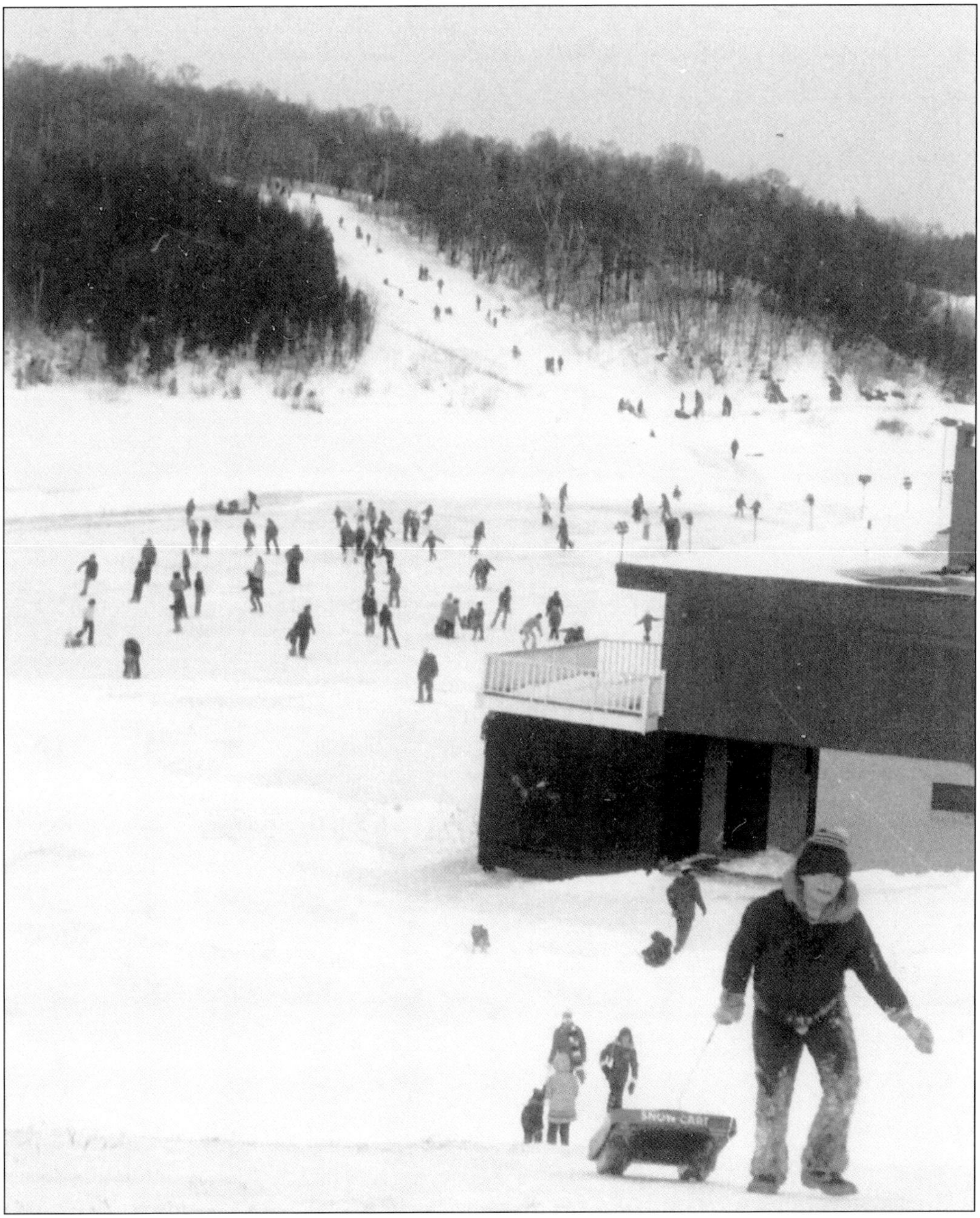

The earliest uses of the Rockwood Park in winter was for skating and curling and the harvesting of ice. Sometimes residents fought over who had the rights to the lake surface, even ending up in court. In 1926 the World Championship in speed skating was won on the lake by Charlie Gorman. Close to two-thirds of the population of the city, some 30,000 people, are said to have crowded around the lake to see the event. In 1966 a ski hill was developed in the park as part of the Canadian Centennial and the amalgamation of Saint John, Simonds, and Lancaster. It was meant to be a big winter attraction, yet lasted only a dozen years. The biggest winter event in the park today is the Skate to Care program, which annually raises about $100,000 for mental health in New Brunswick.

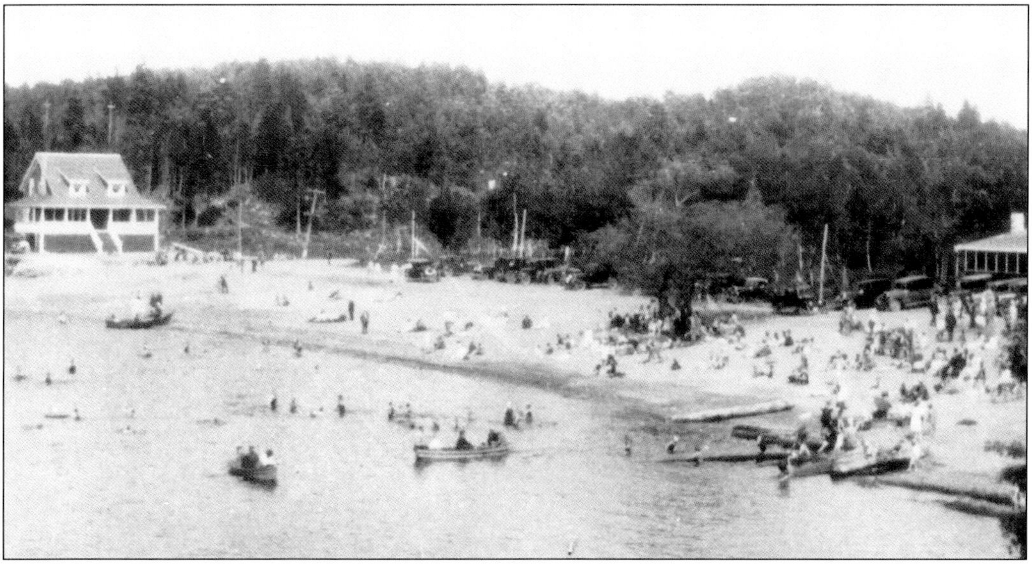

Dominion Park was about an hour's walk from Saint John West, but those who did not wish to bathe in the cold Fundy waters would gladly travel that distance, as it was the nearest place where fresh water swimming could be enjoyed. Located in Sand Cove on the lower reaches of the St. John River, it was known variously as Tippett Beach and Raynes Beach from its early owner's properties. On July 1, 1945, it was bought by the municipality for public use. The beach, with backup services such as the restaurant, dance hall, and bathhouses, became more and more popular as car ownership increased. In the early 1970s, pulpwood drifting onto the beach nearly resulted in its closure, but the problem was cleared up and the beach is the site to this day of the annual west side Days picnic each June. (Courtesy Art Kincade, Gerry Maxwell.)

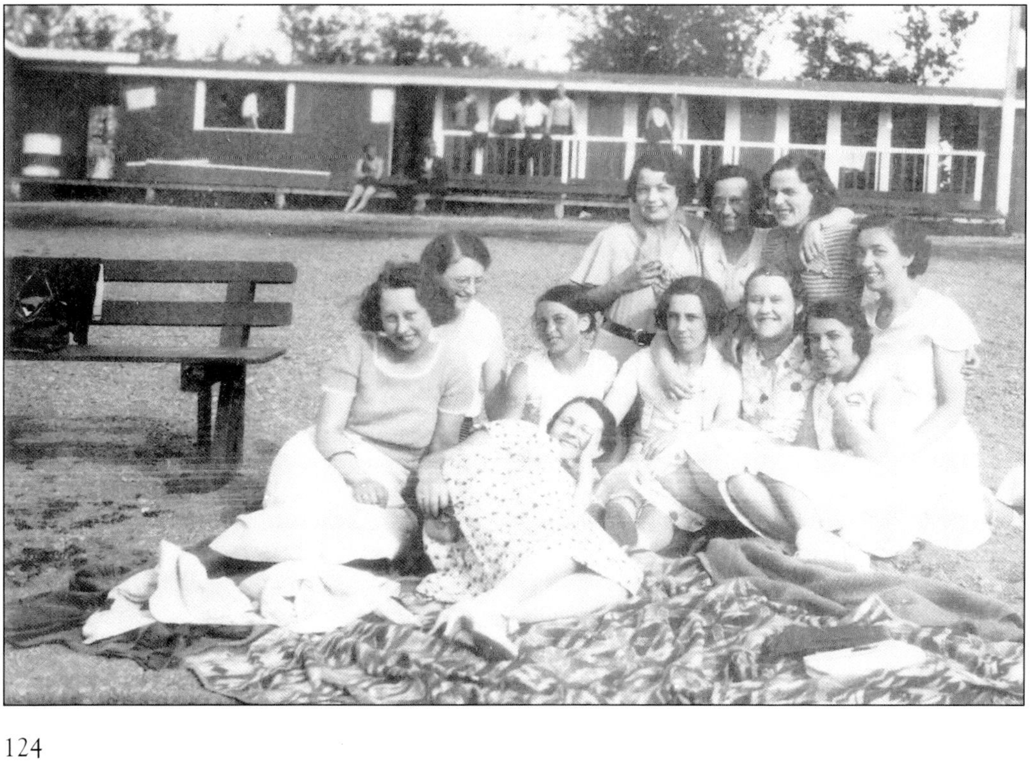

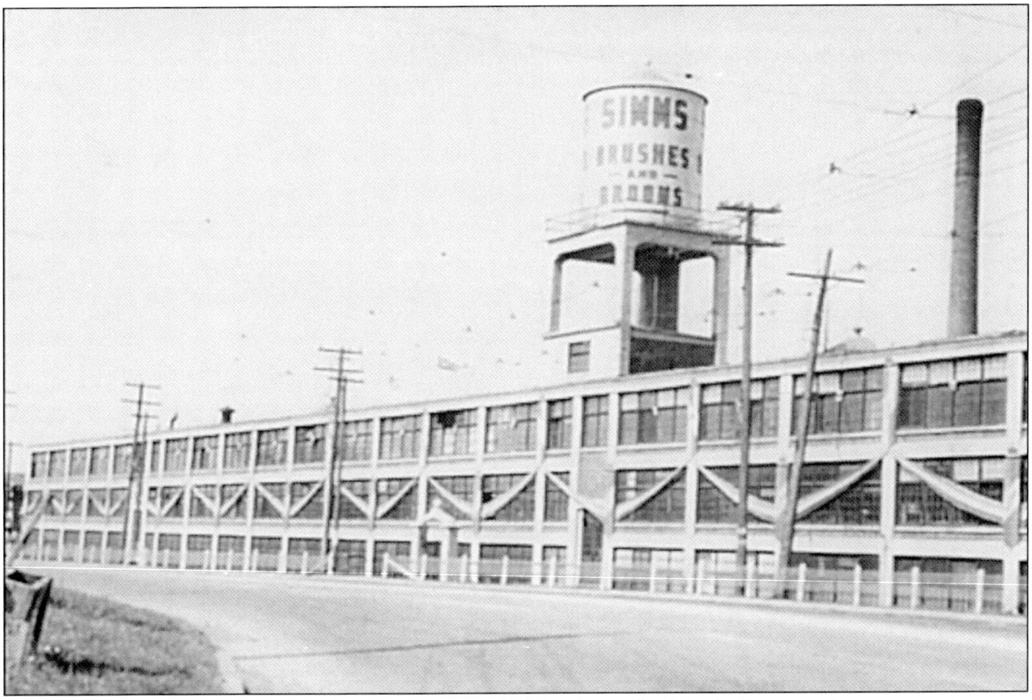

These photos show the decorations that were placed on the Ford plant on Lancaster Avenue and the T.S. Simms Brush Factory on Simms Corner in 1939. Both of these places would have been interesting to Saint Johners as they provided employment. The T.S. Simms Brush Factory has been in business since 1912 at what was called Avery Corner. Their nearby neighbour, the Ford plant was built in 1937, and at 216 feet by 166 feet with natural light roofing, it was, at the time, a real boost for Saint John coming as it did right at the end of the Depression. It cost $200,000 to build.

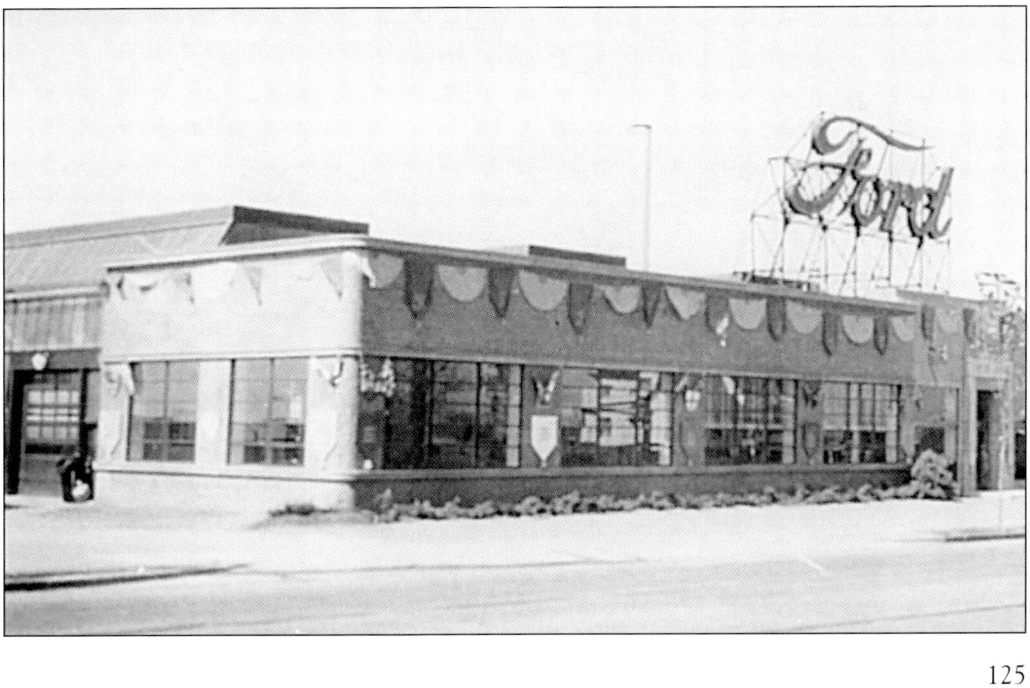

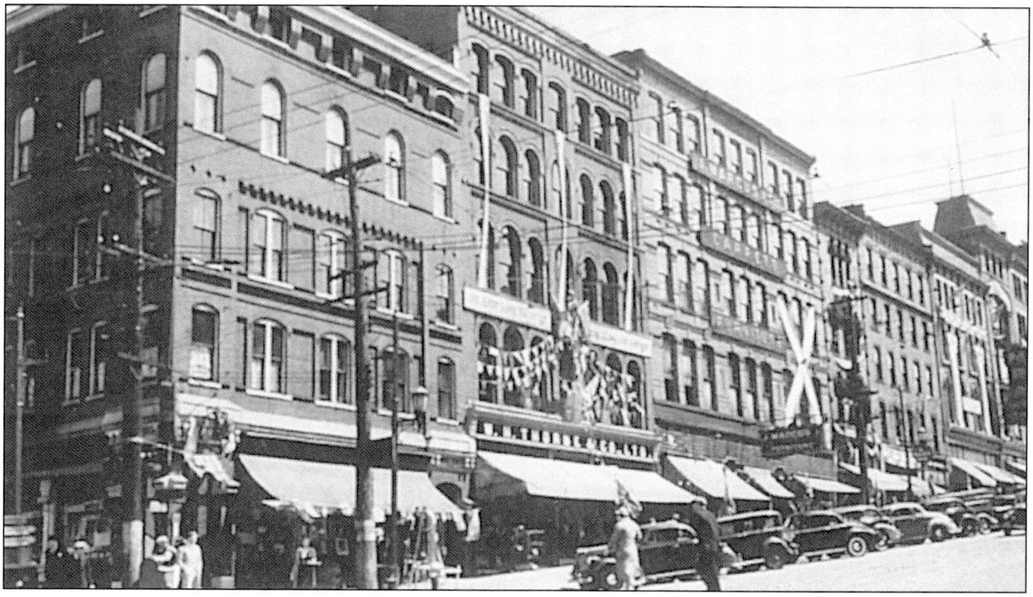

Next to their own King Street in Saint John West, this was the most popular shopping area in Saint John. This is the shortest, widest, steepest main street in Canada. To walk from the bottom to the top is like climbing up an eight-storey building. Streets like this are why Saint John women are said to have the shapeliest legs in Canada.

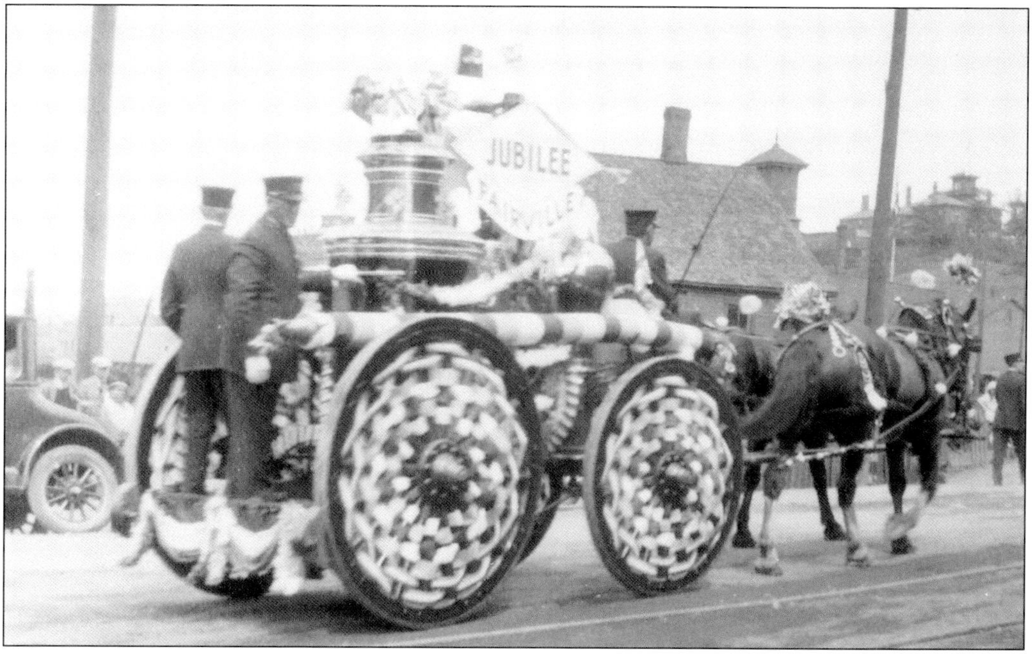

This photo was found in the Provincial Hospital Archives, likely because someone thought the Fairville Firemen shown on parade were at Simms Corner near their station, as it appears the Provincial Hospital in the background. We thought so too, until we had a good look, and discovered they are on Wall Street in central Saint John. Still, West Siders would have been there, too, giving the Fairville Firemen a good cheer, as they readily answered alarms in Carleton if called.

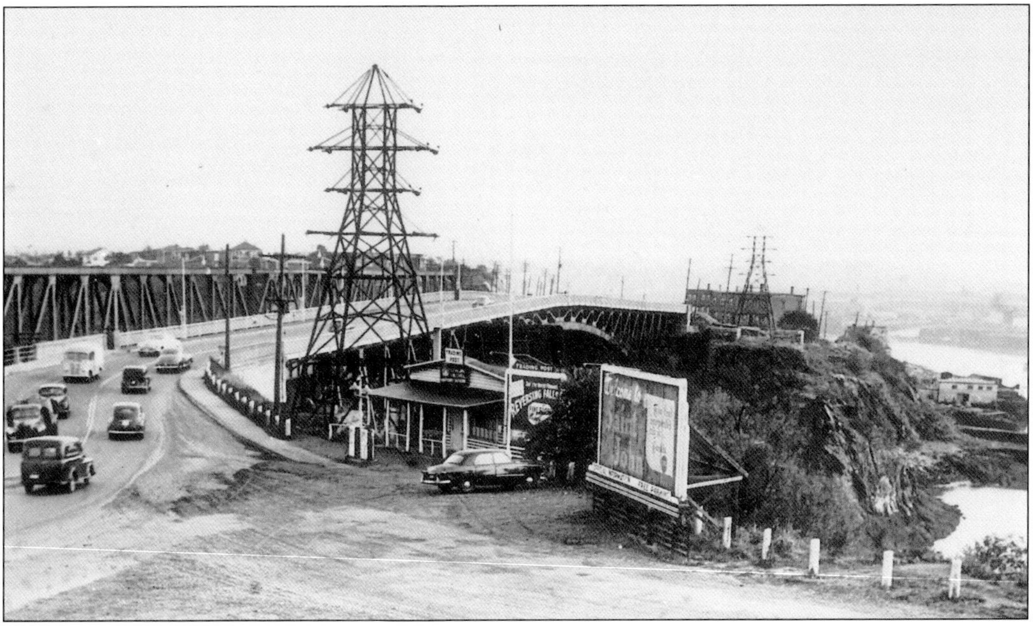

Since 1525 when Estavan Gomez recorded the Reversing Falls as "Rio de la Beulta", or "River of the Return", the falls have been a curiosity to visitors. In this photo by Dyson Thomas, we see the west side of the bridge when it was known as the Reversing Falls Outpost likely about 1948. It was run by the Saint John Merchants Association and besides selling postcards and providing tourist information, it also sold gasoline and served meals. Sometimes dances were held in the building, so it was an attractive place for West Siders to visit. The current structure, much changed, is built on the pillars of the suspension bridge of 1853 and dates from 1974.

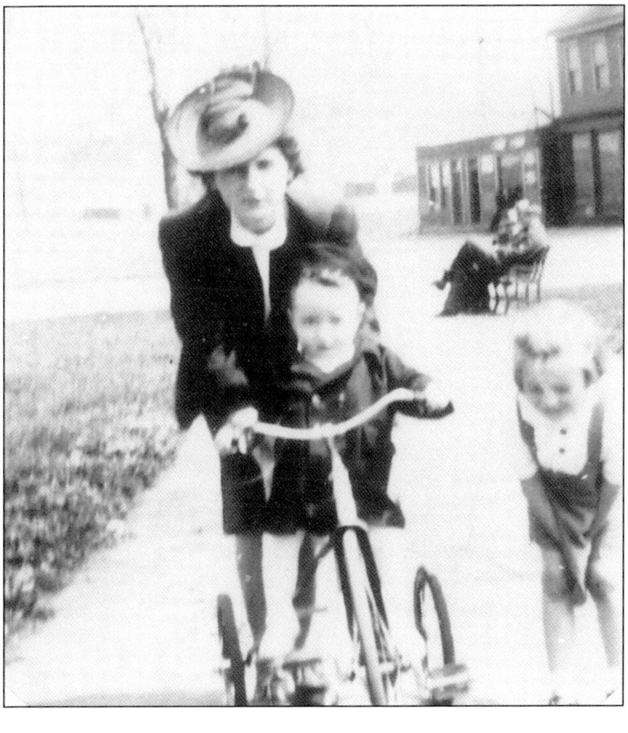

No matter how far a West Sider might travel he always came back to the "best side", as he will say for, "Once a west sider always a west sider", is a popular motto of the area. This mother obviously agrees, as she has chosen to spend her leisure time in a park on Market Place, which, surprisingly, seems to have no official (or unofficial) name. It may be Tilley Square, or Market Square, though nothing designates it as such on any of the maps. In the background, though, is a well-known corner, and though it too has no official name, all West Siders knew it as "The Board". It was where longshoremen got their orders for the day from a chalk board.

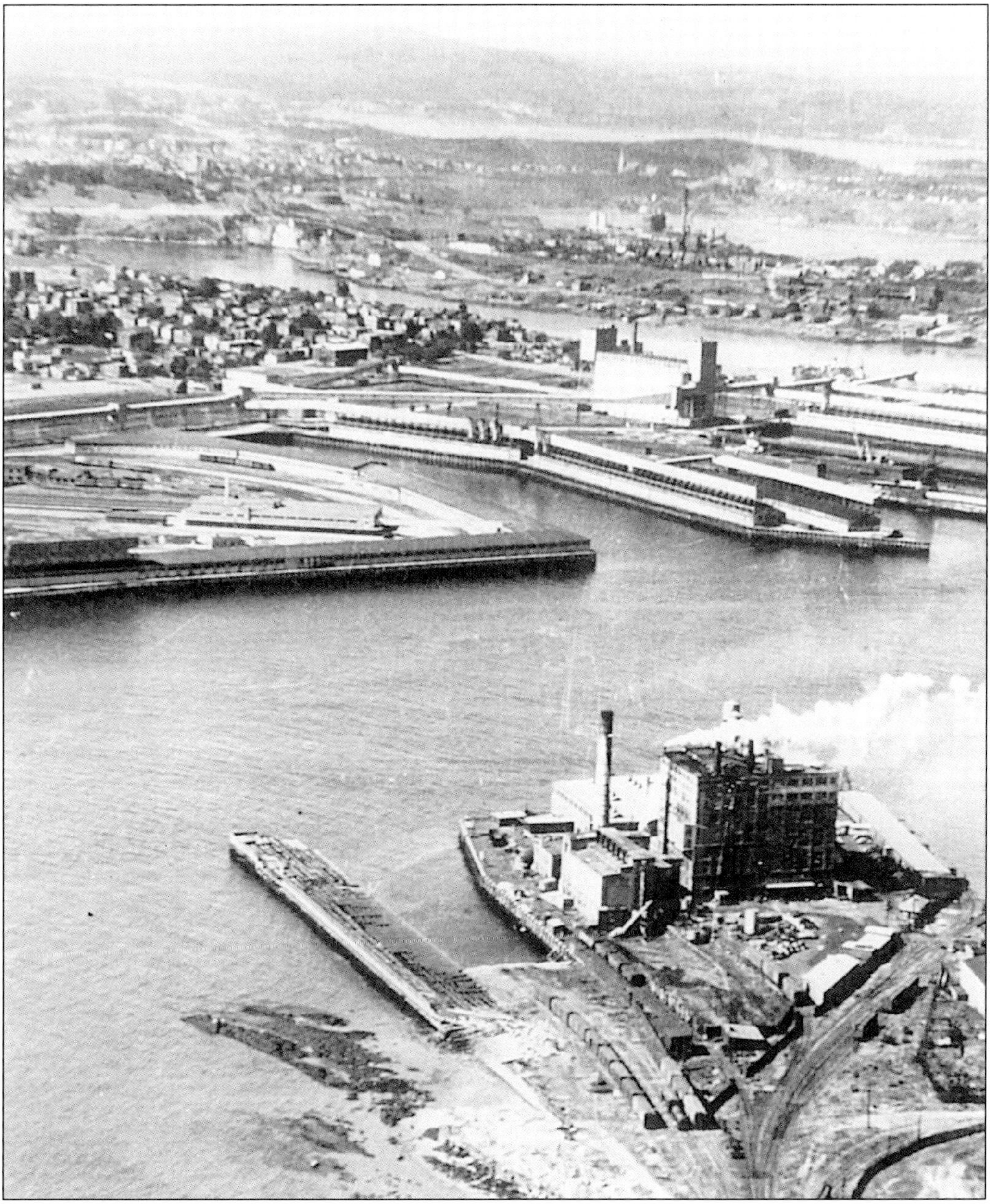

Now we say goodbye with this view from high over the centre of Saint John, looking towards the West Side. Many of the buildings and places we've identified are now gone, and others are disappearing as you read this. Sadly, in the foreground of this picture is Lantic Sugar, which once employed 1,200 Saint Johners and will close forever on December 31, 1999. Such is the course of history. We've provided you with a small piece of it in this latest book and in doing so, we hope it has brought many memories your way, and that you've enjoyed the experience to the same degree that Fred and I did while working on it.